C-3315

CAREER EXAMINATION SERIES

THIS IS YOUR **PASSBOOK**® FOR ...

CLEANER, CUSTODIAN USPS

NATIONAL LEARNING CORPORATION®
passbooks.com

COPYRIGHT NOTICE

This book is SOLELY intended for, is sold ONLY to, and its use is RESTRICTED to individual, bona fide applicants or candidates who qualify by virtue of having seriously filed applications for appropriate license, certificate, professional and/or promotional advancement, higher school matriculation, scholarship, or other legitimate requirements of educational and/or governmental authorities.

This book is NOT intended for use, class instruction, tutoring, training, duplication, copying, reprinting, excerption, or adaptation, etc., by:

1) Other publishers
2) Proprietors and/or Instructors of «Coaching» and/or Preparatory Courses
3) Personnel and/or Training Divisions of commercial, industrial, and governmental organizations
4) Schools, colleges, or universities and/or their departments and staffs, including teachers and other personnel
5) Testing Agencies or Bureaus
6) Study groups which seek by the purchase of a single volume to copy and/or duplicate and/or adapt this material for use by the group as a whole without having purchased individual volumes for each of the members of the group
7) Et al.

Such persons would be in violation of appropriate Federal and State statutes.

PROVISION OF LICENSING AGREEMENTS. — Recognized educational, commercial, industrial, and governmental institutions and organizations, and others legitimately engaged in educational pursuits, including training, testing, and measurement activities, may address request for a licensing agreement to the copyright owners, who will determine whether, and under what conditions, including fees and charges, the materials in this book may be used them. In other words, a licensing facility exists for the legitimate use of the material in this book on other than an individual basis. However, it is asseverated and affirmed here that the material in this book CANNOT be used without the receipt of the express permission of such a licensing agreement from the Publishers. Inquiries re licensing should be addressed to the company, attention rights and permissions department.

All rights reserved, including the right of reproduction in whole or in part, in any form or by any means, electronic or mechanical, including photocopying, recording, or by any information storage and retrieval system, without permission in writing from the Publisher.

Copyright © 2018 by

National Learning Corporation

212 Michael Drive, Syosset, NY 11791
(516) 921-8888 • www.passbooks.com
E-mail: info@passbooks.com

PUBLISHED IN THE UNITED STATES OF AMERICA

PASSBOOK® SERIES

THE *PASSBOOK® SERIES* has been created to prepare applicants and candidates for the ultimate academic battlefield – the examination room.

At some time in our lives, each and every one of us may be required to take an examination – for validation, matriculation, admission, qualification, registration, certification, or licensure.

Based on the assumption that every applicant or candidate has met the basic formal educational standards, has taken the required number of courses, and read the necessary texts, the *PASSBOOK® SERIES* furnishes the one special preparation which may assure passing with confidence, instead of failing with insecurity. Examination questions – together with answers – are furnished as the basic vehicle for study so that the mysteries of the examination and its compounding difficulties may be eliminated or diminished by a sure method.

This book is meant to help you pass your examination provided that you qualify and are serious in your objective.

The entire field is reviewed through the huge store of content information which is succinctly presented through a provocative and challenging approach – the question-and-answer method.

A climate of success is established by furnishing the correct answers at the end of each test.

You soon learn to recognize types of questions, forms of questions, and patterns of questioning. You may even begin to anticipate expected outcomes.

You perceive that many questions are repeated or adapted so that you can gain acute insights, which may enable you to score many sure points.

You learn how to confront new questions, or types of questions, and to attack them confidently and work out the correct answers.

You note objectives and emphases, and recognize pitfalls and dangers, so that you may make positive educational adjustments.

Moreover, you are kept fully informed in relation to new concepts, methods, practices, and directions in the field.

You discover that you arre actually taking the examination all the time: you are preparing for the examination by "taking" an examination, not by reading extraneous and/or supererogatory textbooks.

In short, this PASSBOOK®, used directedly, should be an important factor in helping you to pass your test.

CLEANER, CUSTODIAN (USPS)

DUTIES
Cleans in and about post office facilities. Performs related duties.

SCOPE OF THE EXAMINATION
The written test is designed to test for knowledge, skills, and/or abilities in such areas as:
1. Janitorial principles and practices;
2. Cleaning products and methods; and
3. General and mental abilities.

HOW TO TAKE A TEST

I. YOU MUST PASS AN EXAMINATION

A. *WHAT EVERY CANDIDATE SHOULD KNOW*

Examination applicants often ask us for help in preparing for the written test. What can I study in advance? What kinds of questions will be asked? How will the test be given? How will the papers be graded?

As an applicant for a civil service examination, you may be wondering about some of these things. Our purpose here is to suggest effective methods of advance study and to describe civil service examinations.

Your chances for success on this examination can be increased if you know how to prepare. Those "pre-examination jitters" can be reduced if you know what to expect. You can even experience an adventure in good citizenship if you know why civil service exams are given.

B. *WHY ARE CIVIL SERVICE EXAMINATIONS GIVEN?*

Civil service examinations are important to you in two ways. As a citizen, you want public jobs filled by employees who know how to do their work. As a job seeker, you want a fair chance to compete for that job on an equal footing with other candidates. The best-known means of accomplishing this two-fold goal is the competitive examination.

Exams are widely publicized throughout the nation. They may be administered for jobs in federal, state, city, municipal, town or village governments or agencies.

Any citizen may apply, with some limitations, such as the age or residence of applicants. Your experience and education may be reviewed to see whether you meet the requirements for the particular examination. When these requirements exist, they are reasonable and applied consistently to all applicants. Thus, a competitive examination may cause you some uneasiness now, but it is your privilege and safeguard.

C. *HOW ARE CIVIL SERVICE EXAMS DEVELOPED?*

Examinations are carefully written by trained technicians who are specialists in the field known as "psychological measurement," in consultation with recognized authorities in the field of work that the test will cover. These experts recommend the subject matter areas or skills to be tested; only those knowledges or skills important to your success on the job are included. The most reliable books and source materials available are used as references. Together, the experts and technicians judge the difficulty level of the questions.

Test technicians know how to phrase questions so that the problem is clearly stated. Their ethics do not permit "trick" or "catch" questions. Questions may have been tried out on sample groups, or subjected to statistical analysis, to determine their usefulness.

Written tests are often used in combination with performance tests, ratings of training and experience, and oral interviews. All of these measures combine to form the best-known means of finding the right person for the right job.

II. HOW TO PASS THE WRITTEN TEST

A. NATURE OF THE EXAMINATION

To prepare intelligently for civil service examinations, you should know how they differ from school examinations you have taken. In school you were assigned certain definite pages to read or subjects to cover. The examination questions were quite detailed and usually emphasized memory. Civil service exams, on the other hand, try to discover your present ability to perform the duties of a position, plus your potentiality to learn these duties. In other words, a civil service exam attempts to predict how successful you will be. Questions cover such a broad area that they cannot be as minute and detailed as school exam questions.

In the public service similar kinds of work, or positions, are grouped together in one "class." This process is known as *position-classification*. All the positions in a class are paid according to the salary range for that class. One class title covers all of these positions, and they are all tested by the same examination.

B. FOUR BASIC STEPS

1) Study the announcement

How, then, can you know what subjects to study? Our best answer is: "Learn as much as possible about the class of positions for which you've applied." The exam will test the knowledge, skills and abilities needed to do the work.

Your most valuable source of information about the position you want is the official exam announcement. This announcement lists the training and experience qualifications. Check these standards and apply only if you come reasonably close to meeting them.

The brief description of the position in the examination announcement offers some clues to the subjects which will be tested. Think about the job itself. Review the duties in your mind. Can you perform them, or are there some in which you are rusty? Fill in the blank spots in your preparation.

Many jurisdictions preview the written test in the exam announcement by including a section called "Knowledge and Abilities Required," "Scope of the Examination," or some similar heading. Here you will find out specifically what fields will be tested.

2) Review your own background

Once you learn in general what the position is all about, and what you need to know to do the work, ask yourself which subjects you already know fairly well and which need improvement. You may wonder whether to concentrate on improving your strong areas or on building some background in your fields of weakness. When the announcement has specified "some knowledge" or "considerable knowledge," or has used adjectives like "beginning principles of..." or "advanced ... methods," you can get a clue as to the number and difficulty of questions to be asked in any given field. More questions, and hence broader coverage, would be included for those subjects which are more important in the work. Now weigh your strengths and weaknesses against the job requirements and prepare accordingly.

3) Determine the level of the position

Another way to tell how intensively you should prepare is to understand the level of the job for which you are applying. Is it the entering level? In other words, is this the position in which beginners in a field of work are hired? Or is it an intermediate or advanced level? Sometimes this is indicated by such words as "Junior" or "Senior" in the class title. Other jurisdictions use Roman numerals to designate the level – Clerk I, Clerk II, for example. The word "Supervisor" sometimes appears in the title. If the level is not indicated by the title, check the description of duties. Will you be working under very close supervision, or will you have responsibility for independent decisions in this work?

4) Choose appropriate study materials

Now that you know the subjects to be examined and the relative amount of each subject to be covered, you can choose suitable study materials. For beginning level jobs, or even advanced ones, if you have a pronounced weakness in some aspect of your training, read a modern, standard textbook in that field. Be sure it is up to date and has general coverage. Such books are normally available at your library, and the librarian will be glad to help you locate one. For entry-level positions, questions of appropriate difficulty are chosen – neither highly advanced questions, nor those too simple. Such questions require careful thought but not advanced training.

If the position for which you are applying is technical or advanced, you will read more advanced, specialized material. If you are already familiar with the basic principles of your field, elementary textbooks would waste your time. Concentrate on advanced textbooks and technical periodicals. Think through the concepts and review difficult problems in your field.

These are all general sources. You can get more ideas on your own initiative, following these leads. For example, training manuals and publications of the government agency which employs workers in your field can be useful, particularly for technical and professional positions. A letter or visit to the government department involved may result in more specific study suggestions, and certainly will provide you with a more definite idea of the exact nature of the position you are seeking.

III. KINDS OF TESTS

Tests are used for purposes other than measuring knowledge and ability to perform specified duties. For some positions, it is equally important to test ability to make adjustments to new situations or to profit from training. In others, basic mental abilities not dependent on information are essential. Questions which test these things may not appear as pertinent to the duties of the position as those which test for knowledge and information. Yet they are often highly important parts of a fair examination. For very general questions, it is almost impossible to help you direct your study efforts. What we can do is to point out some of the more common of these general abilities needed in public service positions and describe some typical questions.

1) General information

Broad, general information has been found useful for predicting job success in some kinds of work. This is tested in a variety of ways, from vocabulary lists to questions about current events. Basic background in some field of work, such as sociology or economics, may be sampled in a group of questions. Often these are principles which have become familiar to most persons through exposure rather than through formal training. It is difficult to advise you how to study for these questions; being alert to the world around you is our best suggestion.

2) Verbal ability

An example of an ability needed in many positions is verbal or language ability. Verbal ability is, in brief, the ability to use and understand words. Vocabulary and grammar tests are typical measures of this ability. Reading comprehension or paragraph interpretation questions are common in many kinds of civil service tests. You are given a paragraph of written material and asked to find its central meaning.

3) Numerical ability

Number skills can be tested by the familiar arithmetic problem, by checking paired lists of numbers to see which are alike and which are different, or by interpreting charts and graphs. In the latter test, a graph may be printed in the test booklet which you are asked to use as the basis for answering questions.

4) Observation

A popular test for law-enforcement positions is the observation test. A picture is shown to you for several minutes, then taken away. Questions about the picture test your ability to observe both details and larger elements.

5) Following directions

In many positions in the public service, the employee must be able to carry out written instructions dependably and accurately. You may be given a chart with several columns, each column listing a variety of information. The questions require you to carry out directions involving the information given in the chart.

6) Skills and aptitudes

Performance tests effectively measure some manual skills and aptitudes. When the skill is one in which you are trained, such as typing or shorthand, you can practice. These tests are often very much like those given in business school or high school courses. For many of the other skills and aptitudes, however, no short-time preparation can be made. Skills and abilities natural to you or that you have developed throughout your lifetime are being tested.

Many of the general questions just described provide all the data needed to answer the questions and ask you to use your reasoning ability to find the answers. Your best preparation for these tests, as well as for tests of facts and ideas, is to be at your physical and mental best. You, no doubt, have your own methods of getting into an exam-taking mood and keeping "in shape." The next section lists some ideas on this subject.

IV. KINDS OF QUESTIONS

Only rarely is the "essay" question, which you answer in narrative form, used in civil service tests. Civil service tests are usually of the short-answer type. Full instructions for answering these questions will be given to you at the examination. But in case this is your first experience with short-answer questions and separate answer sheets, here is what you need to know:

1) Multiple-choice Questions

Most popular of the short-answer questions is the "multiple choice" or "best answer" question. It can be used, for example, to test for factual knowledge, ability to solve problems or judgment in meeting situations found at work.

A multiple-choice question is normally one of three types—

- It can begin with an incomplete statement followed by several possible endings. You are to find the one ending which *best* completes the statement, although some of the others may not be entirely wrong.
- It can also be a complete statement in the form of a question which is answered by choosing one of the statements listed.
- It can be in the form of a problem – again you select the best answer.

Here is an example of a multiple-choice question with a discussion which should give you some clues as to the method for choosing the right answer:

When an employee has a complaint about his assignment, the action which will *best* help him overcome his difficulty is to

    A. discuss his difficulty with his coworkers
    B. take the problem to the head of the organization
    C. take the problem to the person who gave him the assignment
    D. say nothing to anyone about his complaint

In answering this question, you should study each of the choices to find which is best. Consider choice "A" – Certainly an employee may discuss his complaint with fellow employees, but no change or improvement can result, and the complaint remains unresolved. Choice "B" is a poor choice since the head of the organization probably does not know what assignment you have been given, and taking your problem to him is known as "going over the head" of the supervisor. The supervisor, or person who made the assignment, is the person who can clarify it or correct any injustice. Choice "C" is, therefore, correct. To say nothing, as in choice "D," is unwise. Supervisors have and interest in knowing the problems employees are facing, and the employee is seeking a solution to his problem.

2) True/False Questions

The "true/false" or "right/wrong" form of question is sometimes used. Here a complete statement is given. Your job is to decide whether the statement is right or wrong.

SAMPLE: A roaming cell-phone call to a nearby city costs less than a non-roaming call to a distant city.

This statement is wrong, or false, since roaming calls are more expensive.
This is not a complete list of all possible question forms, although most of the others are variations of these common types. You will always get complete directions for

answering questions. Be sure you understand *how* to mark your answers – ask questions until you do.

V. RECORDING YOUR ANSWERS

Computer terminals are used more and more today for many different kinds of exams.

For an examination with very few applicants, you may be told to record your answers in the test booklet itself. Separate answer sheets are much more common. If this separate answer sheet is to be scored by machine – and this is often the case – it is highly important that you mark your answers correctly in order to get credit.

An electronic scoring machine is often used in civil service offices because of the speed with which papers can be scored. Machine-scored answer sheets must be marked with a pencil, which will be given to you. This pencil has a high graphite content which responds to the electronic scoring machine. As a matter of fact, stray dots may register as answers, so do not let your pencil rest on the answer sheet while you are pondering the correct answer. Also, if your pencil lead breaks or is otherwise defective, ask for another.

Since the answer sheet will be dropped in a slot in the scoring machine, be careful not to bend the corners or get the paper crumpled.

The answer sheet normally has five vertical columns of numbers, with 30 numbers to a column. These numbers correspond to the question numbers in your test booklet. After each number, going across the page are four or five pairs of dotted lines. These short dotted lines have small letters or numbers above them. The first two pairs may also have a "T" or "F" above the letters. This indicates that the first two pairs only are to be used if the questions are of the true-false type. If the questions are multiple choice, disregard the "T" and "F" and pay attention only to the small letters or numbers.

Answer your questions in the manner of the sample that follows:

32. The largest city in the United States is
    A. Washington, D.C.
    B. New York City
    C. Chicago
    D. Detroit
    E. San Francisco

1) Choose the answer you think is best. (New York City is the largest, so "B" is correct.)
2) Find the row of dotted lines numbered the same as the question you are answering. (Find row number 32)
3) Find the pair of dotted lines corresponding to the answer. (Find the pair of lines under the mark "B.")
4) Make a solid black mark between the dotted lines.

VI. BEFORE THE TEST

Common sense will help you find procedures to follow to get ready for an examination. Too many of us, however, overlook these sensible measures. Indeed, nervousness and fatigue have been found to be the most serious reasons why applicants fail to do their best on civil service tests. Here is a list of reminders:

- Begin your preparation early – Don't wait until the last minute to go scurrying around for books and materials or to find out what the position is all about.
- Prepare continuously – An hour a night for a week is better than an all-night cram session. This has been definitely established. What is more, a night a week for a month will return better dividends than crowding your study into a shorter period of time.
- Locate the place of the exam – You have been sent a notice telling you when and where to report for the examination. If the location is in a different town or otherwise unfamiliar to you, it would be well to inquire the best route and learn something about the building.
- Relax the night before the test – Allow your mind to rest. Do not study at all that night. Plan some mild recreation or diversion; then go to bed early and get a good night's sleep.
- Get up early enough to make a leisurely trip to the place for the test – This way unforeseen events, traffic snarls, unfamiliar buildings, etc. will not upset you.
- Dress comfortably – A written test is not a fashion show. You will be known by number and not by name, so wear something comfortable.
- Leave excess paraphernalia at home – Shopping bags and odd bundles will get in your way. You need bring only the items mentioned in the official notice you received; usually everything you need is provided. Do not bring reference books to the exam. They will only confuse those last minutes and be taken away from you when in the test room.
- Arrive somewhat ahead of time – If because of transportation schedules you must get there very early, bring a newspaper or magazine to take your mind off yourself while waiting.
- Locate the examination room – When you have found the proper room, you will be directed to the seat or part of the room where you will sit. Sometimes you are given a sheet of instructions to read while you are waiting. Do not fill out any forms until you are told to do so; just read them and be prepared.
- Relax and prepare to listen to the instructions
- If you have any physical problem that may keep you from doing your best, be sure to tell the test administrator. If you are sick or in poor health, you really cannot do your best on the exam. You can come back and take the test some other time.

VII. AT THE TEST

The day of the test is here and you have the test booklet in your hand. The temptation to get going is very strong. Caution! There is more to success than knowing the right answers. You must know how to identify your papers and understand variations in the type of short-answer question used in this particular examination. Follow these suggestions for maximum results from your efforts:

1) Cooperate with the monitor

The test administrator has a duty to create a situation in which you can be as much at ease as possible. He will give instructions, tell you when to begin, check to see that you are marking your answer sheet correctly, and so on. He is not there to guard you, although he will see that your competitors do not take unfair advantage. He wants to help you do your best.

2) Listen to all instructions

Don't jump the gun! Wait until you understand all directions. In most civil service tests you get more time than you need to answer the questions. So don't be in a hurry. Read each word of instructions until you clearly understand the meaning. Study the examples, listen to all announcements and follow directions. Ask questions if you do not understand what to do.

3) Identify your papers

Civil service exams are usually identified by number only. You will be assigned a number; you must not put your name on your test papers. Be sure to copy your number correctly. Since more than one exam may be given, copy your exact examination title.

4) Plan your time

Unless you are told that a test is a "speed" or "rate of work" test, speed itself is usually not important. Time enough to answer all the questions will be provided, but this does not mean that you have all day. An overall time limit has been set. Divide the total time (in minutes) by the number of questions to determine the approximate time you have for each question.

5) Do not linger over difficult questions

If you come across a difficult question, mark it with a paper clip (useful to have along) and come back to it when you have been through the booklet. One caution if you do this – be sure to skip a number on your answer sheet as well. Check often to be sure that you have not lost your place and that you are marking in the row numbered the same as the question you are answering.

6) Read the questions

Be sure you know what the question asks! Many capable people are unsuccessful because they failed to *read* the questions correctly.

7) Answer all questions

Unless you have been instructed that a penalty will be deducted for incorrect answers, it is better to guess than to omit a question.

8) Speed tests

It is often better NOT to guess on speed tests. It has been found that on timed tests people are tempted to spend the last few seconds before time is called in marking answers at random – without even reading them – in the hope of picking up a few extra points. To discourage this practice, the instructions may warn you that your score will be "corrected" for guessing. That is, a penalty will be applied. The incorrect answers will be deducted from the correct ones, or some other penalty formula will be used.

9) Review your answers

If you finish before time is called, go back to the questions you guessed or omitted to give them further thought. Review other answers if you have time.

10) Return your test materials

If you are ready to leave before others have finished or time is called, take ALL your materials to the monitor and leave quietly. Never take any test material with you. The monitor can discover whose papers are not complete, and taking a test booklet may be grounds for disqualification.

VIII. EXAMINATION TECHNIQUES

1) Read the general instructions carefully. These are usually printed on the first page of the exam booklet. As a rule, these instructions refer to the timing of the examination; the fact that you should not start work until the signal and must stop work at a signal, etc. If there are any *special* instructions, such as a choice of questions to be answered, make sure that you note this instruction carefully.

2) When you are ready to start work on the examination, that is as soon as the signal has been given, read the instructions to each question booklet, underline any key words or phrases, such as *least, best, outline, describe* and the like. In this way you will tend to answer as requested rather than discover on reviewing your paper that you *listed without describing*, that you selected the *worst* choice rather than the *best* choice, etc.

3) If the examination is of the objective or multiple-choice type – that is, each question will also give a series of possible answers: A, B, C or D, and you are called upon to select the best answer and write the letter next to that answer on your answer paper – it is advisable to start answering each question in turn. There may be anywhere from 50 to 100 such questions in the three or four hours allotted and you can see how much time would be taken if you read through all the questions before beginning to answer any. Furthermore, if you come across a question or group of questions which you know would be difficult to answer, it would undoubtedly affect your handling of all the other questions.

4) If the examination is of the essay type and contains but a few questions, it is a moot point as to whether you should read all the questions before starting to answer any one. Of course, if you are given a choice – say five out of seven and the like – then it is essential to read all the questions so you can eliminate the two that are most difficult. If, however, you are asked to answer all the questions, there may be danger in trying to answer the easiest one first because you may find that you will spend too much time on it. The best technique is to answer the first question, then proceed to the second, etc.

5) Time your answers. Before the exam begins, write down the time it started, then add the time allowed for the examination and write down the time it must be completed, then divide the time available somewhat as follows:

- If 3-1/2 hours are allowed, that would be 210 minutes. If you have 80 objective-type questions, that would be an average of 2-1/2 minutes per question. Allow yourself no more than 2 minutes per question, or a total of 160 minutes, which will permit about 50 minutes to review.
- If for the time allotment of 210 minutes there are 7 essay questions to answer, that would average about 30 minutes a question. Give yourself only 25 minutes per question so that you have about 35 minutes to review.

6) The most important instruction is to *read each question* and make sure you know what is wanted. The second most important instruction is to *time yourself properly* so that you answer every question. The third most important instruction is to *answer every question*. Guess if you have to but include something for each question. Remember that you will receive no credit for a blank and will probably receive some credit if you write something in answer to an essay question. If you guess a letter – say "B" for a multiple-choice question – you may have guessed right. If you leave a blank as an answer to a multiple-choice question, the examiners may respect your feelings but it will not add a point to your score. Some exams may penalize you for wrong answers, so in such cases *only*, you may not want to guess unless you have some basis for your answer.

7) Suggestions
   a. Objective-type questions
      1. Examine the question booklet for proper sequence of pages and questions
      2. Read all instructions carefully
      3. Skip any question which seems too difficult; return to it after all other questions have been answered
      4. Apportion your time properly; do not spend too much time on any single question or group of questions
      5. Note and underline key words – *all, most, fewest, least, best, worst, same, opposite,* etc.
      6. Pay particular attention to negatives
      7. Note unusual option, e.g., unduly long, short, complex, different or similar in content to the body of the question
      8. Observe the use of "hedging" words – *probably, may, most likely,* etc.
      9. Make sure that your answer is put next to the same number as the question
      10. Do not second-guess unless you have good reason to believe the second answer is definitely more correct
      11. Cross out original answer if you decide another answer is more accurate; do not erase until you are ready to hand your paper in
      12. Answer all questions; guess unless instructed otherwise
      13. Leave time for review

   b. Essay questions
      1. Read each question carefully
      2. Determine exactly what is wanted. Underline key words or phrases.
      3. Decide on outline or paragraph answer

4. Include many different points and elements unless asked to develop any one or two points or elements
5. Show impartiality by giving pros and cons unless directed to select one side only
6. Make and write down any assumptions you find necessary to answer the questions
7. Watch your English, grammar, punctuation and choice of words
8. Time your answers; don't crowd material

8) Answering the essay question

Most essay questions can be answered by framing the specific response around several key words or ideas. Here are a few such key words or ideas:

M's: manpower, materials, methods, money, management
P's: purpose, program, policy, plan, procedure, practice, problems, pitfalls, personnel, public relations

a. Six basic steps in handling problems:
   1. Preliminary plan and background development
   2. Collect information, data and facts
   3. Analyze and interpret information, data and facts
   4. Analyze and develop solutions as well as make recommendations
   5. Prepare report and sell recommendations
   6. Install recommendations and follow up effectiveness

b. Pitfalls to avoid
   1. *Taking things for granted* – A statement of the situation does not necessarily imply that each of the elements is necessarily true; for example, a complaint may be invalid and biased so that all that can be taken for granted is that a complaint has been registered
   2. *Considering only one side of a situation* – Wherever possible, indicate several alternatives and then point out the reasons you selected the best one
   3. *Failing to indicate follow up* – Whenever your answer indicates action on your part, make certain that you will take proper follow-up action to see how successful your recommendations, procedures or actions turn out to be
   4. *Taking too long in answering any single question* – Remember to time your answers properly

IX. AFTER THE TEST

Scoring procedures differ in detail among civil service jurisdictions although the general principles are the same. Whether the papers are hand-scored or graded by machine we have described, they are nearly always graded by number. That is, the person who marks the paper knows only the number – never the name – of the applicant. Not until all the papers have been graded will they be matched with names. If other tests, such as training and experience or oral interview ratings have been given, scores will be combined. Different parts of the examination usually have different weights. For example, the written test might count 60 percent of the final grade, and a rating of training and experience 40 percent. In many jurisdictions, veterans will have a certain number of points added to their grades.

After the final grade has been determined, the names are placed in grade order and an eligible list is established. There are various methods for resolving ties between those who get the same final grade – probably the most common is to place first the name of the person whose application was received first. Job offers are made from the eligible list in the order the names appear on it. You will be notified of your grade and your rank as soon as all these computations have been made. This will be done as rapidly as possible.

People who are found to meet the requirements in the announcement are called "eligibles." Their names are put on a list of eligible candidates. An eligible's chances of getting a job depend on how high he stands on this list and how fast agencies are filling jobs from the list.

When a job is to be filled from a list of eligibles, the agency asks for the names of people on the list of eligibles for that job. When the civil service commission receives this request, it sends to the agency the names of the three people highest on this list. Or, if the job to be filled has specialized requirements, the office sends the agency the names of the top three persons who meet these requirements from the general list.

The appointing officer makes a choice from among the three people whose names were sent to him. If the selected person accepts the appointment, the names of the others are put back on the list to be considered for future openings.

That is the rule in hiring from all kinds of eligible lists, whether they are for typist, carpenter, chemist, or something else. For every vacancy, the appointing officer has his choice of any one of the top three eligibles on the list. This explains why the person whose name is on top of the list sometimes does not get an appointment when some of the persons lower on the list do. If the appointing officer chooses the second or third eligible, the No. 1 eligible does not get a job at once, but stays on the list until he is appointed or the list is terminated.

X. HOW TO PASS THE INTERVIEW TEST

The examination for which you applied requires an oral interview test. You have already taken the written test and you are now being called for the interview test – the final part of the formal examination.

You may think that it is not possible to prepare for an interview test and that there are no procedures to follow during an interview. Our purpose is to point out some things you can do in advance that will help you and some good rules to follow and pitfalls to avoid while you are being interviewed.

What is an interview supposed to test?
The written examination is designed to test the technical knowledge and competence of the candidate; the oral is designed to evaluate intangible qualities, not readily measured otherwise, and to establish a list showing the relative fitness of each candidate – as measured against his competitors – for the position sought. Scoring is not on the basis of "right" and "wrong," but on a sliding scale of values ranging from "not passable" to "outstanding." As a matter of fact, it is possible to achieve a relatively low score without a single "incorrect" answer because of evident weakness in the qualities being measured.

Occasionally, an examination may consist entirely of an oral test – either an individual or a group oral. In such cases, information is sought concerning the technical knowledges and abilities of the candidate, since there has been no written examination for this purpose. More commonly, however, an oral test is used to supplement a written examination.

Who conducts interviews?

The composition of oral boards varies among different jurisdictions. In nearly all, a representative of the personnel department serves as chairman. One of the members of the board may be a representative of the department in which the candidate would work. In some cases, "outside experts" are used, and, frequently, a businessman or some other representative of the general public is asked to serve. Labor and management or other special groups may be represented. The aim is to secure the services of experts in the appropriate field.

However the board is composed, it is a good idea (and not at all improper or unethical) to ascertain in advance of the interview who the members are and what groups they represent. When you are introduced to them, you will have some idea of their backgrounds and interests, and at least you will not stutter and stammer over their names.

What should be done before the interview?

While knowledge about the board members is useful and takes some of the surprise element out of the interview, there is other preparation which is more substantive. It *is* possible to prepare for an oral interview – in several ways:

1) Keep a copy of your application and review it carefully before the interview

This may be the only document before the oral board, and the starting point of the interview. Know what education and experience you have listed there, and the sequence and dates of all of it. Sometimes the board will ask you to review the highlights of your experience for them; you should not have to hem and haw doing it.

2) Study the class specification and the examination announcement

Usually, the oral board has one or both of these to guide them. The qualities, characteristics or knowledges required by the position sought are stated in these documents. They offer valuable clues as to the nature of the oral interview. For example, if the job involves supervisory responsibilities, the announcement will usually indicate that knowledge of modern supervisory methods and the qualifications of the candidate as a supervisor will be tested. If so, you can expect such questions, frequently in the form of a hypothetical situation which you are expected to solve. NEVER go into an oral without knowledge of the duties and responsibilities of the job you seek.

3) Think through each qualification required

Try to visualize the kind of questions you would ask if you were a board member. How well could you answer them? Try especially to appraise your own knowledge and background in each area, *measured against the job sought*, and identify any areas in which you are weak. Be critical and realistic – do not flatter yourself.

4) Do some general reading in areas in which you feel you may be weak

For example, if the job involves supervision and your past experience has NOT, some general reading in supervisory methods and practices, particularly in the field of human relations, might be useful. Do NOT study agency procedures or detailed manuals. The oral board will be testing your understanding and capacity, not your memory.

5) Get a good night's sleep and watch your general health and mental attitude

You will want a clear head at the interview. Take care of a cold or any other minor ailment, and of course, no hangovers.

What should be done on the day of the interview?

Now comes the day of the interview itself. Give yourself plenty of time to get there. Plan to arrive somewhat ahead of the scheduled time, particularly if your appointment is in the fore part of the day. If a previous candidate fails to appear, the board might be ready for you a bit early. By early afternoon an oral board is almost invariably behind schedule if there are many candidates, and you may have to wait. Take along a book or magazine to read, or your application to review, but leave any extraneous material in the waiting room when you go in for your interview. In any event, relax and compose yourself.

The matter of dress is important. The board is forming impressions about you – from your experience, your manners, your attitude, and your appearance. Give your personal appearance careful attention. Dress your best, but not your flashiest. Choose conservative, appropriate clothing, and be sure it is immaculate. This is a business interview, and your appearance should indicate that you regard it as such. Besides, being well groomed and properly dressed will help boost your confidence.

Sooner or later, someone will call your name and escort you into the interview room. *This is it.* From here on you are on your own. It is too late for any more preparation. But remember, you asked for this opportunity to prove your fitness, and you are here because your request was granted.

What happens when you go in?

The usual sequence of events will be as follows: The clerk (who is often the board stenographer) will introduce you to the chairman of the oral board, who will introduce you to the other members of the board. Acknowledge the introductions before you sit down. Do not be surprised if you find a microphone facing you or a stenotypist sitting by. Oral interviews are usually recorded in the event of an appeal or other review.

Usually the chairman of the board will open the interview by reviewing the highlights of your education and work experience from your application – primarily for the benefit of the other members of the board, as well as to get the material into the record. Do not interrupt or comment unless there is an error or significant misinterpretation; if that is the case, do not hesitate. But do not quibble about insignificant matters. Also, he will usually ask you some question about your education, experience or your present job – partly to get you to start talking and to establish the interviewing "rapport." He may start the actual questioning, or turn it over to one of the other members. Frequently, each member undertakes the questioning on a particular area, one in which he is perhaps most competent, so you can expect each member to participate in the examination. Because time is limited, you may also expect some rather abrupt switches in the direction the questioning takes, so do not be upset by it. Normally, a board member will not pursue a single line of questioning unless he discovers a particular strength or weakness.

After each member has participated, the chairman will usually ask whether any member has any further questions, then will ask you if you have anything you wish to add. Unless you are expecting this question, it may floor you. Worse, it may start you off on an extended, extemporaneous speech. The board is not usually seeking more information. The question is principally to offer you a last opportunity to present further qualifications or to indicate that you have nothing to add. So, if you feel that a significant qualification or characteristic has been overlooked, it is proper to point it out in a sentence or so. Do not compliment the board on the thoroughness of their examination – they have been sketchy, and you know it. If you wish, merely say, "No thank you, I have nothing further to add." This is a point where you can "talk yourself out" of a good impression or fail to present an important bit of information. Remember, *you close the interview yourself.*

The chairman will then say, "That is all, Mr. _____, thank you." Do not be startled; the interview is over, and quicker than you think. Thank him, gather your belongings and take your leave. Save your sigh of relief for the other side of the door.

How to put your best foot forward

Throughout this entire process, you may feel that the board individually and collectively is trying to pierce your defenses, seek out your hidden weaknesses and embarrass and confuse you. Actually, this is not true. They are obliged to make an appraisal of your qualifications for the job you are seeking, and they want to see you in your best light. Remember, they must interview all candidates and a non-cooperative candidate may become a failure in spite of their best efforts to bring out his qualifications. Here are 15 suggestions that will help you:

1) Be natural – Keep your attitude confident, not cocky

If you are not confident that you can do the job, do not expect the board to be. Do not apologize for your weaknesses, try to bring out your strong points. The board is interested in a positive, not negative, presentation. Cockiness will antagonize any board member and make him wonder if you are covering up a weakness by a false show of strength.

2) Get comfortable, but don't lounge or sprawl

Sit erectly but not stiffly. A careless posture may lead the board to conclude that you are careless in other things, or at least that you are not impressed by the importance of the occasion. Either conclusion is natural, even if incorrect. Do not fuss with your clothing, a pencil or an ashtray. Your hands may occasionally be useful to emphasize a point; do not let them become a point of distraction.

3) Do not wisecrack or make small talk

This is a serious situation, and your attitude should show that you consider it as such. Further, the time of the board is limited – they do not want to waste it, and neither should you.

4) Do not exaggerate your experience or abilities

In the first place, from information in the application or other interviews and sources, the board may know more about you than you think. Secondly, you probably will not get away with it. An experienced board is rather adept at spotting such a situation, so do not take the chance.

5) If you know a board member, do not make a point of it, yet do not hide it

Certainly you are not fooling him, and probably not the other members of the board. Do not try to take advantage of your acquaintanceship – it will probably do you little good.

6) Do not dominate the interview

Let the board do that. They will give you the clues – do not assume that you have to do all the talking. Realize that the board has a number of questions to ask you, and do not try to take up all the interview time by showing off your extensive knowledge of the answer to the first one.

7) Be attentive

You only have 20 minutes or so, and you should keep your attention at its sharpest throughout. When a member is addressing a problem or question to you, give him your undivided attention. Address your reply principally to him, but do not exclude the other board members.

8) Do not interrupt

A board member may be stating a problem for you to analyze. He will ask you a question when the time comes. Let him state the problem, and wait for the question.

9) Make sure you understand the question

Do not try to answer until you are sure what the question is. If it is not clear, restate it in your own words or ask the board member to clarify it for you. However, do not haggle about minor elements.

10) Reply promptly but not hastily

A common entry on oral board rating sheets is "candidate responded readily," or "candidate hesitated in replies." Respond as promptly and quickly as you can, but do not jump to a hasty, ill-considered answer.

11) Do not be peremptory in your answers

A brief answer is proper – but do not fire your answer back. That is a losing game from your point of view. The board member can probably ask questions much faster than you can answer them.

12) Do not try to create the answer you think the board member wants

He is interested in what kind of mind you have and how it works – not in playing games. Furthermore, he can usually spot this practice and will actually grade you down on it.

13) Do not switch sides in your reply merely to agree with a board member

Frequently, a member will take a contrary position merely to draw you out and to see if you are willing and able to defend your point of view. Do not start a debate, yet do not surrender a good position. If a position is worth taking, it is worth defending.

14) Do not be afraid to admit an error in judgment if you are shown to be wrong

    The board knows that you are forced to reply without any opportunity for careful consideration. Your answer may be demonstrably wrong. If so, admit it and get on with the interview.

15) Do not dwell at length on your present job

    The opening question may relate to your present assignment. Answer the question but do not go into an extended discussion. You are being examined for a *new* job, not your present one. As a matter of fact, try to phrase ALL your answers in terms of the job for which you are being examined.

Basis of Rating

    Probably you will forget most of these "do's" and "don'ts" when you walk into the oral interview room. Even remembering them all will not ensure you a passing grade. Perhaps you did not have the qualifications in the first place. But remembering them will help you to put your best foot forward, without treading on the toes of the board members.

    Rumor and popular opinion to the contrary notwithstanding, an oral board wants you to make the best appearance possible. They know you are under pressure – but they also want to see how you respond to it as a guide to what your reaction would be under the pressures of the job you seek. They will be influenced by the degree of poise you display, the personal traits you show and the manner in which you respond.

ABOUT THIS BOOK

    This book contains tests divided into Examination Sections. Go through each test, answering every question in the margin. At the end of each test look at the answer key and check your answers. On the ones you got wrong, look at the right answer choice and learn. Do not fill in the answers first. Do not memorize the questions and answers, but understand the answer and principles involved. On your test, the questions will likely be different from the samples. Questions are changed and new ones added. If you understand these past questions you should have success with any changes that arise. Tests may consist of several types of questions. We have additional books on each subject should more study be advisable or necessary for you. Finally, the more you study, the better prepared you will be. This book is intended to be the last thing you study before you walk into the examination room. Prior study of relevant texts is also recommended. NLC publishes some of these in our Fundamental Series. Knowledge and good sense are important factors in passing your exam. Good luck also helps. So now study this Passbook, absorb the material contained within and take that knowledge into the examination. Then do your best to pass that exam.

EXAMINATION SECTION

EXAMINATION SECTION
TEST 1

DIRECTION: Each question or Incomplete statement is followed by several suggested answers or completions. Select the one that BEST answers the question or completes the statement. *PRINT THE LETTER OF THE CORRECT ANSWER IN THE SPACE AT THE RIGHT.*

Questions 1-5.

DIRECTIONS: Column I lists cleaning jobs. Column II lists cleansing agents and devices. Select the PROPER cleansing agent from column II for each job in column I. Place the letter of the cleansing agent select in the space at the right corresponding to the number of the cleaning job.

COLUMN I	COLUMN II
1. Chewing gum	A. Muriatic acid
2. Ink stains	B. Broad bladed knife
3. Fingermarks on glass	C. Kerosene
4. Rust stains on porcelain	D. Oxalic acid
5. Hardened dirt on porcelain	E. Lye
	F. Linseed oil

6. When the bristles of a floor brush have worn short. the brush should be

    A. thrown away and the handles saved
    B. saved and the brush used on rough cement floors
    C. saved and used for high dusting in classrooms
    D. saved and used for the weekly scrubbing of linoleum floors

7. Feather dusters should NOT be used because they

    A. take more time to use than other dusters
    B. cannot be cleaned
    C. do not take up the dust but merely move it from one place to another
    D. do not stir up the dust and streak the furniture with dust rails

8. Floors that are usually NOT waxed are those made of

    A. pine wood   B. mastic tile
    C. rubber tile   D. terrazzo

9. For sweeping under radiators and other inaccessible places, the MOST appropriate tool is the

    A. counter brush   B. dry mop
    C. feather duster   D. 16" floor brush

10. A cleansing agent that should NOT be used in the cleaning of windows is

A. water containing fine pumice
B. water containing a small amount of ammonia
C. water containing a little kerosene
D. a paste cleanser made from water and cleaning powder

11. The BEST way to dust desks is to use a

    A. circular motion with soft dry cloth that has been washed
    B. damp cloth, taking care not to disturb papers on the desk
    C. soft cloth, moistened with oil, using a back and forth motion
    D. back and forth motion with a soft dry cloth

11.____

12. Trisodium phosphate is a substance BEST used In

    A. washing kalsomined walls
    B. polishing of brass
    C. washing mastic tile floors
    D. clearing stoppages

12.____

13. Treated linoleum is PROPERLY cleaned by daily

    A. dusting with a treated mop
    B. sweeping with a floor brush
    C. mopping with a weak soap solution
    D. mopping after removal of dust with a floor brush

13.____

14. Of the following, the MOST proper use for chamois skin is

    A. drying of window glass after washing
    B. washing of window glass
    C. polishing of metal fixtures
    D. drying toilet bowls after washing

14.____

15. A squeegee is a tool which is used in

    A. clearing stoppages in waste lines
    B. the central vacuum cleaning system
    C. cleaning inside boiler surfaces
    D. drying windows after washing

15.____

16. Concrete and cement floors are usually painted a battleship gray color.
    The MOST important reason for painting the floor is

    A. to improve the appearance of the floor
    B. the paint prevents the absorption of too much water when the floor is mopped
    C. the paint makes the floor safer and less slippery
    D. the concrete becomes harder and will not settle

16.____

17. A resin-base floor finish USUALLY

    A. gives the highest lustre of all floor finishes
    B. should be applied in one heavy coat
    C. provides a slip-resistant surface
    D. should not be used on asphalt tile

17.____

18. The one of the following cleaning operations on soft floors that generally requires MOST NEARLY the same amount of time per 1,000 square feet as damp mopping is

   A. applying a thin coat of wax
   B. sweeping
   C. dust mopping
   D. wet mopping

18.____

19. Of the following cleaning jobs, the one that should be allowed the MOST time to complete a 1,000 square foot area is

   A. vacuuming carpets
   B. washing painted walls
   C. stripping and waxing soft floors
   D. machine-scrubbing hard floors

19.____

20. When instructing your staff in the use of sodium silicate, you should tell them that it is MOST commonly used to

   A. seal concrete floors
   B. condition leather
   C. treat boiler water
   D. neutralize acid wastes

20.____

21. Cleaners should be instructed that dust mopping is LEAST appropriate for removing light soil from _____ floors.

   A. terrazzo
   B. unsealed concrete
   C. resin-finished soft
   D. sealed wood

21.____

22. Of the following, the substance that should be recommended for polishing hardwood furniture is

   A. lemon oil polish
   B. neatsfoot oil
   C. paste wax
   D. water-emulsion wax

22.____

23. The use of concentrated acid to remove stains from ceramic tile bathroom floors USUALLY results in making the surface

   A. pitted and porous
   B. clean and shiny
   C. harder and glossier
   D. waterproof

23.____

24. Asphalt tile floors should be protected by coating with

   A. hard-milled soap
   B. water-emulsion wax
   C. sodium metaphosphate
   D. varnish

24.____

25. Of the following, the BEST way to economize on cleaning tools and materials is to

   A. train the cleaners to use them properly
   B. order at least a three-year supply of every item in order to avoid annual price increases
   C. attach a price sticker to every item so that the people using them will realize their high cost
   D. delay ordering material for three months at the beginning of each year to be sure that the old material is used to the fullest extent

25.____

KEY (CORRECT ANSWERS)

1.	B	11.	D
2.	D	12.	C
3.	C	13.	A
4.	A	14.	A
5.	C	15.	D
6.	B	16.	B
7.	C	17.	C
8.	D	18.	A
9.	A	19.	C
10.	A	20.	A

21. B
22. C
23. A
24. B
25. A

TEST 2

DIRECTIONS: Each question or incomplete statement is followed by several suggested answers or completions. Select the one that BEST answers the question or completes the statement. *PRINT THE LETTER OF THE CORRECT ANSWER IN THE SPACE AT THE RIGHT.*

1. Of the following office cleaning jobs performed during the year, the one which should be done MOST frequently is   1.____

   A. cleaning the fluorescent lights
   B. dusting the Venetian blinds
   C. cleaning the bookcase glass
   D. carpetsweeping the rug

2. The BEST polishing agent to use on wood furniture is   2.____

   A. pumice
   B. paste wax
   C. water emulsion wax
   D. neatsfoot oil

3. Lemon oil polish is used BEST to polish   3.____

   A. exterior bronze
   B. marble walls
   C. leather seats
   D. lacquered metal

4. Cleaning with trisodium phosphate is MOST likely to damage   4.____

   A. toilet bowls
   B. drain pipes
   C. polished marble floors
   D. rubber tile floors

5. Of the following cleaning agents, the one which should NOT be used to remove stains from urinals is   5.____

   A. caustic lye
   B. detergent
   C. oxalic acid
   D. muriatic acid

6. The one of the following cleaners which GENERALLY contains an abrasive is   6.____

   A. caustic lye
   B. trisodium phosphate
   C. scouring powder
   D. ammonia

7. The instructions on a box of cleaning powder say: *Mix one pound of cleaning powder in four gallons of water.* According to these instructions, how many ounces of cleaning powder should be mixed in one gallon of water?   7.____

   A. 4   B. 8   C. 12   D. 16

8. In accordance with recommended practice, a dust mop, when not being used, should be stored   8.____

   A. hanging, handle end down
   B. hanging, handle end up
   C. standing on the floor, handle end down
   D. standing on the floor, handle end up

9. The two types of floors found in public buildings are classified as hard floors and soft floors.
An example of a hard floor is one made of

   A. linoleum
   B. cork
   C. ceramic tile
   D. asphalt tile

10. A squeegee is a tool that is MAINLY used to clean

    A. painted walls
    B. radiator covers
    C. window glass
    D. ceramic tile floors

11. The BEST way to determine whether a cleaner is doing his work well is by

    A. observing the cleaner at work for several hours
    B. asking the cleaner questions about the work
    C. asking other cleaners to rate his work
    D. inspecting the cleanliness of the spaces assigned to the cleaner

12. The PRIMARY purpose of using a disinfectant material is to

    A. kill germs
    B. destroy odors
    C. remove stains
    D. kill insects

13. Windows should be washed by using a solution of warm water mixed with

    A. chlorine bleach
    B. kerosene
    C. ammonia
    D. soft soap

14. Of the following, the MOST effective way to reduce waste of cleaning tools is to

    A. keep careful records of how often tools are issued
    B. require that the old tool be returned before issuing a new one
    C. require that all tools be used for a fixed number of hours before replacing them
    D. train the cleaners to use the tools properly

15. The number of square feet of unobstructed corridor floor space that a cleaner should sweep in an hour is MOST NEARLY

    A. 1200   B. 2400   C. 4000   D. 6000

16. Sweeping compound is used on concrete floors MAINLY to

    A. polish the floor
    B. keep the dust down
    C. soften the encrusted dirt
    D. provide a non-slip surface

17. The BEST attachment to use on an electric scrubbing machine when stripping waxed resilient flooring is a

    A. nylon disk
    B. soft brush
    C. steel wool pad
    D. pumice wheel

18. A counter brush is BEST suited to cleaning

    A. water cooler drains
    B. radiators
    C. light fixtures
    D. lavatory fixtures

19. In high dusting of walls and ceilings, the CORRECT procedure is to 19.____

    A. begin with lower walls and process up to the ceiling
    B. remove pictures and window shades only if they are dusty
    C. clean the windows thoroughly before dusting any other part of the room
    D. begin with the ceiling, then dust the walls

20. When cleaning a room, the cleaner should 20.____

    A. dust desks before sweeping
    B. dust desks after sweeeping
    C. open windows wide during the desk dusting process
    D. begin dusting at rows most distant from entrance door

21. Too much water on asphalt tile is objectionable MAINLY because the tile 21.____

    A. will tend to become discolored or spotted
    B. may be loosened from the floor
    C. will be softened and made uneven
    D. colors will tend to run

22. To reduce the slip hazard resulting from waxing linoleum, the MOST practical of the following methods is 22.____

    A. apply the wax in one heavy coat
    B. apply the wax after varnishing the linoleum
    C. buff the wax surface thoroughly
    D. apply the wax in several thin coats

23. Assume that the water emulsion wax needed for routine waxing in your building is 15 gallons per month. This wax is supplied in 55-gallon drums. 23.____
    To cover your needs for a year, the MINIMUM number of drums you would have to request is

    A. two   B. three   C. four   D. six

24. In washing down the walls, the correct procedure is to start at the bottom of the wall and work to the top. 24.____
    The MOST important reason for this is:

    A. Dirt streaking will tend to be avoided or easily removed
    B. Less cleansing agent will be required
    C. Rinse water will not be required
    D. The time for cleaning the wall is less than if washing started at the top of the wall

25. In mopping a wood floor, the cleaner should 25.____

    A. mop against the grain of the wood wherever possible
    B. mop as large an area as possible at one time
    C. wet the floor before mopping with a cleaning agent
    D. mop only aisles and clear areas and use a scrub brush under desks and chairs

KEY (CORRECT ANSWERS)

1. D
2. B
3. A
4. C
5. D

6. C
7. A
8. B
9. C
10. C

11. D
12. A
13. C
14. D
15. D

16. B
17. A
18. B
19. D
20. B

21. B
22. D
23. C
24. A
25. C

TEST 3

DIRECTIONS: Each question or incomplete statement is followed by several suggested answers or completions. Select the one that BEST answers the question or completes the statement. *PRINT THE LETTER OF THE CORRECT ANSWER IN THE SPACE AT THE RIGHT.*

1. The MAIN reason for using a sweeping compound is to 1.____

    A. spot-finish waxed surfaces
    B. retard dust when sweeping floors
    C. loosen accumulations of grease
    D. remove paint spots from tile flooring

2. The one of the following cleaning agents which is recommended for use on marble floors is 2.____

    A. an acid cleaner
    B. a soft soap
    C. trisodium phosphate
    D. a neutral liquid detergent

3. A cleaning solution of one cup of soap chips dissolved in a pail of warm water can be used to wash 3.____

    A. painted walls   B. rubber tile
    C. marble walls   D. terrazzo floors

4. Sodium fluoride is a 4.____

    A. pesticide   B. disinfectant
    C. detergent   D. paint thinner

5. Scratches or burns in linoleum, rubber tile, or cork floors should be removed by rubbing with 5.____

    A. crocus cloth   B. fine steel wool
    C. sandpaper   D. emery cloth

6. A room 12 feet wide by 25 feet long has a floor area of _____ square feet. 6.____

    A. 37   B. 200   C. 300   D. 400

7. A cleaning solution should be applied to a painted wall using a 7.____

    A. wool rag   B. brush   C. sponge   D. squeegee

8. When scrubbing a wooden floor, it is ADVISABLE to 8.____

    A. flood the surface with the cleaning solution in order to float the dirt out of all cracks and crevices
    B. hose off the loosened dirt before starting the scrubbing operation
    C. pick up the cleaning solution as soon as possible
    D. mix a mild acid with the cleaning solution in order to clean the surface quickly

9. How many hours will it take a worker to sweep a floor space of 2800 square feet if he sweeps at the of 800 square feet per hour?

   A. 8   B. $6\frac{1}{2}$ C. $3\frac{1}{2}$ D. $2\frac{1}{2}$

10. One gallon of water contains

    A. 2 quarts   B. 4 quarts   C. 2 pints   D. 4 pints

11. A standard cleaning solution is prepared by mixing 4 ounces of detergent powder in 2 gallons of water. The number of ounces of detergent powder needed for the same strength solution in 5 gallons of water is

    A. 4   B. 6   C. 8   D. 10

12. The principal reason why soap should NOT be used in cleaning windows is
    A. it causes loosening of the putty
    B. it may cause rotting of the wood frames
    C. a film is left on the window, requiring additional rinsing
    D. frequent use of soap will cause the glass to become permanently clouded

13. When a window pane is broken, the FIRST step the custodian takes is to
    A. remove broken glass from floors and the window sill
    B. determine the cause
    C. remove the putty with a putty knife
    D. prepare a piece of glass to replace the broken pane

14. Your instructions to a cleaner about the proper sweeping of offices should include the following Instruction:
    A. Do not move chairs and wastebaskets from their places when sweeping
    B. Place chairs and baskets on the desks to get them out of the way
    C. Set aside the loose small furniture and chairs in an orderly manner when sweeping office floors
    D. Move the desks and chairs to the side of the room close to the wall in order to sweep properly

15. To remove dirt accumulations after the completion of the sweeping task, brushes should be
    A. tapped on the floor in the normal sweeping position
    B. struck on the floor against the side of the block
    C. struck on the floor against the end of the block
    D. turned upside down and the handle tapped on the floor

16. To sweep rough cement floors in a basement, the BEST tool to use is a
    A. deck brush   B. new 30" floor brush
    C. corn broom   D. treated mop

17. When a floor is scrubbed, it is NOT correct to

   A. use a steady, even rotary motion
   B. rinse the floor with clean hot water
   C. have the mop strokes follow the boards when drying the floor
   D. wet the floor first by pouring several bucketsful of water on it

18. Flushing with a hose is MOST appropriate as a method of cleaning

   A. terrazzo floors of corridors
   B. untreated wood floors
   C. linoleum floors where not in frequent use
   D. cement floors

19. Improper use of a carbon dioxide type portable fire extinguisher may cause injury to the operator because

   A. handling the nozzle during discharge can cause frostbite to the skin
   B. carbon dioxide is highly poisonous if breathed into the lungs
   C. use of carbon dioxide on an oil fire can cause a chemical explosion
   D. the powdery residue left by the discharge is highly caustic to the skin

20. When using a portable single ladder with ten rungs, the GREATEST number of rungs that a cleaner should climb up is

   A. 7   B. 8   C. 9   D. 10

21. Of the following types of portable fire extinguishers, the one which should be used to control a fire in or around live electrical equipment is the _____ type.

   A. foam
   B. soda acid
   C. carbon dioxide
   D. gas cartridge water

22. The MOST frequent cause of accidental injuries to workers on the job is

   A. unsafe working practices of employees
   B. poor design of buildings and working areas
   C. lack of warning signs in hazardous work areas
   D. lack of adequate safety guards on equipment and machinery

23. Of the following, the MOST important purpose of preparing an accident report on an injury to a cleaner is to help

   A. collect statistics on different types of accidents
   B. calm the feelings of the injured cleaner
   C. prevent similar accidents in the future
   D. prove that the cleaner was at fault

24. The one of the following types of locks that is used on emergency exit doors is the _____ bolt.

   A. panic   B. dead   C. cinch   D. toggle

25. The one of the following types of locks that USUALLY contains both a live bolt and a dead bolt is a _____ lock.   25._____

    A. mortise
    C. loose pin butt
    B. double-hung window
    D. window frame

KEY (CORRECT ANSWERS)

1.	B	11.	D
2.	D	12.	C
3.	A	13.	A
4.	A	14.	C
5.	B	15.	A
6.	C	16.	C
7.	C	17.	D
8.	C	18.	D
9.	C	19.	A
10.	B	20.	B

21. C
22. A
23. C
24. A
25. A

EXAMINATION SECTION
TEST 1

DIRECTIONS: Each question or incomplete statement is followed by several suggested answers or completions. Select the one that BEST answers the question or completes the Statement. *PRINT THE LETTER OF THE CORRECT ANSWER IN THE SPACE AT THE RIGHT.*

1. Which of the following substances causes asphalt tile to turn spongy? 1.____
   A. Oil B. Varnish C. Water D. Dust

2. Which of the following would NOT cause asphalt tile to turn yellow? 2.____
   A. A layer of dust B. Varnish
   C. Lacquer D. Water

3. Which one of the following is LEAST likely to be an advantage of waxing a floor? 3.____
   A. Helps to make a room quieter
   B. Helps to reduce wear on the floor
   C. Gives a pleasant shine to the floor
   D. Improves the stain resistance of the floor

4. The action of liquid cleaner on a floor with built-up wax is to 4.____
   A. make the wax disappear into the air
   B. turn the wax into little grains that must be swept up in a vacuum cleaner
   C. soften the wax, which has to be scrubbed away and then rinsed off
   D. make the floor waterproof

5. After how many waxings should built-up wax be removed from a floor? Every 5.____
   A. waxing B. 3 waxings C. 6 waxings D. 12 waxings

6. Manuals on floor cleaning describe methods of cleaning *resilient flooring*. Which of the following kinds of flooring surfaces is NOT resilient? _____ tile. 6.____
   A. Cork B. Asphalt C. Vinyl D. Terrazzo

7. In buffing a floor, it is NOT desirable to use a polishing brush because the 7.____
   A. brush will scratch the surface you are trying to polish
   B. strands of the brush fall out easily
   C. brush is often used for other purposes
   D. brush does not usually remove deep scuff marks

8. *Rolling* results when only the upper parts of a wax coat dry, leaving the lower parts wet. In waxing a floor, this condition comes from 8.____
   A. putting on too thick a coat of wax
   B. putting on too thin a coat of wax
   C. rinsing the floor before applying the wax
   D. leaving soap on the floor before applying the wax

13

9. After a cork or linoleum floor is installed, how long should you wait before you mop the floor for the FIRST time?

    A. 1 days   B. 3 days   C. 12 hours   D. 2 weeks

10. On sweeping stairways, you should direct your men to make a practice of sweeping them

    A. when traffic is heavy so that people can see them working
    B. whenever they have free time during the day
    C. during the morning at a time when traffic is lightest
    D. in the middle of the day when the traffic is medium heavy

11. How often must public corridors be swept?

    A. Only when a visible amount of dirt piles up
    B. Every day
    C. Once a week
    D. Every three days

12. You should NOT use an oily mop to sweep floor because it

    A. leaves a sticky film that can catch dust
    B. eats away at the floor like acid
    C. makes the floor completely waterproof
    D. prevents wax from being applied

13. Which of the following would NOT be used on a concrete floor?

    A. Water base wax   B. Oily sweeping compound
    C. Solvent wax   D. Wire brush

14. You should NOT use an alkaline cleaner on linoleum floors because the cleaner

    A. will make the floor shine too brightly
    B. makes the linoleum sticky
    C. makes the linoleum crack and curl
    D. costs too much to be practical

15. The BEST way of wet mopping a large floor area is to mop the floor area

    A. with a circular motion
    B. from side to side or with a figure eight motion
    C. with forward and back strokes
    D. alternate side to side forward and back

16. The type of product to use when cleaning terrazzo floors is

    A. mild cleaner   B. diluted acid solution
    C. scouring powder   D. paste wax

17. A cleaner was wet mopping an asphalt tile floor. He decided to make the floor as wet as possible.
For him to do this is a

   A. *good* idea, because the more water you use, the cleaner the floor will be
   B. *bad* idea, because water should never be wasted
   C. *good* idea, because the floor will not have to be washed as often
   D. *bad* idea, because the excess water will eventually damage the floor surface

17.____

18. When you wet clean a stairway by hand, you need two buckets.
One of them is for the cleaning solution, and the other one is used for

   A. extra ammonia for cleaning
   B. rinsing, and should be filled with clean water
   C. putting out fires, and should be filled with sand
   D. storage of equipment

18.____

19. The cleaning of stairways is USUALLY scheduled to be done with

   A. corridor cleaning
   B. sidewalk cleaning
   C. incinerator work
   D. move-outs

19.____

20. *Dry cleaning* in relation to a building refers to

   A. a reconditioning process that restores the appearance of a floor and protects the surface by buffing
   B. dusting of a wall area with specially treated cloth in order to produce a sheen
   C. patch waxing of a floor with a powdered wax compound
   D. dry mopping only of a floor area

20.____

Questions 21-24.

DIRECTION: Questions 21 through 24, inclusive, are to be answered SOLELY on the basis of the following paragraph.

All cleaning agents and supplies should be kept in a central storeroom which should be kept locked and only the custodian, store keeper, and foreman should have keys. Shelving should be provided for the smaller items, while barrels containing scouring powder or other bulk material should be set on the floor or on special cradles. Each compartment in the shelves should be marked plainly and only the item indicated stored therein. Each barrel should also be marked plainly. It may also be desirable to keep special items such as electric lamps, flashlight batteries, etc. in a locked cabinet or separate room to which only the custodian and the night building foreman have keys.

21. According to the above paragraph, scouring powder

   A. should be kept on shelves
   B. comes in one-pound cans
   C. should be kept in a locked cabinet
   D. is a bulk material

21.____

15

4 (#1)

22. According to the above paragraph,

    A. the storekeeper should not be entrusted with the safekeeping of lightbulbs
    B. flashlight batteries should be stored in barrels
    C. the central storeroom should be kept locked
    D. only special items should be stored under lock and key

23. According to the above paragraph,

    A. each shelf compartment should contain at least four different Items
    B. barrels must be stored in cradles
    C. all items stored should be in marked compartments
    D. crates of lightbulbs should be stored in cradles

24. As used In the above paragraph, the word *cradle* means a

    A. dolly   B. support
    C. doll's bed   D. hand truck

25. The material recommended for removing blood or fruit stains from concrete is

    A. soft soap   B. neatsfoot oil
    C. oxalic acid   D. ammonia

KEY (CORRECT ANSWER)

1.	A	11.	B
2.	A	12.	A
3.	A	13.	B
4.	C	14.	C
5.	C	15.	B
6.	D	16.	A
7.	D	17.	D
8.	A	18.	B
9.	B	19.	A
10.	C	20.	A

21. D
22. C
23. C
24. B
25. D

TEST 2

DIRECTIONS: Each question or incomplete statement is followed by several suggested answers or completions. Select the one that BEST answers the question or completes the statement. *PRINT THE LETTER OF THE CORRECT ANSWER IN THE SPACE AT THE RIGHT.*

1. The wall surface which does NOT have to be washed from the bottom up to avoid streaking is a(n) _____ wall.
   A. semi-gloss painted
   B. enamel painted
   C. glazed tile
   D. unglazed tile

2. The one of the following practices which is GENERALLY recommended to prolong the useful life of a corn broom is
   A. soaking a new broom overnight before using it for the first time to remove brittleness
   B. storing the broom with the tips of the straws resting on the floor to keep the edges even
   C. keeping the straws moistened when sweeping
   D. storing the broom in a warm humid enclosure to prevent drying of the bristles

3. While a cleaner is sweeping the public corridors and stairways, he notices some crayon marks on walls and stains on the floors.
   He should
   A. stop sweeping and remove the stains immediately
   B. finish sweeping and then return to remove the stains
   C. make note of the marks and stains in his building and remove them once a month
   D. make a note of the marks and stains and report them to the superintendent so that the cause can be eliminated before the stains are removed

4. When transporting the equipment required for mopping stairhalls and corridors, a cleaner should NOT
   A. attempt to do it alone
   B. carry water in the pails because spillage may cause a tenant to slip and fall
   C. use the elevator
   D. carry the equipment in both hands when climbing stairs

5. A cleaner should apply washing solution to a portion of a painted wall and should rinse the same area before applying the solution to another area.
   In order to allow sufficient time for the solution to take effect on the soil, the area covered each time should be APPROXIMATELY _____ square feet.
   A. 20   B. 60   C. 160   D. 600

6. Asphalt tile floors should be maintained by coating them with
   A. water emulsion wax
   B. paste wax
   C. oil emulsion wax
   D. neatsfoot oil

1.____
2.____
3.____
4.____
5.____
6.____

7. The broom with which a cleaner should sweep an asphalt-paved playground is the _____ broom.

   A. hair   B. corn   C. garage   D. Scotch

8. The central vacuum cleaning system should be cleaned

   A. weekly
   B. twice weekly
   C. daily
   D. when necessary

9. The FIRST thing a window cleaner should do is

   A. test window bolts
   B. see that cleaning tools are good
   C. cheak window belt
   D. nit lean too heavily on glass

10. During a shortage of custodial help in a public building, the cleaning task which will probably receive LEAST attention is

    A. picking up sweepings
    B. emptying ashtrays
    C. washing walls
    D. dust-mopping offices

11. Of the following substances commonly used on floors, the MOST flammable is

    A. resin-based floor finish
    B. floor sealer
    C. water emulsion wax
    D. trisodium phosphate

12. The MOST effective method for cleaning badly soiled carpeting is

    A. wet shampooing
    B. vacuum cleaning
    C. dry shampooing
    D. wire brushing

13. Painted walls and ceilings should be brushed down

    A. daily
    B. weekly
    C. every month, especially during the winter
    D. two or three times a year

14. If an asphalt tile floor become excessively dirty, the method of cleaning should include

    A. the use of kerosene or benzine as a solvent
    B. the use of a solution of modified laundry soda
    C. sanding down the spotted areas with a sanding machine on the wet floor
    D. use of a light oil and treated mop

15. To remove light stains from marble walls, the BEST method is to

    A. use steel wool and a scouring powder, then rinse with clear warm water
    B. was the stained area with a dilute acid solution
    C. sand down the spot first, then wash with mild soap solution
    D. wet marble first, then scrub with mild soap solution using a soft fiber brush

16. To rid a toilet room of objectionable odors, the PROPER method is to

   A. spread some chloride of lime on the floor
   B. place deodorizer cubes in a box hung on the wall
   C. wash the floor with hot water containing a little kerosene
   D. wash the floor with hot water into which some disinfectant has been poured

17. Toilet rooms, to be cleaned properly, should be swept

   A. daily
   B. and mopped daily
   C. daily and mopped twice a week
   D. daily and mopped thoroughly at the end of the

18. In waxing a floor, it is usually BEST to

   A. start the waxing under stationary furniture and then do the aisles
   B. pour the wax on the floor, spreading it under the desks with a wax mop
   C. remove the old wax coat before rewaxing
   D. wet mop the floor after the second coat has dried to obtain a high polish

19. Of the following, the MOST important reason why a wet mop should NOT be wrung out by hand is that

   A. the strings of the mop will be damaged by hand-wringing
   B. sharp objects picked up by the mop may injure the hands
   C. the mop cannot be made dry enough by hand-wringing
   D. fine dirt will become embedded in the strings of the mop

20. When a painted wall is washed by hand, the wall should be washed from the

   A. top down, with a soaking wet sponge
   B. bottom up, with a soaking wet sponge
   C. top down, with a damp sponge
   D. bottom up, with a damp sponge

21. When a painted wall is brushed with a clean lambswool duster, the duster should be drawn _____ with a _____ pressure.

   A. downward; light
   B. upward; light
   C. downward; firm
   D. upward; firm

22. The one of the following terms which BEST describes the size of a floor brush is

   A. 72 cubic inch
   B. 32 ounce
   C. 24 inch
   D. 10 square foot

23. Terrazzo floors should be mopped periodically with a(n)

   A. acid solution
   B. neutral detergent in warm water
   C. mop treated with kerosene
   D. strong alkaline solution

24. The MAIN reason why the handle of a reversible floor brush should be shifted from one side of the brush block to the opposite side is to

    A. change the angle at which the brush sweeps the floor
    B. give equal wear to both sides of the brush
    C. permit the brush to sweep hard-to-reach areas
    D. make it easier to sweep backward

24.____

25. When a long corridor is swept with a floor brush, it is good practice to

    A. push the brush with moderately long strokes and flick it after each stroke
    B. press on the brush and push it the whole length of the corridor in one sweep
    C. pull the brush inward with short, brisk strokes
    D. sweep across rather than down the length of the corridor

25.____

KEY (CORRECT ANSWERS)

1.	C	11.	B
2.	A	12.	A
3.	B	13.	D
4.	D	14.	D
5.	C	15.	D
6.	A	16.	D
7.	C	17.	B
8.	B	18.	A
9.	C	19.	B
10.	C	20.	D

21. A
22. C
23. B
24. B
25. A

TEST 3

DIRECTIONS: Each question or incomplete statement is followed by several suggested answers or completions. Select the one that BEST answers the question or completes the Statement. *PRINT THE LETTER OF THE CORRECT ANSWER IN THE SPACE AT THE RIGHT.*

1. The MOST common cause of slipperiness of a terrazzo floor after it has been washed is the

    A. failure to rinse the floor clean of the cleaning agent
    B. destruction of the floor seal by the cleaning agent
    C. incomplete removal of dirt from the floor
    D. use of oil in the cleaning process

    1._____

2. When electric lighting fixtures are washed, a precaution that should be observed is:

    A. The metal part of the fixture should be washed with a warm mild ammonia solution
    B. Holding screws of the glass globe should be loosened about one-half turn after they have all been applied to the cleaned globe
    C. Trisodium phosphate should not be used in washing glass globes because it dulls the glass
    D. Chain links of the fixture should be loosened to enable removal of the entire fixture for cleaning

    2._____

3. A cleaner will make the BEST impression on the office staff if he

    A. impresses them with the importance of his job
    B. says little and is cold and distant
    C. is easy-going and good-natured
    D. is courteous and performs his duties with as little delay as possible

    3._____

4. If it is necessary to wash stairways, this should be done during the

    A. day
    B. night
    C. weekend
    D. morning rush hour

    4._____

5. A detergent is GENERALLY used in

    A. waterproofing walls
    B. killing crabgrass
    C. cleaning floor and walls
    D. exterminating rodents

    5._____

6. Many new products are used in new buildings for floors, walls, and other surfaces. A cleaner should determine the BEST procedure to be used to clean such new surfaces by

    A. referring to the manual of procedures
    B. obtaining information on the cleaning procedure from the manufacturer
    C. asking the advice of the mechanics who installed the new material
    D. asking the district supervisor how to clean the surfaces

    6._____

7. A window cleaner should carefully examine his safety belt

    A. once a week
    B. before he puts it on each time
    C. once a month
    D. once before he enters a building

    7._____

8. One of your cleaners was injured as a result of slipping on an oily floor. This type of accident is MOST likely due to

   A. defective equipment
   B. the physical condition of the cleaner
   C. failure to use proper safety appliances
   D. poor housekeeping

9. For wet mopping the floor of a corridor by hand, the MINIMUM number of pails needed is

   A. one   B. two   C. three   D. four

10. A comparison of wet mopping by hand with scrubbing by hand indicates that mopping

    A. needs more cleaning solution
    B. is more time-consuming
    C. requires twice as much water
    D. is less effective on hardened soil

11. Chrome fixtures should be cleaned by

    A. using a mild soap solution then polishing with a soft cloth
    B. dusting lightly, then wax with an oil base wax
    C. polishing with a scouring pad
    D. washing with a solution of water and ammonia, then rinsing with a detergent

12. The BEST way for a building custodian to tell if the night cleaners have done their work well is to check

    A. on how much cleaning material has been used
    B. on how much wastepaper was collected
    C. the building for cleanliness
    D. the floor mops to see if they are still wet

13. THe one of the following items which ordinarily requires the MOST time to wash is a(n)

    A. 5 ft x 10 ft. Venetian blind
    B. 4 ft fluorescent fixture
    C. incandescent fixture
    D. 5 ft x 10 ft ceramic tile floor

14. A broom that has been properly used should GENERALLY be replaced after

    A. it has been used for one month
    B. its bristles have been worn down by more than one-third of their original length
    C. it has been used for two months
    D. its bristles have been worn down by more than two-thirds of their original length

15. Carbon tetrachloride is NOT recommended for cleaning purposes because of

    A. the poisonous nature of its fumes
    B. its limited cleaning value
    C. the damaging effects it has on equipment
    D. the difficulty of application

16. Proper care of floor brushes includes

    A. washing brushes daily after each use with warm soap solution
    B. dipping brushes in kerosene periodically to remove dirt
    C. washing with warm soap solution at least once a month
    D. avoiding contact with soap or soda solutions to prevent drying of bristles

17. Of the following, the cleaning assignment which you would LEAST prefer to have performed during school hours is

    A. sweeping of corridors and stairs
    B. cleaning and polishing of brass fixtures
    C. cleaning toilets
    D. dusting of offices, halls, and special rooms

18. A cleaning detergent is composed of

    A. cleaning acids   B. salts
    C. sodium compounds   D. alkaline compounds

19. Neatsfoot oil is commonly used to

    A. oil light machinery
    B. prepare sweeping compound
    C. clean metal fixtures
    D. treat leather-covered chairs

20. The one of the following terms which BEST describes the size of a floor mop is

    A. 10 quart   B. 32 ounce
    C. 24 inch O.D.   D. 10 square feet

21. Cleaners will USUALLY be motivated to do a good job by a custodian who

    A. lets them get away with poor performance
    B. treats them fairly
    C. treats some of them more favorably than others
    D. lets them take a nap in the afternoon

22. When changing brushes on a scrubbing machine, of the following, the FIRST step to take is to

    A. lock the switch in the *off* position
    B. be sure the power cable electric plug supplying the machine is disconnected from the wall outlet
    C. place the machine on top of the positioned brushes
    D. dip the brushes in water

23. The BEST method or tool to use for cleaning dust from an unplastered cinderblock wall is

    A. a tampico brush with stock cleaning solution
    B. a vacuum cleaner
    C. water under pressure from hose and nozzle
    D. a feather duster

24. The BEST reason for cleaning lightbulbs is 24.____
    A. the bulb willlast longer
    B. removing dust
    C. obtaining optimum light
    D. preventing electrical shock

25. Effluorescence may BEST be removed from brickwork by washing with a solution of _____ acid. 25.____
    A. muriatic   B. citric   C. carbonic   D. nitric

KEY (CORRECT ANSWERS)

1.	A	11.	A
2.	B	12.	C
3.	D	13.	A
4.	C	14.	B
5.	C	15.	A
6.	B	16.	C
7.	B	17.	C
8.	D	18.	C
9.	B	19.	D
10.	D	20.	B

21. B
22. B
23. B
24. C
25. A

EXAMINATION SECTION
TEST 1

DIRECTIONS: Each question or incomplete statement is followed by several suggested answers or completions. Select the one that BEST answers the question or completes the statement. *PRINT THE LETTER OF THE CORRECT ANSWER IN THE SPACE AT THE RIGHT.*

1. Of the following, the FIRST thing a custodian should do when he enters the boiler room to check on the operation of the boiler is to

   A. check the boiler water level
   B. blow down the boiler
   C. check the boiler water temperature
   D. check the fuel supply

   1.____

2. Cleaners will usually be motivated to do a GOOD job by a custodian who

   A. lets them get away with poor performance
   B. treats them fairly
   C. treats some of them more favorably than others
   D. lets them take a nap in the afternoon

   2.____

3. The MOST important aim of a training program in fire prevention is to train the custodial staff to

   A. be constantly alert to fire hazards
   B. assist the city fire department in extinguishing fires
   C. maintain the sprinkler system
   D. climb ladders safely

   3.____

4. The one of the following which is NOT recommended for prolonging the useful life of a hair broom is to

   A. rotate the brush to avoid wear on one side only
   B. wash the brush by using it as a mop once a week
   C. comb the brush weekly
   D. hang the brush in storage to avoid resting on the bristles

   4.____

5. A GOOD indication of the quality of the cleaning operation in a building is the

   A. amount of cleaning material used each month
   B. number of cleaners employed
   C. number of complaints of unsanitary conditions received
   D. number of square feet of hall space cleaned daily

   5.____

6. Spontaneous ignition is MOST likely to occur in a

   A. pile of oily rags
   B. vented fuel oil tank
   C. metal file cabinet filled with papers in file folders
   D. covered metal container containing clean rags

   6.____

7. A boiler test kit is used to test

   A. boiler water
   B. fuel oil
   C. pressure gauges
   D. steam consumption

8. The MOST common cause of a dripping faucet is a

   A. broken stem
   B. cracked bonnet
   C. worn washer
   D. loose retaining screw on the handle

9. The lighting systems in public buildings usually operate MOST NEARLY on _____ volts.

   A. 6   B. 24   C. 115   D. 220

10. A type of hammer which can be used to remove nails from wood is the

    A. ball-peen   B. mallet   C. sledge   D. claw

11. A vacuum pump is used in a(n) _____ heating system.

    A. steam
    B. hot air
    C. hot water
    D. electric

12. An expansion tank is used in a(n) heating system.

    A. steam
    B. hot air
    C. hot water
    D. electric

13. The thermostat in the office area of a public building should have a winter daytime setting of about _____ ° F.

    A. 50   B. 60   C. 70   D. 80

14. The fuel oil which USUALLY requires preheating before it enters an oil burner is known as

    A. #1   B. #2   C. #4   D. #6

15. The domestic hot water in a large public building is circulated by

    A. gravity flow
    B. a pump which runs continuously
    C. a pump which is controlled by water pressure
    D. a pump which is controlled by water temperature

16. The vaporstat on a rotary-cup boil burner senses

    A. oil temperature
    B. primary air pressure
    C. secondary air pressure
    D. oil pressure

17. The emergency switch for a fully automatic oil burner is USUALLY located

    A. at the entrance to the boiler room
    B. on the burner
    C. at the electrical distribution panel in the boiler room
    D. at the electric service meter panel

18. The try-cocks on a steam boiler are used to 18.____

   A. drain the boiler
   B. check the operation of the safety valves
   C. check the water level in the boiler
   D. drain the pressure gauge

19. The draft in a natural draft furnace is USUALLY measured in 19.____

   A. pounds B. inches of mercury
   C. inches of water D. cubic feet

20. The stack temperature in a low pressure oil-fired steam boiler installation should be about _____ ° F. 20.____

   A. 212 B. 275 C. 350 D. 875

21. A material that transmits heat VERY POORLY is a good 21.____

   A. insulator B. conductor
   C. radiator D. convector

22. The asbestos covering on steam lines 22.____

   A. increases the flow of steam
   B. reduces the loss of heat
   C. increases the loss of heat
   D. prevents leaks

23. The air in a closed room that is heated by a radiator USUALLY 23.____

   A. settles to the floor B. rises
   C. remains stationary D. contracts

24. A gallon of water which is changed to steam at atmosphere pressure will increase in volume about _____ times. 24.____

   A. 5 B. 15 C. 150 D. 1500

25. The humidity of the air means its 25.____

   A. clarity B. weight
   C. dust content D. moisture content

26. The safety device which opens automatically to release excessive steam pressure in a boiler is the _____ valve. 26.____

   A. check B. safety
   C. gate D. quick opening

27. Of the following devices, the one which is NOT usually found on a natural draft coal-fired boiler is the 27.____

   A. feedwater regulator B. low-water cutout
   C. safety valve D. water column

28. The number of degree days for two days in the city when the temperature for these two days averages 55° F is

   A. 2 B. 10 C. 20 D. 30

29. A detergent is GENERALLY used in

   A. waterproofing walls
   B. killing crabgrass
   C. cleaning floor and walls
   D. exterminating rodents

30. The MAIN reason for using a sweeping compound is to

   A. spot-finish waxed surfaces
   B. retard dust when sweeping floors
   C. loosen accumulations of grease
   D. remove paint spots from tile flooring

31. The one of the following cleaning agents which is RECOMMENDED for use on marble floors is

   A. an acid cleaner
   B. a soft soap
   C. trisodium phosphate
   D. a neutral liquid detergent

32. A cleaning solution of one cup of soap chips dissolved in a pail of warm water can be used to wash

   A. painted walls   B. rubber tile
   C. marble walls   D. terrazzo floors

33. Sodium fluoride is a

   A. pesticide   B. disinfectant
   C. detergent   D. paint thinner

34. Scratches or burns in linoleum, rubber tile, or cork floors should be removed by rubbing with

   A. crocus cloth   B. fine steel wool
   C. sandpaper   D. emery cloth

35. A room 12 feet wide by 25 feet long has a floor area of _____ square feet.

   A. 37 B. 200 C. 300 D. 400

36. A cleaning solution should be applied to a painted wall using a

   A. wool rag B. brush C. sponge D. squeegee

37. When scrubbing a wooden floor, it is advisable to 37.____
    A. flood the surface with the cleaning solution in order to float the dirt out of all cracks and crevices
    B. hose off the loosened dirt before starting the scrubbing operation
    C. pick up the cleaning solution as soon as possible
    D. mix a mild acid with the cleaning solution in order to clean the surface quickly

38. How many hours will it take a worker to sweep a floor space of 2800 square feet if he sweeps at the rate of 800 square feet per hour? 38.____
    A. 8   B. 6 1/2   C. 3 1/2   D. 2 1/2

39. One gallon of water contains 39.____
    A. 2 quarts   B. 4 quarts   C. 2 pints   D. 4 pints

40. A standard cleaning solution is prepared by mixing 4 ounces of detergent powder in 2 gallons of water. 40.____
    The number of ounces of detergent powder needed, for the same strength solution, in 5 gallons of water is
    A. 4   B. 6   C. 8   D. 10

KEY (CORRECT ANSWERS)

1. A	11. A	21. A	31. D
2. B	12. C	22. B	32. A
3. A	13. C	23. B	33. A
4. B	14. D	24. D	34. B
5. C	15. D	25. D	35. C
6. A	16. B	26. B	36. C
7. A	17. A	27. B	37. C
8. C	18. C	28. C	38. C
9. C	19. C	29. C	39. B
10. D	20. C	30. B	40. D

TEST 2

DIRECTIONS: Each question or incomplete statement is followed by several suggested answers or completions. Select the one that BEST answers the question or completes the statement. *PRINT THE LETTER OF THE CORRECT ANSWER IN THE SPACE AT THE RIGHT.*

1. A custodian should know approximately how long it takes to do each job so that he can 1.____

    A. judge correctly if the person doing the job is working too slowly
    B. tell how much time to take if he has to do it himself
    C. retrain experienced employees in better work habits
    D. tell how much time to dock a worker if he skips that part of the work

2. In order to have building employees willing to follow standardized cleaning procedures, the custodian must be prepared to 2.____

    A. demonstrate the advantages of the procedures
    B. do part of the cleaning work each day until the employees learn the procedures
    C. let the employees go home early if they save time using the procedures
    D. offer incentive pay to encourage their use

3. The BEST agent to use to remove chewing gum from fabric is 3.____

    A. ammonia   B. chlorine bleach
    C. a degreaser   D. water

4. Water emulsion wax should NOT be used on 4.____

    A. linoleum   B. cork tile flooring
    C. furniture   D. rubber tile flooring

5. Tops of desks, file cabinets, and bookcases are BEST dusted with a 5.____

    A. damp cloth   B. treated cotton cloth
    C. damp sponge   D. feather duster

6. The one of the following which is NOT a material used in scrub brushes is 6.____

    A. tampico   B. terrazzo   C. palmetto   D. bassine

7. A chamois is PROPERLY used to 7.____

    A. wash enamel surfaces   B. wash window glass
    C. dry enamel surfaces   D. dry window glass

8. The PROPER sequence of operations used in cleaning an office, when the floor is to be swept with a broom, is 8.____

    A. clean ashtrays, empty wastebaskets, sweep, dust
    B. sweep, dust, clean ashtrays, empty wastebaskets
    C. dust, sweep, clean ashtrays, empty wastebaskets
    D. clean ashtrays, empty wastebaskets, dust, sweep

9. Of the following, the MOST common result of accidents occurring while using hand tools is

   A. loss of limbs
   B. loss of eyesight
   C. infection of wounds
   D. loss of life

10. A twenty-four foot long extension ladder is placed with its top resting against a vertical wall.
    The SAFEST procedure would be to place the base of the ladder a distance from the wall of _____ feet.

    A. 3   B. 6   C. 9   D. 12

11. The one of the following extinguishing agents which should NOT be used on an oil fire is

    A. foam
    B. sand
    C. water
    D. carbon dioxide

12. The extinguishing agent in a portable soda-acid fire extinguisher is

    A. sodium bicarbonate
    B. sulphuric acid
    C. carbon dioxide
    D. water

13. The information on an accident report which is MOST useful toward prevention of similar accidents is the

    A. name of the victim
    B. cause of the accident
    C. type of injury sustained
    D. date of the accident

14. A fusible link is used to

    A. weld two pieces of chain together
    B. solder an electric wire to a terminal
    C. attach a ground wire to a water pipe
    D. hold a fire door open

15. When making up a pipe joint in the shop, between a nipple and a valve, the _____ should be held in a _____ vise and the _____ .

    A. valve; square-jawed; pipe screwed into it
    B. pipe; square-jawed; valve screwed onto it
    C. valve; pipe; pipe screwed into it
    D. pipe; pipe; valve screwed onto it

16. A city water meter is USUALLY read in

    A. pounds
    B. cubic feet
    C. pounds per square inch
    D. degrees

17. The valve which AUTOMATICALLY prevents back flow in a water pipe is called a _____ valve.

    A. check   B. globe   C. gate   D. by-pass

18. The BEST wrench to use to tighten a galvanized iron pipe valve or fitting which has hexagonal ends is _____ wrench.

    A. stillson   B. strap   C. monkey   D. socket

19. A flushometer would be connected to a

    A. water meter   B. toilet bowl
    C. garden hose   D. fire hose

20. Electric service meters are read in

    A. kilowatt hours   B. electrons
    C. amperes   D. volts

21. The device used to reduce the voltage of an electric circuit is the

    A. voltmeter   B. fuse
    C. circuit breaker   D. transformer

22. Ordinary light bulbs are USUALLY rated in

    A. watts   B. ohms   C. amperes   D. filaments

23. The electric plug on a scrubbing machine should be plugged into a

    A. light socket   B. wall outlet
    C. fuse receptacle   D. dimmer switch

24. The device which should be used to connect the output shaft of an electric motor to the input shaft of the centrifugal pump is the

    A. flexible coupling   B. petcock
    C. alemite fitting   D. clutch

25. The type of wood screw which is used to attach a hinge to a door jamb is the _____ screw.

    A. flat head   B. lag
    C. round head   D. square head

26. Of the following bolt sizes, the one which identifies the bolt that has the LARGEST diameter is

    A. 4 - 40   B. 6 - 32   C. 8 - 32   D. 10 - 24

27. The tool MOST commonly used with a mitre box to cut wooden molding is the _____ saw.

    A. hack   B. rip   C. keyhole   D. back

28. The type of lock which can be opened ONLY from the lock side of a door is the

    A. cylinder lock   B. spring latch
    C. padlock   D. mortise lock

29. A key which will open many locks of the same type is USUALLY called a _____ key.

    A. tumbler   B. master   C. magnetic   D. cotter

30. Of the following, the BEST lubricant to use on locks is

    A. grease
    B. graphite
    C. mineral oil
    D. talc

31. A device which allows an exit door to be opened from the inside by pressing on a horizontal bar is known as a

    A. door pull
    B. double bolt bar lock
    C. cross bolt dead lock
    D. panic bolt

32. The MOST useful information for preventing future vandalism which should be included in a vandalism report is

    A. a list of damaged items
    B. how the vandals got into the building
    C. a list of stolen items
    D. how many hours it took to clean up the mess

33. A custodian should tour his assigned building a short time after the closing time MAINLY to see that

    A. any office workers who are on overtime are really working
    B. no unauthorized persons are in the building
    C. all the hall lights are turned off
    D. all the typewriters have dust covers on

34. As a custodian, if you want to be sure that a worker understands some difficult job instructions you just gave him, it is MOST important for you to

    A. ask him questions about the instructions
    B. ask him to write the instructions down and show them to you
    C. ask an experienced man to check on his work
    D. check on his work yourself after he has finished

35. The BEST way for a custodian to keep control of his work assignments is to

    A. inspect the building weekly
    B. make a written schedule and check it against the work being done each day
    C. have the men report to him at the completion of each job and then give them a new assignment
    D. leave the men on their own until complaints are received

36. The MOST important thing a custodian must do is to

    A. plan ahead
    B. keep stock records
    C. put out the lights when leaving the building
    D. answer the telephone

37. One of the ways in which a custodian can maintain proper control of his subordinates is to

    A. punish every minor infraction of the rules
    B. deny making any mistakes himself

C. criticize his own supervisor to show his own superiority
D. instill the idea that he keeps an eye on everything in his department

38. You see that one of your workers is not doing a job according to the safety rules. You should

   A. correct him so that he will know how to work
   B. take him off the job and send him to training class
   C. let it go and wait to see if he works this way all the time
   D. bawl him out

39. The BEST action a custodian can take to promote the security of his building is to

   A. depend on the police department to constantly patrol the area
   B. turn out all outside lights so that it will be difficult for intruders to find entry at night
   C. be sure all doors and windows are locked securely before the last person leaves the building at night
   D. allow only employees to enter the building during the day

40. The one thing a custodian should NOT do after his building has been broken into is to

   A. notify the police
   B. report the incident to his supervisor
   C. leave the damage to doors or windows unrepaired until his supervisor can inspect them on his regularly scheduled visit
   D. make the point of entry more secure than it was before the break-in

KEY (CORRECT ANSWERS)

1.	A	11.	C	21.	D	31.	D
2.	A	12.	D	22.	A	32.	B
3.	C	13.	B	23.	B	33.	B
4.	C	14.	D	24.	A	34.	A
5.	B	15.	D	25.	A	35.	B
6.	B	16.	B	26.	D	36.	A
7.	D	17.	A	27.	D	37.	D
8.	A	18.	C	28.	C	38.	A
9.	C	19.	B	29.	B	39.	C
10.	B	20.	A	30.	B	40.	C

EXAMINATION SECTION
TEST 1

DIRECTIONS: Each question or incomplete statement is followed by several suggested answers or completions. Select the one that BEST answers the question or completes the statement. *PRINT THE LETTER OF THE CORRECT ANSWER IN THE SPACE AT THE RIGHT.*

1. A foreman who <u>expedites</u> a job

   A. abolishes it
   B. makes it bigger
   C. slows it down
   D. speeds it up

2. If a man is working at a <u>uniform</u> speed, it means he is working at a speed which is

   A. changing
   B. fast
   C. slow
   D. steady

3. To say that a caretaker is <u>obstinate</u> means that he is

   A. cooperative
   B. patient
   C. stubborn
   D. willing

4. To say that a caretaker is <u>negligent</u> means that he is

   A. careless
   B. neat
   C. nervous
   D. late

5. To say that something is <u>absurd</u> means that it is

   A. definite
   B. not clear
   C. ridiculous
   D. unfair

6. To say that a foreman is <u>impartial</u> means that he is

   A. fair
   B. improving
   C. in a hurry
   D. watchful

7. A foreman who is <u>lenient</u> is one who is

   A. careless
   B. harsh
   C. inexperienced
   D. mild

8. A foreman who is <u>punctual</u> is one who is

   A. able
   B. polite
   C. prompt
   D. sincere

9. If you think one of your men is too <u>awkward</u> to do a job, it means you think he is too

   A. clumsy
   B. lazy
   C. old
   D. weak

10. A man who is <u>seldom</u> late, is late

    A. always
    B. never
    C. often
    D. rarely

11. In lifting a heavy can, a caretaker should keep his

   A. back and knees straight
   B. back bent and knees straight
   C. knees and back bent
   D. knees bent and back straight

12. If a man is injured on the job and it is *likely* that he has broken bones, the foreman should

   A. call for an ambulance
   B. call the superintendent
   C. take him to the hospital in his car
   D. tell the injured man to go to the hospital immediately

13. The MAIN reason for not letting dust cloths or oily rags pile up in storage closets is that

   A. a fire may start from this material
   B. the closet will not look neat and orderly
   C. the oil may soak into the floor and stain it
   D. they take up valuable space which may be put to better uses

14. Suppose, in making your rounds, you come upon a small oil and grease fire in a basement. After putting in a fire alarm, you find the fire extinguisher is out of order. The BEST thing for you to do is to

   A. do nothing since you have put in an alarm
   B. open all the doors and windows
   C. throw earth and sand on the fire
   D. throw water on the fire

15. The BEST thing to do for a man who feels he is about to faint is to

   A. apply a cold compress to his forehead
   B. give him some cold water to drink
   C. lower his head between his knees
   D. move him out to the fresh air

16. In removing the end of a broken bulb from a socket, the caretaker should stick a hard rubber wedge into the socket and

   A. pull the wedge down
   B. push the wedge up
   C. turn the wedge to the right
   D. turn the wedge to the left

17. At the end of the day, all ash is raked from the incinerator firebox. This is done *mainly* to

   A. get it ready for re-use
   B. leave the firebox ready for firing the next day
   C. prevent the fire from relighting itself
   D. put the ash in cans for removal by the Sanitation Department

18. Black smoke from the furnace will indicate

    A. a lack of draft
    B. that the incinerator fire door is closed
    C. that the incinerator fire door is open
    D. too much draft

19. The time for burning materials in incinerators is limited to the hours between

    A. 7 a.m. and 4 p.m.   B. 8 a.m. and 6 p.m.
    C. 5 p.m. and 7 a.m.   D. 6 p.m. and 8 a.m.

20. The BEST way to remove chewing gum from the floor is with a

    A. cloth wet with acid   B. bristle brush
    C. putty knife   D. rubber sponge

21. The 16-inch hair broom is BEST used on

    A. basement areas   B. cement walks
    C. stair risers   D. stair halls

22. It is MOST important that the slot in the floor saddle of the elevator be kept free of dirt since, otherwise,

    A. a fire may start   B. it will be unsightly
    C. someone may slip   D. the door will not close

23. Wall panels in elevators should be cleaned with a cloth dipped in

    A. ammonia in water   B. gasoline
    C. hot water   D. neutral soap solution

24. Before lighting-off the incinerator, material such as rubber should be removed because it

    A. can be used in cleaning work
    B. may cause a lot of smoke
    C. may clog the incinerator
    D. will not burn well

25. Of the following, the one that would be dangerous to burn in an incinerator is

    A. camphor balls   B. empty fruit cans
    C. glass   D. paper

KEY (CORRECT ANSWERS)

1. D
2. D
3. C
4. A
5. C

6. A
7. D
8. C
9. A
10. D

11. D
12. A
13. A
14. C
15. C

16. D
17. C
18. A
19. A
20. C

21. D
22. D
23. A
24. B
25. A

TEST 2

DIRECTIONS: Each question or incomplete statement is followed by several suggested answers or completions. Select the one that BEST answers the question or completes the statement. *PRINT THE LETTER OF THE COREECT ANSWER IN THE SPACE AT THE RIGHT.*

1. Before the incinerator is lit, it is BEST that the fire door be _____ with the peephole _____.

    A. closed, closed
    B. closed, open
    C. open, closed
    D. open, open

2. A spark arrestor in the incinerator is located

    A. at the top of the flue
    B. between the fire door and the ash door
    C. in the refractory chamber
    D. on the second floor hopper

3. Elevator cleaning is BEST done between

    A. 8 a.m. and 9 a.m.
    B. 9 a.m. and 10 a.m.
    C. 12 noon and 1 p.m.
    D. 2:30 p.m. and 3:30 p.m.

4. The wax solution that is put on floors of elevators once a week is made of _____ part(s) wax and _____ part(s) water.

    A. 1, 1   B. 1, 2   C. 2, 1   D. 3, 2

5. The cleaning of an elevator cab should take *approximately*

    A. 15 minutes
    B. 40 minutes
    C. one hour for every 225 square feet
    D. one hour for every 300 square feet

6. In washing windows, the blade of the squeegee should always be

    A. dried after each stroke
    B. held straight against the glass
    C. used with as much water as possible
    D. wet after each stroke

7. Caretakers are instructed to leave a 4-inch space between the material in an incinerator can and the top of the can. This is done *mainly* to

    A. follow Sanitation Department rules
    B. make it possible to pile cans on top of each other
    C. make the can easier to lift
    D. prevent spilling over of the material

8. A new corn broom should be soaked overnight before using it for the first time. This is done to

   A. help the broom to keep its shape
   B. make it possible to use the broom for scrubbing
   C. make the broom to wear evenly
   D. remove the brittleness of the broom's straws

9. After each day's use of the mop tank, the

   A. compartments and wringer should be rinsed and wiped dry
   B. compartments should be half-filled with clean water
   C. mop wringer should be left in the unreleased position
   D. wheels-should-be oiled and the excess oil wiped off

10. Elevator cab walls should be cleaned with a solution of water and

    A. ammonia   B. carbon tetrachloride
    C. kerosene   D. oil

11. A caretaker received $700.00 for having worked from Monday through Friday, 9 a.m. to 5 p.m. with one hour a day for lunch. The number of hours the caretaker would have to work to earn $120.00 is

    A. 10   B. 6
    C. 700 divided by 120 D. 700 minus 120

12. If the cost of a broom went up from $4.00 to $6.00, the per cent INCREASE in the original cost is

    A. 20   B. 25   C. 33 1/3   D. 50

13. The *average* of the numbers 3, 5, 7, 8, 12 is

    A. 5   B. 6   C. 7   D. 8

14. The cost of 100 bags of cotton cleaning cloths, 89 pounds per bag, at 7 cents per pound, is

    A. $549.35   B. $623.00   C. $700.00   D. $890.00

15. If 5 1/2 bags of sweeping compound cost $55.00, then 6 1/2 bags would cost

    A. $60.00   B. $62.50   C. $65.00   D. $67.00

16. The cost of cleaning supplies in a project averaged $330.00 a month during the first 8 months of the year. How much can be spent each month for the last four months if the total amount that can be spent for cleaning supplies for the year is $3,880?

    A. $124.00   B. $220.00   C. $310.00   D. $330.00

17. A shelf in a supply closet can safely hold only 100 pounds. A package of paper towels weighs 2 pounds, a carton of disinfectant weighs 8 pounds, and a box of soap weighs 1 pound. There are already 6 cartons of disinfectant and 6 boxes of soap on the shelf. How many packages of towels can be *safely* placed there?

    A. 20   B. 23   C. 25   D. 27

18. A cleaning solution is made up of 4 gallons of water, 1 pint of liquid soap, and 1 pint of ammonia. How many gallons of water is needed to use up a gallon of ammonia?

    A. 8   B. 16   C. 24   D. 32

18.____

19. Suppose a caretaker has 50 stair halls to clean. If he cleans 74% of them, the number of stair halls still UNCLEANED is

    A. 38   B. 26   C. 24   D. 13

19.____

20. If a man has a 12 foot piece of wood and wishes to cut it into two pieces so that one piece is twice as long as the other, the LONGER piece should be _____ feet.

    A. 7   B. 7 1/2   C. 8   D. 8 1/2

20.____

KEY (CORRECT ANSWERS)

1.	D	11.	B
2.	A	12.	D
3.	B	13.	C
4.	C	14.	B
5.	A	15.	C
6.	A	16.	C
7.	D	17.	B
8.	D	18.	D
9.	A	19.	D
10.	A	20.	C

EXAMINATION SECTION
TEST 1

DIRECTIONS: Each question or incomplete statement is followed by several suggested answers or completions. Select the one that BEST answers the question or completes the statement. *PRINT THE LETTER OF THE CORRECT ANSWER IN THE SPACE AT THE RIGHT.*

1. An electrical device whose function is to keep boiler steam pressure from exceeding the predetermined pressure is the

    A. relief valve
    B. vaporstat
    C. pressure gage
    D. pressuretrol

    1.____

2. Sodium sulphite is used to

    A. treat boiler water
    B. detect leaks in a gas system
    C. remove ink stains
    D. seal wood

    2.____

3. Boiler water should have a pH value between

    A. 5 and 7   B. 9 and 11   C. 13 and 14   D. 15 and 17

    3.____

4. The percentage of dryness of steam is called steam

    A. purity   B. ratio   C. priming   D. quality

    4.____

5. A bottom blowdown on a boiler is used to

    A. decrease the amount of fuel consumed
    B. increase the boiler steam pressure
    C. decrease the water intake
    D. eliminate impurities from the mud drum

    5.____

6. The flow of oil to a rotary cup oil burner is generally controlled by a(n)

    A. aquastat
    B. steam coil
    C. solenoid valve
    D. venturi

    6.____

7. The unit of a rotary cup oil burner that senses primary air failure is the

    A. remote switch
    B. modutrol
    C. vaporstat
    D. stackmeter

    7.____

8. The quantity of water delivered by a centrifugal pump varies _____ pump speed.

    A. directly as the cube of the
    B. directly as the square of the
    C. directly as the
    D. inversely as the

    8.____

9. The volute casing of a centrifugal pump serves the MAIN purpose of

    A. a priming chamber
    B. venting the pump head
    C. converting velocity head into pressure head
    D. making the pump run quieter

    9.____

10. The amount of water vapor mixed with dry air in the atmosphere is known as

   A. saturation ratio
   B. humidity
   C. vapor density
   D. dew point

11. When water freezes at 32° F, the amount of heat lost, per lb. of water is _____ BTU.

   A. 212   B. 180   C. 144   D. 100

12. The one of the following factors which does NOT affect human comfort in air conditioning is air

   A. temperature
   B. purity
   C. motion
   D. absorption

13. The element of a mechanical compression refrigerating system in which the refrigerant absorbs heat is the

   A. evaporator
   B. receiver
   C. condenser
   D. carnot

14. When the water level in a boiler falls below a specified level, the oil burner is shut off by the action of a

   A. magnetic gas valve
   B. purge control
   C. low water cut-out
   D. bellows feed

15. A small by-pass line would be installed around a large gate valve in a water line in order to

   A. measure the flow accurately
   B. show the direction of the flow
   C. alter the liquid flow in case of valve failure
   D. make it easier to open the gate valve

16. Flanged butterfly valves are operated by bringing them from closed to full-open position in _____ turn(s).

   A. 3 full
   B. 2 full
   C. one-half
   D. one-quarter

17. A monometer measures

   A. electrical energy
   B. revolutions per minute
   C. difference in pressure
   D. fluid volume

18. The difference between a compound gage and a standard gage is that the compound gage measures

   A. only pressures less than atmospheric
   B. pressures above and below atmospheric
   C. only pressures greater than atmospheric
   D. only pressures greater than absolute

19. The absolute pressure indicated by a gage reading of 14 psi is *approximately* _____ psi.

   A. 18.0   B. 24.0   C. 28.0   D. 32.0

20. A boiler steam gage should be graduated so that, when indicating the normal operating pressure, its pointer is nearly

   A. horizontal
   B. vertical
   C. 45 off the vertical position
   D. 60 off the vertical position

21. The packing generally used in the expansion points of a firebrick wall is

   A. sand   B. tar
   C. asbestos   D. high-temperature cement

22. The carbon dioxide (CO_2) content of the flue gases of an efficiently fired boiler should measure about

   A. 4%   B. 6%   C. 8%   D. 12%

23. Pre-heaters are generally installed when burning fuel oil number

   A. 6   B. 4   C. 2   D. 1

24. A typical boiler heat balance would show that the GREATEST amount of heat loss in boiler operation is

   A. in the slag   B. in the flue gases
   C. by radiation   D. by moisture in the air

25. When a boiler setting leaks air, there is an increase in the

   A. amount of heat lost
   B. boiler output
   C. quantity of flue gas impurities
   D. blow down

26. The 2 in a concrete mix of 1:2:4 refers to the quantity of

   A. cement   B. sand   C. water   D. filler

27. When roofing material is specified as *5 ply 70 lbs.*, it means that, as laid, the total of 5 plies weighs 70 lbs. per 100

   A. square feet   B. yards length
   C. square inches   D. feet length

28. The choice that shows which type of equipment is designed to prevent an elevator car from starting before the hatchway door is closed and locked is the

   A. hoistway access switch   B. interlocks
   C. spring buffer   D. counterweight

29. The piping through which water from private wells is delivered to swimming pools must be painted   29.____

   A. red   B. purple   C. orange   D. black

30. A chemical commonly used to disinfect swimming pools is   30.____

   A. ammonium nitrate
   B. chloraseptic
   C. ammonium bicarbonate
   D. calcium hypochorite

31. Shades and Venetian blinds are cleaned BEST with a   31.____

   A. dry cloth
   B. scouring powder
   C. vacuum cleaner
   D. paradry.

32. The surfaces of water coolers and door kick plates are cleaned BEST by using a cleaning solution and a   32.____

   A. brush
   B. wet cloth
   C. cellulose sponge
   D. wad of paper

33. The BEST technique to use when washing the outside surface of the upper sash of double hung windows that are not equipped with safety belt anchors is to work from a   33.____

   A. standing position on the outside of the sill
   B. sitting position on the sill with the feet inside the room
   C. standing position on the inside of the sill
   D. standing position on the top of a stepladder

34. The one of the following that should be used to clean an acoustical ceiling is a   34.____

   A. dry mop
   B. water wet cloth
   C. waxed cloth
   D. vacuum cleaner

35. The BEST procedure to follow to determine the actual cleaning ability of a specific material is to   35.____

   A. test its performance
   B. read the specifications
   C. ask the manufacturer
   D. examine trade literature

36. The one of the following statements that is CORRECT concerning the application of wax by the use of a twine mop with handle is that   36.____

   A. infrequent heavy coats are preferred
   B. the mop used for waxing must be hard
   C. the wax should be poured from a pail onto the floor
   D. the wax should be applied in thin coats

37. One coat of floor sealer applied to a hardwood floor usually lasts   37.____

   A. at least 2 years
   B. a maximum of 1 year
   C. no more than 6 months
   D. no more than 3 months

38. The material recommended for removing blood or fruit stains from concrete is   38._____

    A. soft soap   B. neatsfoot oil
    C. oxalic acid   D. ammonia

39. To order wet mop filler replacements, you should specify the   39._____

    A. number of strands   B. girth
    C. weight   D. wet test strength

40. You should use chlordane in a building to control   40._____

    A. water seepage   B. kitchen odors
    C. mildew   D. roaches

KEY (CORRECT ANSWERS)

1. D	11. C	21. C	31. C
2. A	12. D	22. D	32. C
3. B	13. A	23. A	33. B
4. C	14. C	24. B	34. D
5. D	15. D	25. A	35. A
6. C	16. D	26. B	36. D
7. C	17. C	27. A	37. B
8. C	18. B	28. B	38. D
9. C	19. C	29. A	39. C
10. B	20. B	30. D	40. D

TEST 2

DIRECTIONS: Each question or incomplete statement is followed by several suggested answers or completions. Select the one that BEST answers the question or completes the statement. *PRINT THE LETTER OF THE CORRECT ANSWER IN THE SPACE AT THE RIGHT.*

1. Safety belts worn by window cleaners must meet the approval of the

    A. National Safety Council
    B. American Safety Council
    C. American National Standards Institute
    D. State Department of Labor

2. After a snowfall has stopped, all snow must be removed from sidewalks (the time between 9 P.M. and 7 A.M. excluded) within _____ hour(s).

    A. 4   B. 3   C. 2   D. 1

3. Little white insects that look like small shrimps and feed on the roots of grass are called

    A. grubs
    B. ricks
    C. praying mantes
    D. crabs

4. A term used to indicate a lawn chemical weed killer is

    A. germicide
    B. emulsified
    C. herbicide
    D. vitrified

5. A device installed in a drainage system to prevent gases from flowing into a building is called a

    A. trap   B. stall   C. cleanout   D. bidet

6. The plumbing fixture that contains a ball cock is the

    A. trap
    B. water closet
    C. sprinkler
    D. dishwasher

7. In a plumbing installation, an escutcheon is a

    A. metal collar
    B. reducing tee
    C. valve
    D. single sweep

8. A leaking faucet stem can be repaired by replacing the

    A. flange or the seat
    B. nipple
    C. o-ring or the packing
    D. cock

9. The abbreviation *O.S. and Y.*, as used in plumbing, applies to a(n)

    A. hot well
    B. radiator
    C. injector
    D. gate valve

10. Gas range piping should have a minimum diameter of _____ inch.

    A. 3/4   B. 1/2   C. 1/4   D. 1/8

11. The pipe fitting that would be used to connect a 2" pipe at a 45-degree angle to another 2" pipe is called a(n)

    A. tee
    B. orifice flange
    C. reducer
    D. elbow

12. An instrument that measures relative humidity is called a(n)

    A. manometer
    B. interferometer
    C. hygrometer
    D. petrometer

13. The one of the following flat drive belts that gives the BEST service in dry places is a(n) _____ belt.

    A. rawhide
    B. oak-tanned
    C. chrome-tanned
    D. semirawhide

14. The letter representing the standard V-belt section which has the LOWEST horsepower-per-belt rating is

    A. E
    B. C
    C. B
    D. A

15. A 6 x 19 wire rope has

    A. 6 strands
    B. 6 wires in each strand
    C. 19 strands
    D. 25 strands arranged in a 6 x 19 pattern

16. A water tank that is 5 feet in diameter and 30 feet high has a volume of *most nearly* _____ cu.ft.

    A. 150
    B. 250
    C. 600
    D. 1200

17. The circumference of a circle with a radius of 5 inches is *most nearly* _____ in.

    A. 31.3
    B. 30.0
    C. 20.1
    D. 13.4

18. A flexible coupling should be used to connect two shafts that

    A. have centerlines at right angles to each other
    B. may be slightly out of line
    C. start and stop too fast
    D. have different speeds

19. Of the following materials used to make pipe, the one that is MOST brittle is

    A. lead
    B. aluminum
    C. copper
    D. cast iron

20. Mechanical equipment is generally tested and inspected on regular schedule in order to

    A. avoid breakdowns
    B. train new personnel
    C. maintain inventory
    D. give employees something to do

21. The *united inches* for a pane of glass that measures 14 inches by 20 inches is

    A. 14   B. 34   C. 40   D. 54

22. The one of the following that should NOT be lubricated is a(n)

    A. spur gear train   B. motor commutator
    C. roller chain drive   D. automobile axle

23. The one of the following oils that has the LOWEST viscosity is S.A.E.

    A. 70   B. 50   C. 20   D. 10W

24. A neoprene gasket would normally be used in a pipeline carrying

    A. steam   B. compressed air
    C. carbon dioxide D. light oil

25. The one of the following that would NOT be used in cleaning toilet bowls is

    A. a cleaning cloth   B. oxalic acid
    C. muriatic acid   D. a detergent

26. An electric motor-driven air compressor is automatically started and stopped by a

    A. thermostat   B. line air valve
    C. pressure switch D. float trap

27. The term *kilowatt hours* describes the consumption of

    A. energy   B. radiation
    C. cooling capacity D. conductance

28. AC voltage may be converted to DC voltage by means of a

    A. magneto   B. rectifier
    C. voltage regulator D. transducer

29. When replacing a blown fuse, it is BEST to

    A. install another one of slightly larger size
    B. seek the cause of the fuse failure before replacing it
    C. install another one of size smaller
    D. read the electric meters as a check on the condition of the circuit

30. A 208 volt, 3 phase, 4 wire circuit power supply has a line to grounded neutral voltage of approximately _____ volts.

    A. 120   B. 208   C. 220   D. 240

31. An interlock is generally installed on electronic equipment to

    A. prevent loss of power
    B. maintain vhf frequencies
    C. keep the vacuum tubes lit
    D. prevent electric shock during maintenance operations

4 (#2)

32. A flame should NOT be used to inspect the electrolyte level in a lead acid battery because the battery cells give off highly flammable   32._____

   A. hydrogen
   B. lead oxide
   C. lithium
   D. xenon

33. The purpose of the third prong in a three-prong male electric plug used in a 120-volt circuit is to   33._____

   A. make a firm connection
   B. strengthen the plug
   C. prevent electric shock
   D. get more electricity

34. You are informed that an employee under your supervision has just been injured in the building. The FIRST course of action you should take is to   34._____

   A. inform your superior
   B. aid the injured employee
   C. call a meeting of all the men
   D. order an investigation

35. In the prevention of accidental injuries, the MOST effective procedure is to   35._____

   A. install safety guards
   B. alert the workers to the hazard
   C. install lighting for easy sight
   D. eliminate the accident hazard

36. The one of the following practices that will INCREASE the possibility of fires occurring is the   36._____

   A. using of understairs areas for storage of all kinds
   B. wiping of machinery shafts with lubricating oil
   C. ventilating of all storage spaces
   D. cleaning of lockers at frequent intervals

37. When evaluating a building for fire hazards, the MOST important considerations are the   37._____

   A. number of stories and the height of each story
   B. location in the neighborhood and the accessibility
   C. interior lighting and the furniture
   D. number of residents and the use of the building

38. The one of the following that is a basic safety requirement for operating a power mower is: 38._____

   A. Fill gasoline-driven mowers indoors
   B. Do not operate power mowers on wet grass
   C. Keep the motor running when you leave the mower unattended for only a short while
   D. Fill the tank while the engine is running

39. You observe a red truck making a fuel delivery. The fuel being delivered is probably   39._____

   A. gasoline
   B. #2 fuel oil
   C. #4 fuel oil
   D. #5 fuel oil

40. The one of the following steps that is NOT taken when operating a carbon dioxide fire extinguisher is to   40.____

   A. carry the extinguisher to the fire and set it on the ground
   B. unhook the hose
   C. pull the pin in the valve wheel
   D. turn the valve and direct the gas to the top of the fire

KEY (CORRECT ANSWERS)

1.	D	11.	D	21.	B	31.	D
2.	B	12.	C	22.	B	32.	A
3.	A	13.	B	23.	D	33.	C
4.	C	14.	D	24.	D	34.	B
5.	A	15.	A	25.	C	35.	D
6.	B	16.	C	26.	C	36.	A
7.	A	17.	A	27.	A	37.	D
8.	C	18.	B	28.	B	38.	B
9.	D	19.	D	29.	B	39.	A
10.	A	20.	A	30.	A	40.	D

EXAMINATION SECTION
TEST 1

DIRECTIONS: Each question or incomplete statement is followed by several suggested answers or completions. Select the one that BEST answers the question or completes the statement. *PRINT THE LETTER OF THE CORRECT ANSWER IN THE SPACE AT THE RIGHT.*

1. There are a considerable number of forms and reports to be submitted on schedule by a building custodian.
   The ADVISABLE method of accomplishing this duty is to

   A. fill out the reports at odd times during the days when you have free time
   B. schedule a definite period of the work week for completing these forms and reports
   C. assign your foreman or cleaner to handle all these forms for you and to have them available on time
   D. classify or group the forms and reports and fill out only one of each group and refer the other forms or reports to the ones completed

   1.____

2. In enforcing compliance with safety regulations, you should take the attitude that they must be complied with because

   A. every accident can be prevented
   B. safety regulations are based on reason and experience with the best methods of accident prevention
   C. compliance with safety regulations will make other safety efforts unnecessary
   D. they are the law, and law enforcement is an end in itself

   2.____

3. The use of trisodium phosphate in cleaning marble should be avoided because

   A. it discolors the surface of the marble
   B. the salt crystals get in the pores, expand, and crack the marble
   C. it pits the glazed surface and bleaches the marble
   D. it builds up a slick surface on the marble

   3.____

4. The use of a concentrated cleaning solution on painted or varnished woodwork

   A. results in burning the pigments of paint or varnish, causing dull, streaky surfaces
   B. cuts down on time and energy in maintaining clean, unblemished surfaces
   C. insures spotless, clean, bright surfaces
   D. is detrimental to the health of the cleaners

   4.____

5. A building custodian will make the BEST impression on the office staff if he

   A. impresses them with the importance of his job
   B. says little and is cold and distant
   C. is easy-going and good-natured
   D. is courteous and performs his duties with as little delay as possible

   5.____

6. Domestic hot water storage reservoirs should be thoroughly cleaned once

   A. a week   B. a month
   C. a year   D. every two years

   6.____

7. A *pH* value of 4 would indicate a(n)

    A. acid solution
    B. neutral solution
    C. alkaline solution
    D. low pressure heating system

8. When the diaphragm or bellows of a thermostatic radiator trap is found to be dirty, it is USUALLY cleaned with

    A. turpentine
    B. carbon tetrachloride
    C. kerosene
    D. mild soap and water

9. The CHIEF purpose of a plumbing trap is to

    A. permit air to enter the sewer
    B. prevent the entrance of sewer gas into the building
    C. break the shock of the water draining off
    D. siphon off the waste water

10. The safety device on the gas pilot flame of a gas-fired apparatus should operate on pilot flame failure to

    A. bypass the main gas supply directly to the flue
    B. switch over to auxiliary bottled gas pilot flame
    C. shut off the gas supply
    D. introduce sufficient excess air to keep the furnace below the lower explosive limit

11. When instructing employees in regard to their duties in case of fire, a supervisor should

    A. tell employees to take no action until the fire department equipment has arrived
    B. tell all employees to go to the scene of the fire
    C. assign each employee specific duties
    D. tell employees to extinguish the fire before calling the supervisor or the fire department

12. The PRINCIPAL value of a good report is that it

    A. is always available for reference
    B. impresses department heads with the need for immediate action
    C. reflects upon the writer of the report
    D. expedites official business

13. The quality of work performed by personnel engaged in building cleaning is BEST evaluated by

    A. studying building cleaning expenditures
    B. studying time records of personnel
    C. analyzing complaints by building occupants
    D. inspecting the building periodically

14. Of the following, a building custodian need NOT be kept informed on

    A. departmental management policies
    B. terms of union contracts covering his subordinates
    C. developments of current interest in custodial operations
    D. current rate of interest on municipal bonds

15. The BEST way to make work assignments to persons required to clean a multi-story building is to

   A. allow the persons to pick their room or area assignments out of a hat
   B. make specific room or area assignments to each person separately
   C. rotate room and area assignments daily according to a chart posted on the bulletin board
   D. each week let a different member of the group make the room or area assignment

16. One important use of accident reports is to provide information that may be used to reduce the possibility of similar accidents.
The MOST valuable entry on the report for this purpose is the

   A. name of the victim
   B. injury sustained by the victim
   C. cause of the accident
   D. location of the accident

17. Suppose that an emergency has arisen which requires you to cancel some of the jobs scheduled for that day.
Of the following jobs, the one that can be eliminated for that day with LEAST effect on the proper operation and maintenance of the building is

   A. mopping and cleaning toilet rooms
   B. checking public stairs and corridors for hazards
   C. improving the location of supplies in the storeroom
   D. replacing broken window panes in offices

18. Of the following, a building custodian's attitude toward grievances should be to

   A. pay little attention to little grievances
   B. be very alert to grievances and make adjustments in existing conditions to appease all of them
   C. know the most frequent causes of grievances and strive to prevent them from arising
   D. maintain rigid discipline of a nature that *smoothes out* all grievances

19. A heavy snowfall must be removed from the sidewalks around the building. You, as building custodian, have assigned two men to shovel snow from the walks. After an interval, you check and find they are bickering as to how much each is shoveling, and no snow is being removed.
In this situation, you should

   A. stand with them to supervise the snow removal and to be sure the work is divided evenly
   B. assign two other men to snow removal and send the original two back to their usual chores
   C. put the man with seniority in full charge of the other man
   D. separate the men by sending them to opposite ends of the walks to shovel alone, with a warning that you will be checking on their progress at short intervals

20. Of the following, safety on the job is BEST assured by 20._____
    A. keeping alert
    B. following every rule
    C. working very slowly
    D. never working alone

KEY (CORRECT ANSWERS)

1. B	11. C
2. B	12. D
3. B	13. D
4. A	14. D
5. D	15. B
6. C	16. C
7. A	17. C
8. C	18. C
9. B	19. D
10. C	20. A

TEST 2

DIRECTIONS: Each question or incomplete statement is followed by several suggested answers or completions. Select the one that BEST answers the question or completes the statement. *PRINT THE LETTER OF THE CORRECT ANSWER IN THE SPACE AT THE RIGHT.*

1. A foam-type fire extinguisher extinguishes fires by 1.____

    A. cooling *only*
    B. drenching *only*
    C. smothering *only*
    D. cooling and smothering

2. The extinguishing agent in a soda-acid fire extinguisher is 2.____

    A. carbon dioxide
    B. water
    C. carbon tetrachloride
    D. calcium chloride solution

3. The PROPER extinguisher to use on an electrical fire in an operating electric motor is 3.____

    A. foam
    B. carbon dioxide
    C. soda and acid
    D. water

4. When an extension ladder is in place and ready to be used, the rope used to extend the ladder should be 4.____

    A. left hanging free out of the way of the climber's feet
    B. used to raise and lower tools to the man on the ladder
    C. used as a means of steadying the climber
    D. tied securely around a lower rung

5. The PRINCIPAL characteristic of panic locks or bolts on doors of places of public assembly is that they 5.____

    A. allow the doors to open outwardly with sufficient pressure on the bars of the lock
    B. allow the doors to open inwardly with sufficient pressure on the bars of the lock
    C. prevent the door from opening under impact load
    D. may be opened with any tumbler lock key

6. The MAIN purpose of periodic inspections and tests of electrical equipment is to 6.____

    A. encourage the men to take better care of the equipment
    B. make the men familiar with the equipment
    C. discover minor faults before they develop into major faults
    D. keep the men busy during otherwise slack periods

7. Standard, extra strong, and double extra strong welded steel pipe of a given size all have the SAME 7.____

    A. outside diameter
    B. inside diameter
    C. average diameter
    D. flow capacity for any given flow velocity

8. In reference to domestic gas piping,

   A. couplings with running threads are used to join pipes
   B. risers must have a drip leg and cap at bottom
   C. gasketed unions may be used in joining pipe
   D. composition disc globe valves are used to throttle the gas

9. Chewing gum should be removed from rubber, asphalt, or linoleum flooring with

   A. a putty knife   B. steel wool
   C. gritty compounds   D. a solvent

10. Which one of the following is the BEST procedure to follow when the linoleum floor of a meeting room containing movable furniture is to be mopped?

    A. The furniture should be moved by sliding it along the floor to prevent injury to the cleaners.
    B. The furniture should not be moved.
    C. The furniture should be moved by lifting it and carrying it to a clear spot to prevent damage to the linoleum.
    D. Very little water should be used in order to prevent the legs of the furniture from getting wet.

11. Asphalt tile flooring that has been subjected to oily compounds

    A. may last indefinitely
    B. must be removed and replaced with new asphalt tile immediately
    C. may be restored to hardness and lustre by several moppings with hot water and several applications of water wax
    D. must be restored to original condition by several moppings with kerosene

12. The use of alcohol in water for washing windows is NOT recommended because it

    A. is a hazard to the cleaner in that he may be affected by the fumes
    B. will damage the paint around the edges of the glass
    C. pits the surface of the glass
    D. destroys the bristles of the brush applying the solution to the pane

13. Of the following, the BEST material to use for removing grass stains on marble or wood is

    A. oxalic acid   B. chloride of lime
    C. sodium silicate   D. sodium hypochlorite

14. Shades or Venetian blinds are PREFERABLY cleaned with a

    A. feather duster   B. counter brush
    C. damp sponge   D. vacuum cleaner

15. Asphalt tile floors are PREFERABLY polished with

    A. water emulsion wax   B. wax in solution with benzol
    C. a high fatty acid soap   D. sodium metaphosphate

16. Washing soda is used to

    A. eliminate the need for rinse mopping or wiping
    B. make the cleaning compound abrasive
    C. decrease the wetting power of water
    D. increase the wetting power of water

16.____

17. Varnish or lacquer may be used as a sealer on floors finished with

    A. asphalt tiles
    B. linoleum
    C. rubber tiles
    D. cork tiles

17.____

18. A long-handled deck scrub brush is MOST effective when scrubbing

    A. large open areas
    B. stair treads
    C. small flat areas
    D. long corridors

18.____

19. The BEST method for preventing the infestation of a building by rats is to

    A. use cats
    B. use rat traps
    C. eliminate rat harborages in the building
    D. use poisoned bait

19.____

20. The one of the following foodstuffs which, if allowed to remain on ordinary asphalt tile, will MOST likely be most injurious to it is

    A. milk
    B. maple syrup
    C. ketchup
    D. salad oil

20.____

KEY (CORRECT ANSWERS)

1.	D	11.	C
2.	B	12.	B
3.	B	13.	D
4.	D	14.	D
5.	A	15.	A
6.	C	16.	D
7.	A	17.	D
8.	B	18.	C
9.	A	19.	C
10.	C	20.	D

TEST 3

DIRECTIONS: Each question or incomplete statement is followed by several suggested answers or completions. Select the one that BEST answers the question or completes the statement. *PRINT THE LETTER OF THE CORRECT ANSWER IN THE SPACE AT THE RIGHT.*

1. Employees engaged in cleaning operations who are issued rubber gloves to protect their hands against caustic solutions should be warned that

    A. such solution allowed to spill over the glove top into the space between the glove and the hand may damage the skin of the hand
    B. rubber gloves have a very short life in contact with caustic solutions
    C. harmful gases can penetrate the rubber and harm even dry hands
    D. contact of the hands with glove-type rubber for over an hour is harmful

2. Pyrethrins are used as

    A. insecticides
    B. germicides
    C. waxes
    D. detergents

3. Water hammer is

    A. a special hammer used to remove scale from a radiator
    B. caused by water in steam lines
    C. caused by excessive boiler pressure
    D. caused by low water level in the boiler

4. Which of the following is USUALLY used in the construction of a steam pressure gauge?

    A. Perfect circle tube
    B. Venturi tube
    C. Bourdon tube
    D. Elastic linkage

5. Usually when a large room is gradually filled with people, the room temperature

    A. and humidity both decrease
    B. increases and the humidity decreases
    C. and humidity increase
    D. decreases and humidity increases

6. A foot valve at the intake end of the suction line of a pump serves MAINLY to

    A. maintain pump prime
    B. filter out large particles in the fluid
    C. increase the maximum suction lift of the pump
    D. increase pump flow rate

7. A pressure gauge attached to a standpipe system shows a pressure of 36 pounds per sq. in.
   The head of water, in feet, above the gauge is MOST NEARLY

    A. 24   B. 36   C. 60   D. 83

8. Of the following, the term *vapor barrier* would MOST likely be associated with

   A. electric service installation
   B. insulation materials
   C. fuel oil tank installation
   D. domestic gas piping

9. Pitot tubes are used to

   A. test feed water for impurities
   B. measure air or gas flow in a duct
   C. prevent overheating of elements of a steam gauge
   D. control the ignition system of an oil burner

10. In warm air heating and in ventilating systems, laboratories and kitchens should NOT be equipped with return ducts in order to

    A. keep air velocities in other returns as high as possible
    B. reduce fire hazards
    C. reduce the possibility of circulating odors through the system
    D. keep the temperature high in these rooms

11. One square foot of equivalent direct steam radiation (EDR) is equivalent to a heat emission of _____ BTU per _____.

    A. 150; hour
    B. 240; minute
    C. 150; minute
    D. 240; hour

12. Of the following, the one which is LEAST likely to cause continuous vibration of an operating motor is

    A. a faulty starting circuit
    B. excessive belt tension
    C. the misalignment of motor and driven equipment
    D. loose bearings

13. The function of a steam trap is to

    A. remove sediment and dirt from steam
    B. remove air and non-condensible gases from steam
    C. relieve excessive steam pressure to the atmosphere
    D. remove condensate from a pipe or an apparatus

14. The temperature at which air is just saturated with the moisture present in it is called its

    A. relative humidity
    B. absolute humidity
    C. humid temperature
    D. dew point

15. If scale forms on the seat of a float-operated boiler feed water regulator, the MOST likely result is

    A. internal corrosion of the boiler shell
    B. insufficient supply of water to the boiler
    C. flooding of the boiler
    D. shutting down of the oil burner by the low water cut-out

16. The compound gauge in the oil suction line shows a high vacuum. This is USUALLY an indication of

    A. a dirty oil strainer
    B. low oil level in the fuel oil storage tank
    C. a leak in the fuel oil preheater
    D. an obstruction in the fuel oil preheater

17. Of the following, the information which is LEAST important on a boiler room log sheet is the

    A. stack temperature readings
    B. CO_2 readings
    C. number of boilers in operation
    D. boiler room humidity

18. Pitting and corrosion of the water side of the boiler heating surfaces is due MAINLY to the boiler water containing dissolved

    A. oxygen
    B. hydrogen
    C. soda-ash
    D. sodium sulphite

19. The combustion efficiency of a boiler can be determined with a CO_2

    A. flue gas temperature
    B. boiler room humidity
    C. outside air temperature
    D. under fire draft

20. The try-cocks of steam boilers are used to

    A. find the height of water in the boiler
    B. test steam pressure in the boiler
    C. empty the boiler of water
    D. act as safety valves

KEY (CORRECT ANSWERS)

1.	A	11.	D
2.	A	12.	A
3.	B	13.	D
4.	C	14.	D
5.	C	15.	C
6.	A	16.	A
7.	D	17.	D
8.	B	18.	A
9.	B	19.	A
10.	C	20.	A

TEST 4

DIRECTIONS: Each question or incomplete statement is followed by several suggested answers or completions. Select the one that BEST answers the question or completes the statement. *PRINT THE LETTER OF THE CORRECT ANSWER IN THE SPACE AT THE RIGHT.*

1. The reason for sweating inside a refrigerator cabinet is

    A. high percent running time of compressor unit
    B. high cabinet air temperature
    C. defective expansion valve
    D. a poor door seal

2. Of the following ingredients, the ones to be mixed with water to *point-up* the brickwork of a building are: 1 part cement,

    A. 2 parts sand, 3 parts gravel
    B. 3 parts sand, 4 parts gravel
    C. 3 parts sand
    D. 5 parts sand

3. Acid soils can BEST be neutralized by liberal applications of

    A. manure
    B. salt
    C. lime
    D. powdered-basalt

4. Summer blooming flower bulbs should be stored in a _____ place.

    A. warm, dry
    B. warm, moist
    C. cool, moist
    D. cool, dry

5. A certain 31-day month had an average temperature of 45 Fahrenheit. The number of degree days for this month is

    A. 31   B. 450   C. 620   D. 1395

6. While concrete is *curing*, it is MOST desirable to

    A. expose the concrete to sun and air as much as possible
    B. keep the concrete surface moist
    C. maintain a temperature of not more than 60°F
    D. maintain a temperature of at least 80°F

7. To join two lengths of pipe together in a solid straight run, the fitting to use is a

    A. coupling
    B. tee
    C. hickey
    D. shoulder nipple

8. New copper flashing that has been soldered should be

    A. muriatic acid
    B. plain water
    C. benzine
    D. washing soda or lye

63

9. The intercooler of a two-stage air compressor is connected to the compressor between the

   A. two stages
   B. filter and the first stage
   C. second stage and the receiver
   D. receiver and point of usage of the air

9.____

10. Both terms *tank* and *close* apply USUALLY to

    A. electric generator couplings
    B. freon storage units
    C. pipe nipples
    D. ventilation plenum chambers

10.____

11. The commercial fertilizer *5-10-5* refers to

    A. 5% nitrogen, 10% phosphoric acid, 5% potash
    B. 5% rotted manure, 10% calcium chloride, 5% bone meal
    C. 5% soda, 10% tobacco dust, 5% bone meal
    D. 5% tobacco dust, 10% rotted manure, 5% sulphur

11.____

12. The slope or slant of a soil line is 1/4" per foot. If this drainage line is 50' long, the difference in elevation from one end to the other is, in feet, MOST NEARLY

    A. 0.55   B. 1.04   C. 2.08   D. 12.5

12.____

13. Oil is used with sharpening stones when sharpening wood chisels in order to

    A. reduce the effort needed to move the blade over the stone
    B. maintain the oil temper of the steel used for the chisel
    C. flush off the small metal chips and clear the cutting edges of the abrasive grit
    D. reduce the temperature due to friction

13.____

14. A maintenance man checking a refrigerator for a freon leak would use a

    A. soap and water solution
    B. halide torch
    C. glycerine solution
    D. linseed oil and whiting solution

14.____

15. A basement floor area of 5000 square feet is under 9 inches of water.
    If this 9 inches of water is to be pumped out of the basement in one hour, the required capacity of the portable pump, in gallons per minute, is MOST NEARLY

    A. 63   B. 470   C. 1020   D. 2810

15.____

16. A MAJOR advantage of keeping a perpetual inventory of supplies is that it

    A. gives a current record of the supplies available at all times
    B. reduces the work required to distribute supplies
    C. avoids the need for periodic physical inventories
    D. shows who is using excessive supplies

16.____

17. Employees generally do NOT object to strict rules and regulations if they

 A. are enforced without bias or favor
 B. result in more material gain
 C. deal with relatively unimportant phases of the work
 D. affect the supervisors more than their subordinates

18. In order to have building employees willing to follow standardized cleaning and maintenance procedures, the supervisor MUST be prepared to

 A. work alongside the employees
 B. demonstrate the reasonableness of the procedures
 C. offer incentive pay for their use
 D. be adamant in opposing changes in the standardized procedures

19. Of the following, the MOST important step when accepting incoming shipments of standard items normally carried in stock is to check the items for

 A. electrical performance
 B. chemical composition
 C. quantity delivered
 D. mechanical performance

20. The orderly arrangement of supplies in storage USUALLY

 A. takes too much time to be worthwhile
 B. is important only in large warehouses
 C. is essential for stock selection and inventory purposes
 D. cannot be accomplished when package sizes vary

KEY (CORRECT ANSWERS)

1.	D	11.	A
2.	C	12.	B
3.	C	13.	C
4.	D	14.	B
5.	C	15.	B
6.	B	16.	A
7.	A	17.	A
8.	D	18.	B
9.	A	19.	C
10.	C	20.	C

EXAMINATION SECTION
TEST 1

DIRECTIONS: Each question or incomplete statement is followed by several suggested answers or completions. Select the one that BEST answers the question or completes the statement. *PRINT THE LETTER OF THE CORRECT ANSWER IN THE SPACE AT THE RIGHT.*

1. If you can't come to work in the morning because you do not feel well, you should

    A. call your supervisor and let him know that you are sick
    B. try to get someone else to take your place
    C. have your doctor call your office as proof that you are sick
    D. come to work anyway so that you won't lose your job

    1._____

2. Many machines have certain safety devices for the operators.
The MOST important reason for having these safety devices is to

    A. increase the amount of work that the machines can do
    B. permit repairs to be made on the machines without shutting them down
    C. help prevent accidents to people who use the machines
    D. reduce the cost of electric power needed to run the machines

    2._____

3. While working on the job, you accidentally break a window pane. No one is around, and you are able to clean up the broken pieces of glass.
It would then be BEST for you to

    A. leave a note near the window that a new glass has to be put in because it was accidentally broken
    B. forget about the whole thing because the window was not broken on purpose
    C. write a report to your supervisor telling him that you saw a broken window pane that has to be fixed
    D. tell your supervisor that you accidentally broke the window pane while working

    3._____

4. There is a two-light fixture in the room where you are working. One of the light bulbs goes out, and you need more light to work by.
You should

    A. change the fuse in the fuse box
    B. have a new bulb put in
    C. call for an electrician and stop work until he comes
    D. find out what is causing the short circuit

    4._____

5. The BEST way to remove some small pieces of broken glass from a floor is to

    A. use a brush and dust pan
    B. pick up the pieces carefully with your hands
    C. use a wet mop and a wringer
    D. sweep the pieces into the corner of the room

    5._____

6. When you are not sure about some instructions that your supervisor has given you on how to do a certain job, it would be BEST for you to

   A. start doing the work and stop when you come to the part that you do not understand
   B. ask the supervisor to go over the instructions which are not clear to you
   C. do the job immediately from beginning to the end, leaving out the part that you are not sure of
   D. wait until the supervisor leaves and then ask a more experienced worker to explain the job to you

6.____

7. When an employee first comes on the job, he is given a period of training by his supervisor.
The MAIN reason for this training period is to

   A. make sure that the employee will learn to do his work correctly and safely
   B. give the employee a chance to show the supervisor that he can learn quickly
   C. allow the supervisor and the employee a chance to become friendly with each other
   D. find out which employees will make good supervisors later on

7.____

8. After you open a sealed box of supplies, you find that the box is not full and that some of the supplies are missing.
You should

   A. use fewer supplies than you intended to
   B. seal the box and take it back to the storeroom
   C. get signed statements from other employees that when you opened the box, it was not full
   D. tell your supervisor about it

8.____

9. Suppose that after you have been on the job a few months, your supervisor shows you some small mistakes you are making in your work.
You should

   A. tell your supervisor that these mistakes don't keep you from finishing your work
   B. ask your supervisor how you can avoid these mistakes
   C. try to show your supervisor that your way of doing the work is just as good as his way of doing it
   D. check with the other workers to find out if your supervisor is also finding fault with them

9.____

10. If your supervisor gives you an order to do a special job which you do not like to do, you should

    A. take a long time to do the job so that you won't get this job again
    B. do the job the best way you know how even though you don't like it
    C. make believe that you didn't hear your supervisor and do your regular work
    D. say nothing but tell another employee that the supervisor wants him to do this special job

10.____

11. If two employees who are working together on a job do not agree on how to do the job, it would be BEST

    A. for each worker to do the job in his own way until it is finished
    B. to put off doing the job until both workers agree to do it the same way
    C. to ask the supervisor to decide on the way the job is to be done
    D. for each worker to ask for a transfer to another assignment because they can't get along with each other

11._____

12. Suppose that in order to finish your work, you have to lift a heavy box off the floor onto an empty desk.
    You should

    A. leave the box where it is and tell your supervisor that you have finished your work
    B. lift the box by yourself very quickly so that your supervisor will see that you are a strong, willing worker
    C. ask another employee to give you a hand to lift the box off the floor
    D. complain to your supervisor that he should check a job before giving you such a tough assignment

12._____

13. Bulletin boards for the posting of official notices are usually put up near the place where employees check in and out each day.
    For an employee to spend a few minutes each day to read the new notices is

    A. *good;* these notices give him information about the Department and his own work
    B. *bad;* all important information is given to employees by their supervisors
    C. *good;* this is a way to "take a break" during the day
    D. *bad;* the notices can't help him in his work

13._____

14. Suppose that your supervisor gives you a job to do and tells you that he wants you to finish it in three hours.
    If you finish the work at the end of 2 hours, you should

    A. wait until the three hours are up and then tell your supervisor that you are finished
    B. go to your supervisor and tell him that you finished a half-hour ahead of time
    C. spend the next half-hour getting ready for the next job you think your supervisor may give you
    D. take a half-hour rest period because good work deserves a reward

14._____

15. Which one of the following is it LEAST important to include in an accident report?

    A. Name and address of the injured person
    B. Date, time, and place where the accident happened
    C. Name and address of the injured person's family doctor
    D. An explanation of how the accident happened

15._____

16. If, near the end of the day, you realize that you made a mistake in your work and you can't do the work over, you should

    A. forget about it because there is only a small chance that the mistake can be traced back to you
    B. wait a few days and take the blame for the mistake if it is caught
    C. ask the other employees to keep the mistake a secret so that no one can be blamed
    D. tell your supervisor about the mistake right away

16._____

17. Employees should wipe up water spilled on floors immediately.
The BEST reason for this is that water on a floor

   A. is a sign that employees are sloppy
   B. makes for a slippery condition that could cause an accident
   C. will eat into the wax protecting the floor
   D. is against health regulations

17._____

18. Another worker, who is a good friend of yours, leaves work an hour before quitting time to take care of a personal matter. When you leave later, you find that your friend did not sign out on the timesheet.
For you to sign out for your friend would be

   A. *good,* because he will do the same for you some day when you want to leave early
   B. *bad,* because other employees will also want you to do the same favor for them on other days
   C. *good,* because the timesheet should not have any empty spaces on it
   D. *bad,* because timesheets are official records which employees should keep honestly and accurately

18._____

19. While you are working, a person asks you how to get to an office which you know is one floor above you in the building where you work.
It would be BEST for you to tell this person that

   A. you can't answer any questions because you have to finish your work
   B. he should go back to the lobby and check the list of offices
   C. the office he is looking for is on the next floor
   D. he should call the office he is looking for to get exact instructions on how to get there

19._____

20. While you are at work, you find a sealed brown envelope under a desk. The envelope is marked *Personal - Hand Delivery* and is addressed to an official who has an office in the building where you are working.
You should

   A. drop the envelope into the nearest mailbox so that it can be delivered the next day
   B. look up the telephone number of the official and call him up to tell him what you have found
   C. put the envelope in your pocket and come in early the next day to deliver it personally to the official
   D. give the envelope to your supervisor right away and tell him where you found it

20._____

21. A messenger delivered 32 letters on Monday, 47 on Tuesday, 29 on Wednesday, 36 on Thursday, and 41 on Friday.
How many letters did he deliver altogether?

   A. 157   B. 185   C. 218   D. 229

21._____

22. Mr. White paid 4% sales tax on a $95 television set.
The amount of sales tax that he paid was

   A. $9.50   B. $4.00   C. $3.80   D. $.95

22._____

23. How many square feet are there in a room which is 25 feet long and 35 feet wide? 23.____
    _____ square feet.

    A. 600   B. 750   C. 875   D. 925

24. How much would it cost to send a 34 pound package by parcel post if the postage is 24.____
    $1.60 for the first 20 pounds and 7 for each additional pound?

    A. $2.34   B. $2.58   C. $2.66   D. $2.80

25. Adding together 1/2, 3/4, and 1/8, the total is 25.____

    A. 1 1/4   B. 1 1/2   C. 1 3/8   D. 1 3/4

26. If a piece of wood 40 inches long is cut into two pieces so that the larger piece is three 26.____
    times as long as the, smaller piece, the smaller piece is _____ inches.

    A. 4   B. 5   C. 8   D. 10

27. Two friends, Smith and Jones, together spend $1,800 to buy a car. 27.____
    If Smith put up twice as much money as Jones, then Jones' share of the cost of the car
    was

    A. $300   B. $600   C. $900   D. $1,200

28. In a certain agency, two-thirds of the employees are clerks and the remainder are typists. 28.____
    If there are 180 clerks, then the number of typists in this agency is

    A. 270   B. 90   C. 240   D. 60

Questions 29-35.

DIRECTIONS: Answer Questions 29 through 35 ONLY according to the information given in
             the chart below.

EMPLOYEE RECORD

Name of Employee	Where Assigned	Number of Days Absent Vacation	Sick Leave	Yearly Salary
Carey	Laundry	18	4	$18,650
Hayes	Mortuary	24	8	$17,930
Irwin	Buildings	20	17	$18,290
King	Supply	12	10	$17,930
Lane	Mortuary	17	8	$17,750
Martin	Buildings	13	12	$17,750
Prince	Buildings	5	7	$17,750
Quinn	Supply	19	0	$17,250
Sands	Buildings	23	10	$18,470
Victor	Laundry	21	2	$18,150

29. The *only* employee who was NOT absent because of sickness is 29.____
   A. Hayes   B. Lane   C. Victor   D. Quinn

30. The employee with the HIGHEST salary is 30.____
   A. Carey   B. Irwin   C. Sands   D. Victor

31. The employee with the LOWEST salary is assigned to the _____ Bureau. 31.____
   A. Laundry   B. Mortuary   C. Building   D. Supply

32. Which one of these was absent or on vacation more than 20 days? 32.____
   A. Irwin   B. Lane   C. Quinn   D. Victor

33. The number of employees whose salary is LESS than $18,100 a year is 33.____
   A. 4   B. 5   C. 6   D. 7

34. MOST employees are assigned to 34.____
   A. Laundry   B. Mortuary   C. Buildings   D. Supply

35. From the chart, you can figure out for each employee 35.____
   A. how long he has worked in his present assignment
   B. how many days vacation he has left
   C. how many times he has been late
   D. how much he earns a month

KEY (CORRECT ANSWERS)

1.	A		16.	D
2.	C		17.	B
3.	D		18.	D
4.	B		19.	C
5.	A		20.	D
6.	B		21.	B
7.	A		22.	C
8.	D		23.	C
9.	B		24.	B
10.	B		25.	C
11.	C		26.	D
12.	C		27.	B
13.	A		28.	B
14.	B		29.	D
15.	C		30.	A

31. D
32. D
33. C
34. C
35. D

TEST 2

DIRECTIONS: Each question or incomplete statement is followed by several suggested answers or completions. Select the one that BEST answers the question or completes the statement. *PRINT THE LETTER OF THE CORRECT ANSWER IN THE SPACE AT THE RIGHT.*

Questions 1-5.

DIRECTIONS: Answer Questions 1 to 5 ONLY according to the information given in the following passage.

EMPLOYEE LEAVE REGULATIONS

Peter Smith, as a full-time permanent City employee under the Career and Salary Plan, earns an "annual leave allowance" This consists of a certain number of days off a year with pay and may be used for vacation, personal business, and for observing religious holidays. As a newly appointed employee, during his first eight years of City service, he will earn an "annual leave allowance" of twenty days off a year (an average of 1 2/3 days off a month). After he has finished eight full years of working for the City, he will begin earning an additional five days off a year. His "annual leave allowance," therefore, will then be twenty-five days a year and will remain at this amount for seven full years. He will begin earning an additional two days off a year after he has completed a total of fifteen years of City employment. Therefore, in his sixteenth year of working for the City, Mr. Smith will be earning twenty-seven days off a year as his "annual leave allowance" (an average of 2 1/4 days off a month).

A "sick leave allowance" of one day a month is also given to Mr. Smith, but it can be used only in case of actual illness. When Mr. Smith returns to work after using "sick leave allowance," he must have a doctor's note if the absence is for a total of more than three days, but he may also be required to show a doctor's note for absences of one, two, or three days.

1. According to the above passage, Mr. Smith's *annual leave allowance* consists of a certain number of days off a year which he

    A. does not get paid for
    B. gets paid for at time and a half
    C. may use for personal business
    D. may not use for observing religious holidays

    1.____

2. According to the above passage, after Mr. Smith has been working for the City for nine years, his *annual leave allowance* will be _____ days a year.

    A. 20   B. 25   C. 27   D. 37

    2.____

3. According to the above passage, Mr. Smith will begin earning an average of 2 1/4 days off a month as his *annual leave allowance* after he has worked for the City for _____ full years.

    A. 7   B. 8   C. 15   D. 17

    3.____

4. According to the above passage, Mr. Smith is given a *sick leave allowance* of

    A. 1 day every 2 months   B. 1 day per month
    C. 1 2/3 days per month   D. 2 1/4 days a month

    4.____

73

5. According to the above passage, when he uses *sick leave allowance*, Mr. Smith may be required to show a doctor's note

 A. even if his absence is for only 1 day
 B. only if his absence is for more than 2 days
 C. only if his absence is for more than 3 days
 D. only if his absence is for 3 days or more

5.___

Questions 6-9.

DIRECTIONS: Answer Questions 6 to 9 ONLY according to the information given in the following passag

MOPPING FLOORS

When mopping hardened cement floors, either painted or unpainted, a soap and water mixture should be used. This should be made by dissolving 1/2 a cup of soft soap in a pail of hot water. It is not desirable, however, under any circumstances, to use a soap and water mixture on cement floors that are not hardened. For mopping this type of floor, it is recommended that the cleaning agent be made up of two ounces of laundry soda mixed in a pail of water.

Soaps are not generally used on hard tile floors because slippery films may build up on the floor. It is generally recommended that these floors be mopped using a pail of hot water in which has been mixed two ounces of washing powder for each gallon of water. The floors should then be rinsed thoroughly.

After the mopping is finished, proper care should be taken of the mop. This is done by first cleaning the mop in clear, warm water. Then, it should be wrung out, after which the strands of the mop should be untangled. Finally, the mop should be hung by its handle to dry.

6. According to the above passage, you should NEVER use a soap and water mixture when mopping _____ floors.

 A. hardened cement B. painted
 C. unhardened cement D. unpainted

6.___

7. According to the above passage, using laundry soda mixed in a pail of water as a cleaning agent is recommended for

 A. all floors
 B. all floors except hard tile floors
 C. some cement floors
 D. lineoleum floor coverings only

7.___

8. According to the above passage, the generally recommended mixture for mopping hard tile floors is

 A. 1/2 a cup of soft soap for each gallon of hot water
 B. 1/2 a cup of soft soap in a pail of hot water
 C. 2 ounces of washing powder in a pail of hot water
 D. 2 ounces of washing powder for each gallon of hot water

8.___

9. According to the above passage, the proper care of a mop after it is used includes 9._____

   A. cleaning it in clear cold water and hanging it by its handle to dry
   B. wringing it out, untangling and drying it
   C. untangling its strands before wringing it out
   D. untangling its strands while cleaning it in clear water

Questions 10-13.

DIRECTIONS: Answer Questions 10 to 13 ONLY according to the information given in the following passage.

HANDLING HOSPITAL LAUNDRY

In a hospital, care must be taken when handling laundry in order to reduce the chance of germs spreading. There is always the possibility that dirty laundry will be carrying dangerous germs. To avoid catching germs when they are working with dirty laundry, laundry workers should be sure that any cuts or wounds they have are bandaged before they touch the dirty laundry. They should also be careful when handling this laundry not to rub their eyes, nose, or mout. Just like all other hospital workers, laundry workers should also protect themselves against germs by washing and rinsing their hands thoroughly before eating meals and before leaving work at the end of the day.

To be sure that germs from dirty laundry do not pass onto clean laundry and thereby increase the danger to patients, clean and dirty laundry should not be handled near each other or by the same person. Special care also has to be taken with laundry that comes from a patient who has a dangerous, highly contagious disease so that as few people as possible come in direct contact with this laundry. Laundry from this patient, therefore, should be kept separate from other dirty laundry at all times.

10. According to the above passage, when working with dirty laundry, laundry workers should 10._____

    A. destroy laundry carrying dangerous germs
    B. have any cuts bandaged before touching the dirty laundry
    C. never touch the dirty laundry directly
    D. rub their eyes, nose, and mouth to protect them from germs

11. According to the above passage, all hospital workers should wash their hands thoroughly 11._____

    A. after eating meals to remove any trace of food from their hands
    B. at every opportunity to show good example to the patients
    C. before eating meals to protect themselves against germs
    D. before starting work in the morning to feel fresh and ready to do a good day's work

12. According to the above passage, the danger to patients will increase 12._____

    A. unless a worker handles dirty and clean laundry at the same time
    B. unless clean and dirty laundry are handled near each other
    C. when clean laundry is ironed frequently
    D. when germs pass from dirty laundry to clean laundry

13. According to the above passage, laundry from a patient with a dangerous, highly contagious disease should be

   A. given special care so that as few people as possible come in direct contact with it
   B. handled in the same way as any other dirty laundry
   C. washed by hand
   D. separated from the other dirty laundry just before it is washed

Questions 14-17.

DIRECTIONS: Answer Questions 14 to 17 ONLY according to the information given in the following passage.

EMPLOYEE SUGGESTIONS

To increase the effectiveness of the New York City governments the City asks its employees to offer suggestions when they feel an improvement could be made in some government operation. The Employees' Suggestions Program was started to encourage City employees to do this. Through this Program, which is only for City employees, cash awards may be given to those whose suggestions are submitted and approve Suggestions are looked for not only from supervisors but from all City employees as any City employee may get an idea which might be approved and contribute greatly to the solution of some problem of City government.

Therefore, all suggestions for improvement are welcome, whether they be suggestions on how to improve working conditions, or on how to increase the speed with which work is done, or on how to reduce or eliminate such things as waste, time losses, accidents, or fire hazards. There are, however, a few types of suggestions for which cash awards can not be given. An example of this type would be a suggestion to increase salaries or a suggestion to change the regulations about annual leave or about sick leave. The number of suggestions sent in has increased sharply during the past few years. It is hoped that it will keep increasing in the future in order to meet the City's needs for more ideas for improved ways of doing things.

14. According to the above passage, the main reason why the City asks its employees for suggestions about government operations is to

   A. increase the effectiveness of the City government
   B. show that the Employees' Suggestion Program is working well
   C. show that everybody helps run the City government
   D. have the employee win a prize

15. According to the above passage, the Employees' Suggestion Program can approve awards only for those suggestions that come from

   A. City employees
   B. City employees who are supervisors
   C. City employees who are not supervisors
   D. experienced employees of the City

16. According to the above passage, a cash award can not be given through the Employees' Suggestion Program for a suggestion about   16.____

   A. getting work done faster
   B. helping prevent accidents on the job
   C. increasing the amount of annual leave for City employees
   D. reducing the chance of fire where City employees work

17. According to the above passage, the suggestions sent in during the past few years have   17.____

   A. all been approved
   B. generally been well written
   C. been mostly about reducing or eliminating waste
   D. been greater in number than before

Questions 18-21.

DIRECTIONS: Answer Questions 18 to 21 ONLY according to the information given in the following passage.

ACCIDENT PREVENTION

Many accidents and injuries can be prevented if employees learn to be more careful. The wearing of shoes with thin or badly worn soles or open toes can easily lead to foot injuries from tacks, nails, and chair and desk legs. Loose or torn clothing should not be worn near moving machinery. This is especially true of neckties which can very easily become caught in the machine. You should not place objects so that they block or partly block hallways, corridors, or other passageways. Even when they are stored in the proper place, tools, supplies, and equipment should be carefully placed or piled so as not to fall, nor have anything stick out from a pile. Before cabinets, lockers, or ladders are moved, the tops should be cleared of anything which might injure someone or fall of If necessary, use a dolly to move these or other bulky objects.

Despite all efforts to avoid accidents and injuries, however, some will happen. If an employee is injured, no matter how small the injury, he should report it to his supervisor and have the injury treated. A small cut that is not attended to can easily become infected and can cause more trouble than some injuries which at first seem more serious. It never pays to take chances.

18. According to the above passage, the one statement that is NOT true is that   18.____

   A. by being more careful, employees can reduce the number of accidents that happen
   B. women should wear shoes with open toes for comfort when working
   C. supplies should be piled so that nothing is sticking out from the pile
   D. if an employee sprains his wrist at work, he should tell his supervisor about it

19. According to the above passage, you should NOT wear loose clothing when you are   19.____

   A. in a corridor
   B. storing tools
   C. opening cabinets
   D. near moving machinery

20. According to the above passage, before moving a ladder, you should

   A. test all the rungs
   B. get a dolly to carry the ladder at all times
   C. remove everything from the top of the ladder which might fall off
   D. remove your necktie

21. According to the above passage, an employee who gets a slight cut should

   A. have it treated to help prevent infection
   B. know that a slight cut becomes more easily infected than a big cut
   C. pay no attention to it as it can't become serious
   D. realize that it is more serious than any other type of injury

Questions 22-24.

DIRECTIONS: Answer Questions 22 to 24 ONLY according to the information given in the following passage.

GOOD EMPLOYEE PRACTICES

As a City employee, you will be expected to take an interest in your work and perform the duties of your job to the best of your ability and in a spirit of cooperation. Nothing shows an interest in your work more than coming to work on time, not only at the start of the day but also when returning from lunch. If it is necessary for you to keep a personal appointment at lunch hour which might cause a delay in getting back to work on time, you should explain the situation to your supervisor and get his approval to come back a little late before you leave for lunch.

You should do everything that is asked of you willingly and consider important even the small jobs that your supervisor gives you. Although these jobs may seem unimportant, if you forget to do them or if you don't do them right, trouble may develop later.

Getting along well with your fellow workers will add much to the enjoyment of your work. You should respect your fellow workers and try to see their side when a disagreement arises. The better you get along with your fellow workers and your supervisor, the better you will like your job and the better you will be able to do it.

22. According to the above passage, in your job as a City employee, you are expected to

   A. show a willingness to cooperate on the job
   B. get your supervisor's approval before keeping any personal appointments at lunch hour
   C. avoid doing small jobs that seem unimportant
   D. do the easier jobs at the start of the day and the more difficult ones later on

23. According to the above passage, getting to work on time shows that you

   A. need the job
   B. have an interest in your work
   C. get along well with your fellow workers
   D. like your supervisor

24. According to the above passage, the one of the following statements that is NOT true is 24._____
   A. if you do a small job wrong, trouble may develop
   B. you should respect your fellow workers
   C. if you disagree with a fellow worker, you should try to see his side of the story
   D. the less you get along with your supervisor, the better you will be able to do your job

Questions 25-35.   VOCABULARY

25. The porter cleaned the VACANT room. 25._____
   In this sentence, the word VACANT means nearly the same as
   A. empty   B. large   C. main   D. crowded

26. The supervisor gave a BRIEF report to his men. 26._____
   In this sentence, the word BRIEF means nearly the same as
   A. long   B. safety   C. complete   D. short

27. The supervisor told him to CONNECT the two pieces. 27._____
   In this sentence, the word CONNECT means nearly the same as
   A. join   B. paint   C. return   D. weigh

28. Standing on the top of a ladder is RISKY. 28._____
   In this sentence, the word RISKY means nearly the same as
   A. dangerous   B. sensible   C. safe   D. foolish

29. He RAISED the cover of the machine. 29._____
   In this sentence, the word RAISED means nearly the same as
   A. broke   B. lifted   C. lost   D. found

30. The form used for reporting the finished work was REVISED. 30._____
   In this sentence, the word REVISED means nearly the same as
   A. printed   B. ordered   C. dropped   D. changed

31. He did his work RAPIDLY. 31._____
   In this sentence, the word RAPIDLY means nearly the same as
   A. carefully   B. quickly   C. slowly   D. quietly

32. The worker was OCCASIONALLY late 32._____
   In this sentence, the word OCCASIONALLY means nearly the same as
   A. sometimes   B. often   C. never   D. always

33. He SELECTED the best tool for the job. 33._____
   In this sentence, the word SELECTED means nearly the same as
   A. bought   B. picked   C. lost   D. broke

34. He needed ASSISTANCE to lift the package.
    In this sentence, the word ASSISTANCE means nearly the same as

    A. strength   B. time   C. help   D. instructions

35. The tools were ISSUED by the supervisor.
    In this sentence, the word ISSUED means nearly the same as

    A. collected   B. cleaned up
    C. given out   D. examined

KEY (CORRECT ANSWERS)

1. C		16. C
2. B		17. D
3. C		18. B
4. B		19. D
5. A		20. C
6. C		21. A
7. C		22. A
8. D		23. B
9. B		24. D
10. B		25. A
11. C		26. D
12. D		27. A
13. A		28. A
14. A		29. B
15. A		30. D

31. B
32. A
33. B
34. C
35. C

EXAMINATION SECTION
TEST 1

DIRECTIONS: Each question or incomplete statement is followed by several suggested answers or completions. Select the one that BEST answers the question or completes the statement. *PRINT THE LETTER OF THE CORRECT ANSWER IN THE SPACE AT THE RIGHT.*

Questions 1-4.

DIRECTIONS: Questions 1 through 4 are to be answered on the basis of the information provided in the paragraph below.

Rodent control must be planned carefully in order to insure its success. This means that more knowledge is needed about the habits and favorite breeding places of Domestic Rats, than any other kind. A favorite breeding place for Domestic Rats is known to be in old or badly constructed buildings. Rats find these buildings very comfortable for making nests. However, the only way to gain this kind of detailed knowledge about rats is through careful study.

1. According to the above paragraph, rats find comfortable nesting places   1.____
   - A. in old buildings
   - B. in pipes
   - C. on roofs
   - D. in sewers

2. The paragraph states that the BEST way to learn all about the favorite nesting places of rats is by   2.____
   - A. asking people
   - B. careful study
   - C. using traps
   - D. watching ratholes

3. According to the paragraph, in order to insure the success of rodent control, it is necessary to   3.____
   - A. design better bait
   - B. give out more information
   - C. plan carefully
   - D. use pesticides

4. The paragraph states that the MOST important rats to study are _____ rats.   4.____
   - A. African
   - B. Asian
   - C. Domestic
   - D. European

Questions 5-8.

DIRECTIONS: Questions 5 through 8 are to be answered on the basis of the following paragraph.

A few people who live in old tenements have the bad habit of throwing garbage out of their windows, especially if there is an empty lot near their building. Sometimes the garbage is food, sometimes the garbage is half-empty soda cans. Sometimes the garbage is a little bit of both mixed together. These people just don't care about keeping the lot clean.

5. The paragraph states that throwing garbage out of windows is a

   A. bad habit
   B. dangerous thing to do
   C. good thing to do
   D. good way to feed rats

6. According to the paragraph, an empty lot next to an old tenement is sometimes used as a place to

   A. hold local gang meetings
   B. play ball
   C. throw garbage
   D. walk dogs

7. According to the paragraph, which of the following throw garbage out of their windows?

   A. Nobody
   B. Everybody
   C. Most people
   D. Some people

8. According to the paragraph, the kinds of garbage thrown out of windows are

   A. candy and cigarette butts
   B. food and half-empty soda cans
   C. fruit and vegetables
   D. rice and bread

Questions 9-12.

DIRECTIONS: Questions 9 through 12 are to be answered on the basis of the following paragraph.

The game that is recognised all over the world as an all-American game is the game of baseball. As a matter of fact, baseball heroes like Joe DiMaggio, Willie Mays, and Babe Ruth, were as famous in their day as movie stars Robert Redford, Paul Newman, and Clint Eastwood are now. All these men have had the experience of being mobbed by fans whenever they put in an appearance anywhere in the world. Such unusual popularity makes it possible for stars like these to earn at least as much money off the job as on the job. It didn't take manufacturers and advertising men long to discover that their sales of shaving lotion, for instance, increased when they got famous stars to advertise their product for them on radio and television.

9. According to the paragraph, baseball is known everywhere as a(n) _____ game.

   A. all-American
   B. fast
   C. unusual
   D. tough

10. According to the paragraph, being so well known means that it is possible for people like Willie Mays and Babe Ruth to

    A. ask for anything and get it
    B. make as much money off the job as on it
    C. travel anywhere free of charge
    D. watch any game free of charge

11. According to the paragraph, which of the following are known all over the world?

    A. Baseball heroes
    B. Advertising men
    C. Manufacturers
    D. Basketball heroes

12. According to the paragraph, it is possible to sell much more shaving lotion on television and radio if

   A. the commercials are in color instead of black and white
   B. you can get a prize with each bottle of shaving lotion
   C. the shaving lotion makes you smell nicer than usual
   D. the shaving lotion is advertised by famous stars

Questions 13-16.

DIRECTIONS: Questions 13 through 16 are to be answered on the basis of the following paragraph.

People are very suspicious of all strangers who knock at their door. For this reason, every pest control aide, whether man or woman, must carry an identification card at all times on the job. These cards are issued by the agency the aide works for. The aide's picture is on the card. The aide's name is typed in, and the aide's signature is written on the line below. The name, address, and telephone number of the agency issuing the card is also printed on it. Once the aide shows this ID card to prove his or her identity, the tenant's time should not be taken up with small talk. The tenant should be told briefly what pest control means. The aide should be polite and ready to answer any questions the tenant may have on the subject. Then, the aide should thank the tenant for listening and say goodbye.

13. According to the above paragraph, when she visits tenants, the one item a pest control aide must ALWAYS carry with her is a(n)

   A. badge   B. driver's license
   C. identification card D. watch

14. According to the paragraph, a pest control aide is supposed to talk to each tenant he visits

   A. at length about the agency
   B. briefly about pest control
   C. at length about family matters
   D. briefly about social security

15. According to the paragraph, the item that does NOT appear on an ID card is the

   A. address of the agency
   B. name of the agency
   C. signature of the aide
   D. social security number of the aide

16. According to the paragraph, a pest control aide carries an identification card because he must

   A. prove to tenants who he is
   B. provide the tenants with the agency's address
   C. provide the tenant with the agency's telephone number
   D. save the tenant's time

Questions 17-20.

DIRECTIONS: Questions 17 through 20 are to be answered on the basis of the following paragraph.

Very early on a summer's morning, the nicest thing to look at is a beach, before the swimmers arrive. Usually all the litter has been picked up from the sand by the Park Department clean-up crew. Everything is quiet. All you can hear are the waves breaking, and the sea gulls calling to each other. The beach opens to the public at 10 A.M. Long before that time, however, long lines of eager men, women, and children have driven up to the entrance. They form long lines that wind around the beach waiting for the signal to move.

17. According to the paragraph, before 10 A.M., long lines are formed that are made up of   17.____
    - A. cars
    - B. clean-up crews
    - C. men, women, and children
    - D. Park Department trucks

18. The season referred to in the above paragraph is   18.____
    - A. fall
    - B. summer
    - C. winter
    - D. spring

19. The place the paragraph is describing is a   19.____
    - A. beach
    - B. park
    - C. golf course
    - D. tennis court

20. According to the paragraph, one of the things you notice early in the morning is that   20.____
    - A. radios are playing
    - B. swimmers are there
    - C. the sand is dirty
    - D. the litter is gone

Questions 21-30.

DIRECTIONS: In Questions 21 through 30, select the answer which means MOST NEARLY the SAME as the capitalized word in the sentence.

21. He received a large REWARD.
    In this sentence, the word REWARD means   21.____
    - A. capture
    - B. recompense
    - C. key
    - D. praise

22. The aide was asked to TRANSMIT a message. In this sentence, the word TRANSMIT means   22.____
    - A. change
    - B. send
    - C. take
    - D. type

23. The pest control aide REQUESTED the tenant to call the Health Department.
    In this sentence, the word REQUESTED means the pest control aide   23.____
    - A. asked
    - B. helped
    - C. informed
    - D. warned

24. The driver had to RETURN the Health Department's truck. In this sentence, the word RETURN means   24.____
    - A. borrow
    - B. fix
    - C. give back
    - D. load up

25. The aide discussed the PURPOSE of the visit. In this sentence, the word PURPOSE means   25.____

     A. date   B. hour   C. need   D. reason,

26. The tenant SUSPECTED the aide who knocked at her door. In this sentence, the word SUSPECTED means   26.____

     A. answered   B. called
     C. distrusted   D. welcomed

27. The aide was POSITIVE that the child hit her. In this sentence, the word POSITIVE means   27.____

     A. annoyed   B. certain   C. sorry   D. surprised

28. The tenant DECLINED to call the Health Department. In this sentence, the word DECLINED means   28.____

     A. agreed   B. decided   C. refused   D. wanted

29. The aide ARRIVED on time.
In this sentence, the word ARRIVED means   29.____

     A. awoke   B. came   C. left   D. delayed

30. The salesman had to DELIVER books to each person he visited.
In this sentence, the word DELIVER means   30.____

     A. give   B. lend   C. mail   D. sell

KEY (CORRECT ANSWERS)

1.	A	11.	A	21.	B
2.	B	12.	D	22.	B
3.	C	13.	C	23.	A
4.	C	14.	B	24.	C
5.	A	15.	D	25.	D
6.	C	16.	A	26.	C
7.	D	17.	C	27.	B
8.	B	18.	B	28.	C
9.	A	19.	A	29.	B
10.	B	20.	D	30.	A

TEST 2

DIRECTIONS: Each question or incomplete statement is followed by several suggested answers or completions. Select the one that BEST answers the question or completes the statement. *PRINT THE LETTER OF THE CORRECT ANSWER IN THE SPACE AT THE RIGHT.*

Questions 1-10.

DIRECTIONS: In Questions 1 through 10, pick the word that means MOST NEARLY the OPPOSITE of the capitalize word in the sentence.

1. It is possible to CONSTRUCT a rat-proof home. The opposite of CONSTRUCT is   1.____
   A. build   B. erect   C. plant   D. wreck

2. The pest control aide had to REPAIR the flat tire. The opposite of the word REPAIR is   2.____
   A. destroy   B. fix   C. mend   D. patch

3. The pest control aide tried to SHOUT the answer. The opposite of the word SHOUT is   3.____
   A. scream   B. shriek   C. whisper   D. yell

4. Daily VISITS are the best.
   The opposite of the word VISITS is   4.____
   A. absences   B. exercises   C. lessons   D. trials

5. It is important to ARRIVE early in the morning. The opposite of the word ARRIVE is   5.____
   A. climb   B. descend   C. enter   D. leave

6. Jorge is a group LEADER.
   The opposite of the word LEADER is   6.____
   A. boss   B. chief   C. follower   D. overseer

7. The EXTERIOR of the house needs painting.
   The opposite of the word EXTERIOR is   7.____
   A. inside   B. outdoors   C. outside   D. surface

8. He CONCEDED the victory.
   The opposite of the word CONCEDED is   8.____
   A. admitted   B. denied   C. granted   D. reported

9. He watched the team BEGIN.
   The opposite of the word BEGIN is   9.____
   A. end   B. fail   C. gather   D. win

10. Your handwriting is ILLEGIBLE.
    The opposite of the word ILLEGIBLE is   10.____
    A. clear   B. confused   C. jumbled   D. unclear

Questions 11-15.

DIRECTIONS: Questions 11 through 15 are to be answered by following the instructions given in each question. Note that 5 possible answers have been given for these questions ONLY. Therefore, for these questions, your choice may be A, B, C, D, or E.

11. Add:

    $12\frac{1}{2}$

    $2\frac{1}{4}$

    $3\frac{1}{4}$

    The CORRECT answer is

    A. 17 B. 17¼ C. 17½ D. 17 3/4 E. 18

    11.____

12. Subtract: 150

    −80

    The CORRECT answer is

    A. 70 B. 80 C. 130 D. 150 E. 230

    12.____

13. After cleaning up some lots in the East Bronx, five cleanup crews loaded the following amounts of garbage on trucks:
    Crew No. 1 loaded 2 1/4 tons
    Crew No. 2 loaded 3 tons
    Crew No. 3 loaded 1 1/4 tons
    Crew No. 4 loaded 2 1/4 tons
    Crew No. 5 loaded 1/2 ton
    The TOTAL number of tons of garbage loaded was

    A. 8 B. 8 1/4 C. 8 3/4 D. 9 E. 9 1/4

    13.____

14. Subtract: 17 3/4

    − 7 1/4

    The CORRECT answer is

    A. 7 1/2 B. 10 1/2 C. 14 1/4 D. 17 3/4 E. 25

    14.____

15. Yesterday, Tom and Bill each received 10 leaflets about rat control. Each supermarket in the neighborhood was supposed to receive one of these leaflets. When the day was over, Tom had 8 leaflets left. Bill had no leaflets left. How many supermarkets got leaflets yesterday?

    A. 8 B. 10 C. 12 D. 18 E. 20

    15.____

Questions 16-20.

DIRECTIONS: Questions 16 through 20 are to be answered ONLY on the basis of the information in the following statement and chart, DAILY WORK REPORT FORM (Chart A).

Assume that you are a member of the Pest Control Truck Crew Number 1. Julio Rivera is your Crew Chief. The crew is supposed to report to work at nine o'clock in the morning, Since you are the first to show up, at ten minutes before nine, on 5/24 Rivera asks you to help him out by filling in the Daily Work Report Form for him. Driver Hal Williams shows up at nine, and Driver Rick Smith shows up ten minutes after Williams.

DAILY WORK REPORT FORM (Chart A)

Block #1 Crew No.	Block #2 Date	
Block #3 TRUCKS IN USE Truck # ____ # ____ # ____ # ____ # ____ # ____ # ____ # ____ # ____ # ____	Block #4 DRIVER'S NAME ____ ____ ____ ____ ____ ____ ____ ____	Block #5 TIME OF ARRIVAL A.M. P.M.
Block #6 TRUCKS OUT OF ORDER # ____ # ____ # ____ # ____ #	Block #7 ADDRESS OF CLEAN-UP SITE No. ____ Street ____	Block #8 Borough Block #9 Signature of Crew Chief

16. According to the above statement, the entry that belongs in Block #9 is   16. ____
    A. Julio Rivera   B. June Stevens
    C. Jim Watson   D. Hal Williams

17. According to the above statement, the entry that should be made in Block #2 is   17. ____
    A. 9:00 A.M.   B. 9:10 P.M.   C. 5/24   D. 7/24

18. The names of Hal Williams and Rick Smith should appear in Block #   18. ____
    A. 4   B. 6   C. 7   D. 9

19. Rick Smith's time of arrival should be entered in Block #5 as _____ A.M.   19.____

    A. 8:50 B. 8:55 C. 9:00 D. 9:10

20. According to the statement, the entry that should be made in Block #1 is   20.____

    A. zero B. one C. 5/24 D. 6/24

Questions 21-23.

DIRECTIONS: Questions 21 through 23 are to be answered on the basis of the statement shown below. Use DAILY WORK REPORT FORM (Chart A) on Page 3 as a guide.

Pete Marberg showed up at a quarter after nine, in the morning, but his truck, No. 22632441, was in the garage for repairs. Steve Marino showed up a half hour after Pete. He was assigned truck No. 6342003, which was in working order.

21. According to the above statement, truck No. 22632441 should be entered in Block #   21.____

    A. 3 B. 4 C. 6 D. 8

22. According to the above statement, Steve Marino showed up at   22.____

    A. 9:00 A.M. B. 9:15 A.M. C. 9:30 P.M. D. 9:45 A.M.

23. According to the above statement, Steve Marino's truck number belongs in Block #3. The number entered there should be   23.____

    A. 22632441 B. 6342003 C. 6432003 D. 26232441

Questions 24-30.

DIRECTIONS: Questions 24 through 30 are to be answered ONLY on basis of the information in the statements above ea question and the following chart, DAILY GARBAGE COLLECTION REPORT (Chart B).

DAILY GARBAGE COLLECTION REPORT C Chart B)				
Block #1	Block #2	Block #3	Block #4	Block #5
No. of Trucks Used For Collection	Address of Garbage Pick-Up	Amount of Garbage Collected	Amount of Garbage Unloaded	Hours During Which Garbage Was Unloaded
#456	45 Southwest	1/2 ton	1/2 ton	From To 7 AM 8 AM
		Block #6 otal Amount of Garbage Collected By All Trucks	Block #7 Total Amount of Garbage Unloaded By All Trucks	Block #8 Total Amount of Time Spent Unloading Of All Trucks
TOTALS _____				

24. Truck # 2437752 started unloading garbage at ten o'clock Monday morning and finished unloading its garbage that afternoon. The clock looked like this when the job was done.
The time entries that should be recorded in Block #5 are
   A. 10 A.M. and 12:15 P.M.
   B. 10 P.M. and 12:30 A.M.
   C. 10 P.M. and 12:00 A.M.
   D. 10 A.M. and 3:00 P.M.

24._____

25. Truck # 8967432 had to pick up a load of garbage from 911 South Avenue. It took the crew until 11:00 A.M. to load the garbage.
According to this statement, the item 911 South Avenue should be entered in Block #

   A. 1   B. 2   C. 3   D. 4

25._____

26. On Tuesday, truck # 124356 unloaded 4 ton of garbage, truck # 2437752 unloaded J ton of garbage, and truck # 435126 unloaded 1/2 ton of garbage.
The TOTAL amount of garbage unloaded by the three trucks on Tuesday should be entered in Block #

   A. 3   B. 4   C. 5   D. 8

26._____

27. On Wednesday, it took truck # 4050607 from 2 P.M. to 6 P.M. to unload 1 ton of garbage. It took truck # 7040650 from 1 P.M. to 2 P.M. to unload 1/4 ton of garbage. These were the only trucks working that day.
The TOTAL amount of time it took for both trucks to unload garbage was _____ hours.

   A. 5   B. 6   C. 7   D. 8

27._____

28. The amount of garbage collected by one truck should be entered in the DAILY GARBAGE COLLECTION REPORT FORM in Block #

   A. 3   B. 6   C. 7   D. 8

28._____

29. Truck # 557799010 reported to 1020 Hudson River Alley to pick up garbage from an empty lot.
This information should be entered in the DAILY GARBAGE COLLECTION REPORT FORM in Block # _____ and Block # _____.

   A. 1; 4   B. 2; 5   C. 1; 2   D. 2; 3

29._____

30. It took the Pest Control Truck crew from 8 in the morning to 12 noon to unload the garbage it collected the night before.
    This information should be entered in the DAILY GARBAGE COLLECTION REPORT FORM under Block #

    A. 4   B. 5   C. 6   D. 7

30._____

KEY (CORRECT ANSWERS)

1.	D	11.	E	21.	C
2.	A	12.	A	22.	D
3.	C	13.	E	23.	B
4.	A	14.	B	24.	D
5.	D	15.	C	25.	B
6.	C	16.	A	26.	B
7.	A	17.	C	27.	A
8.	B	18.	A	28.	A
9.	A	19.	D	29.	C
10.	A	20.	B	30.	B

ARITHMETICAL REASONING
EXAMINATION SECTION
TEST 1

DIRECTIONS: Each question or incomplete statement is followed by several suggested answers or completions. Select the one that BEST answers the question or completes the statement. *PRINT THE LETTER OF THE CORRECT ANSWER IN THE SPACE AT THE RIGHT.*

1. A custodial assistant takes an average of forty minutes to mop 1,000 square feet of floor. The amount of time this custodial assistant should take to mop the floor of a rectangular corridor eight feet wide by sixty feet long is, on the average, MOST NEARLY _____ minutes.

    A. 10   B. 20   C. 30   D. 40

2. An auditorium eighty feet by 100 feet must be swept in one hour.
If each custodial assistant takes fifteen minutes to sweep 1,000 square feet of auditorium area, the number of custodial assistants that must be assigned to complete the sweeping in one hour is

    A. 1   B. 2   C. 3   D. 4

3. A detergent manufacturer recommends mixing 8 ounces of detergent in one gallon of water to prepare a cleaning solution.
The amount of the same detergent which should be mixed with thirty gallons of water to obtain the same strength cleaning solution is _____ ounces.

    A. 24   B. 30   C. 240   D. 380

4. The floor area of a corridor 8 feet wide and 72 feet long is MOST NEARLY _____ square feet.

    A. 80   B. 420   C. 580   D. 870

5. A water tank that is 5 feet in diameter and 30 feet high has a volume of MOST NEARLY _____ cubic feet.

    A. 150   B. 250   C. 600   D. 1,200

6. The circumference of a circle with a radius of 5 inches is MOST NEARLY _____ inches.

    A. 31.3   B. 30.0   C. 20.1   D. 13.4

7. Suppose that you are the custodian-engineer and an employee works for you at the rate of $8.70 per hour with time and one-half paid for time worked after 40 hours in one week. His gross pay for working 53 hours in one week is MOST NEARLY

    A. $461.10   B. $482.10   C. $487.65   D. $517.65

8. Suppose that you are the custodian-engineer and one of your employees has gotten gross earnings of $437.10 for the week, all of which is subject to deductions at the rate of 4.8%.
The amount which should be deducted from the employee's gross earnings for the week is MOST NEARLY

   A. $2.10   B. $14.70   C. $17.70   D. $20.97

9. The directions on the label of a bottle of detergent call for mixing four ounces of detergent with one gallon of water to make a cleaning solution for washing floors. In order to obtain a larger amount of solution of the same strength, one quart of the detergent should be mixed with _____ gallons of water.

   A. 2   B. 4   C. 6   D. 8

10. The area of a lawn which is 58 feet wide by 96 feet long is MOST NEARLY _____ square feet.

    A. 5,000   B. 5,500   C. 6,000   D. 6,500

11. In a building which is heated by an oil-fired boiler, 2,100 gallons of fuel oil were burned in a period in which the degree days reached a total of 1,400.
If all other conditions remained constant, the number of gallons of fuel oil that would be burned in this building during a period in which the degree days reached a total of 3,600 is

    A. 2,400   B. 2,900   C. 4,800   D. 5,400

12. The instructions for mixing a powdered cleaner in water state, *Mix three ounces of powder in a 14-quart pail three-quarters full of water.* A cleaner asks you how much powdered cleaner he should use in a mop truck containing 28 gallons of water to obtain the same strength solution.
The CORRECT answer is _____ ounces of powder.

    A. 6   B. 8   C. 24   D. 32

13. A custodian-engineer wishes to order sponges in the most economical manner.
Keeping in mind that large sponges can be cut up into many smaller sizes, the one of the following that has the LEAST cost per cubic inch of sponge is

    A. 2" x 4" x 6" sponges @ $.48
    B. 4" x 8" x 12" sponges @ $2.88
    C. 4" x 6" x 36" sponges @ $9.60
    D. 6" x 8" x 32" sponges @ $19.20

14. Two cleaners swept four corridors in 24 minutes. Each corridor measured 12 feet x 176 feet.
The space swept per man per minute was MOST NEARLY _____ square feet.

    A. 50   B. 90   C. 180   D. 350

15. Kerosene costs 60 cents a quart.
At that rate, two gallons would cost

    A. $2.40   B. $3.60   C. $4.80   D. $6.00

16. The instructions on a container of cleaning compound states, *Mix one pound of compound in 5 gallons of water.* Using these instructions, the amount of compound which should be added to 15 quarts of water is MOST likely _____ ounces.

    A. 3   B. 8   C. 12   D. 48

16.____

17. Suppose that you are the custodian-engineer and one of your employees has gross earnings of $582.80 for the week, all of which is subject to Social Security deductions at the rate of 4.8%.
    The amount which should be deducted from the employee's gross earnings for the week is MOST NEARLY

    A. $2.80   B. $19.60   C. $23.60   D. $27.96

17.____

18. Suppose that you are a custodian-engineer and an employee works for you at the rate of $11.60 per hour with time and one-half paid for time worked after 40 hours in one week. His gross pay for working 53 hours in one week is MOST NEARLY

    A. $614.80   B. $642.80   C. $650.20   D. $690.20

18.____

19. The volume, in cubic feet, of a cylindrical tank 6 feet in diameter x 35 feet long is MOST NEARLY

    A. 210   B. 990   C. 1,260   D. 3,960

19.____

20. A room 12 feet wide by 25 feet long has a floor area of _____ square feet.

    A. 37   B. 200   C. 300   D. 400

20.____

21. How many hours will it take a worker to sweep a floor space of 2,800 square feet if he sweeps at the rate of 800 square feet per hour?

    A. 8   B. 6 1/2   C. 3 1/2   D. 2 1/2

21.____

22. One gallon of water contains

    A. 2 quarts   B. 4 quarts   C. 2 pints   D. 4 pints

22.____

23. A standard cleaning solution is prepared by mixing 4 ounces of detergent powder in 2 gallons of water.
    The number of ounces of detergent powder needed for the same strength solution in 5 gallons of water is

    A. 4   B. 6   C. 8   D. 10

23.____

24. The ceiling of a room which measures 20 feet x 30 feet is to be given two coats of paint. If one gallon of paint will cover 500 square feet, the two coats of paint will require a MINIMUM of _____ gallons.

    A. 1.5   B. 2   C. 2.4   D. 3.2

24.____

25. The floor area of a room which measures 10 feet long by 10 feet wide is _____ square feet.

    A. 20   B. 40   C. 100   D. 1,000

25.____

KEY (CORRECT ANSWERS)

1. B
2. B
3. C
4. C
5. C

6. A
7. D
8. D
9. D
10. B

11. D
12. D
13. B
14. C
15. C

16. C
17. D
18. D
19. B
20. C

21. C
22. B
23. D
24. C
25. C

SOLUTIONS TO PROBLEMS

1. (8')(60') = 480 sq.ft. Let x = required time in minutes.

    Then, $\dfrac{40}{1000} = \dfrac{x}{480}$. Solving, x = 19.2 or nearly 20.

2. (80')(100') = 8000 sq.ft. Each custodian can sweep (1000)(4) = 4000 sq.ft. in 1 hour. Then, 8000 ÷ 4000 = 2.

3. (8)(30) = 240 ounces

4. (8')(72') = 576 sq.ft. or nearly 580 sq.ft.

5. Volume = $(\pi)(2.5')^2 (30') \approx$ 589 cu.ft. or nearly 600 cu.ft.

6. Circumference = $(2\pi)(5") \approx$ 31.3 sq.in.

7. ($8.70)(40) + ($13.05)(13) = $517.65

8. ($437.10)(.048) ≈ $20.97

9. 1 quart = 32 oz. Then, 32 ÷ 4 = 8 gallons of water

10. (58')(96') = 5568 sq.ft., which is closest to 5500 sq.ft.

11. Let x = number of gallons. Then, $\dfrac{2100}{1400} = \dfrac{x}{3600}$. Solving, x = 5400

12. (.75)(14)(.25) = 2.625 gallons of water. Let x = number of ounces of powder needed. Then, $\dfrac{3}{2.625} = \dfrac{x}{28}$. Solving, x = 32

13. For selection B, (4")(8")(12") = 384 cu.in., and the cost per cubic inch = $2.88 ÷ 384 = $.0075. This is lower than selections A ($.01), C ($.011), or D ($.015).

14. Two men sweep (4)(12')(176') = 8448 total sq.ft. in 24 min. = 352 sq.ft. per min. Each man sweeps 176 sq.ft. per min ≈ 180 sq.ft. per min.

15. Two gallons = 8 quarts. Then, ($.60)(8) = $4.80

16. 15 quarts = 3.75 gallons of water. Let x = required number of ounces of compound. Then, $\dfrac{16}{5} = \dfrac{x}{3.75}$. Solving, x = 12

17. ($582.80)(.048) ≈ $27.96

18. ($11.60 × 40) + ($17.40)(13) = $690.20

19. Volume = $(\pi)(3')^2 (35') \approx$ 990 cu.ft.

20. (12')(25') = 300 sq.ft.

21. 2800 ÷ 800 = 3 1/2 hours

22. One gallon = 4 quarts

23. Let x = required number of ounces. Then, $\dfrac{4}{2} = \dfrac{x}{5}$. Solving, x = 10

24. 2 coats means (2)(20')(30') = 1200 sq.ft. Then, 1200 ÷ 500 = 2.4 gallons

25. (10')(10') = 100 sq.ft.

TEST 2

DIRECTIONS: Each question or incomplete statement is followed by several suggested answers or completions. Select the one that BEST answers the question or completes the statement. *PRINT THE LETTER OF THE CORRECT ANSWER IN THE SPACE AT THE RIGHT.*

1. Assume that a certain elevator starter is at work 8 hours a day, which includes 1 hour for lunch and two 15-minute relief periods. The rest of the workday the starter is performing his duties.
 If the starter works 4 days, the TOTAL amount of time the starter will actually be performing his duties is _____ hours.

    A. 24   B. 26   C. 28   D. 32

    1._____

2. Assume that a certain bank of 18 elevators operating at full capacity could move 3,240 passengers an hour from the main lobby.
 The number of passengers that one of these elevators could move from the lobby every 15 minutes is, on the average,

    A. 12   B. 22   C. 45   D. 180

    2._____

3. In a certain agency, the amount of absence due to injury or illness was an average of 6 hours a month for each employee.
 If this agency had 335 employees, the TOTAL number of hours lost in a year due to injury or sickness was

    A. 4,020   B. 20,100   C. 24,120   D. 28,140

    3._____

4. Assume that in a certain building the elevators must handle 16% of the building population during a peak traffic period.
 If the building population is 2,825, the TOTAL number of people the elevators must handle during a peak traffic period is

    A. 396   B. 424   C. 436   D. 452

    4._____

5. From his coin bank, a boy took 3 half dollars, 8 quarters, 7 dimes, 6 nickels, and 9 pennies to deposit in his school savings account.
 Express in dollars and cents the TOTAL amount of money he deposited.

    A. $2.82   B. $4.59   C. $6.42   D. $7.52

    5._____

6. If a roast that requires 1 hour and 40 minutes of roasting time has been in the oven for 55 minutes, how many more minutes of roasting time are required?

    A. 30   B. 36   C. 45   D. 55

    6._____

7. On the first day of its drive, a school raised $40, which was 33 1/3% of its Red Cross quota.
 How much was the quota?

    A. $120   B. $130   C. $140   D. $150

    7._____

8. When 0.750 is divided by 0.875, the answer is MOST NEARLY

    A. 0.250   B. 0.312   C. 0.624   D. 0.857

    8._____

9. The circumference of a 6-inch diameter circle is MOST NEARLY _____ feet.

    A. 1.57   B. 2.1   C. 2.31   D. 4.24

10. An 18" piece of cable that weighs 3 pounds per foot has a total weight of _____ pounds.

    A. 5.5   B. 4.5   C. 3.0   D. 1.5

11. The sum of 0.135, 0.040, 0.812, and 0.961 is

    A. 1.424   B. 1.625   C. 1.843   D. 1.948

12. If an elevator carries a load of 1,600 pounds uniformly distributed on a 4 feet by 5 feet floor, the weight per square foot is _____ pounds.

    A. 98   B. 80   C. 65   D. 40

13. If one cubic inch of lead weighs one-quarter of a pound, the weight of a bar of lead 1" high by 2" wide by 8" long is _____ pounds.

    A. 1.8   B. 2.5   C. 3.1   D. 4

14. Assume that 8 mechanics have been assigned to do a job that must be finished in 5 days. At the end of 3 days, the men have completed only half the job.
    In order to complete the job on time in the remaining 2 days, the MINIMUM number of extra men that should be assigned is

    A. 2   B. 3   C. 4   D. 6

15. An elevator supply manufacturer quotes a list price of $625 less 10 and 5 percent for ten contactors.
    The actual cost for these ten contactors is MOST NEARLY

    A. $562   B. $554   C. $534   D. $522

16. To find the largest number of passengers, including the operator, allowed to ride in an elevator, divide the rated capacity of the elevator by 150.
    According to this rule, what is the LARGEST number of passengers NOT counting the operator that may be carried in an elevator with a rated capacity of 3,000 lbs.?

    A. 18   B. 19   C. 20   D. 21

17. Suppose that the work schedule for operators is 5 days a week, 8 hours a day.
    In a period of 4 weeks, with no holidays, how many hours will you be required to be on duty?

    A. 160   B. 180   C. 200   D. 225

18. Mr. Jones takes $200 to cover his expenses for a week. He spends $6.00 for carfare coming to work and $6.00 for carfare going home. He buys a $1 newspaper each day and spends $16.00 for lunch and $5.00 for cigarettes each day.
    How much money does he have left at the end of a 5-day work week?

    A. $30.00   B. $55.00   C. $100.00   D. $170.00

19. Twelve hundred employees work in an office building.
Twenty percent of these employees work on the 4th floor and 25% work on the 5th floor.
The TOTAL number of employees who work on the 4th and 5th floors together is

   A. 240   B. 300   C. 540   D. 660

20. An elevator makes one roundtrip every 5 minutes, on the average.
How many roundtrips does it make between 8:15 A.M. and 9:45 A.M.?

   A. 12   B. 18   C. 20   D. 22

21. The floor of an elevator car measures 7 feet by 8 feet 6 inches.
How many square feet of linoleum would be needed to cover this floor?

   A. 31   B. 42   C. 59 1/2   D. 62 1/2

Questions 22-25.

   DIRECTIONS: Each question consists of a statement. You are to indicate whether the statement is TRUE (T) or FALSE (F).

22. In a city building, there are 20 elevators. If on one day five percent of the elevators are out of order, the number of elevators out of order is 2.

23. An elevator operator puts in 32 hours of overtime in January, 26 hours in February, 10 hours in March, 10 hours in April, and 27 hours in May. The average amount of overtime this operator worked per month for these five months is 21 hours.

24. A large city building normally has 45 elevator operators on its day shift. The vacation rules require that only 1/5 be allowed away at any time. The number of operators that may be on vacation at one time is nine.

25. In a six-story city building, there are 13 offices on the first floor, 19 offices on the second floor, 18 offices on the third floor, 17 offices on the fourth floor, 21 offices on the fifth floor, and 23 offices on the sixth floor. The total number of offices in this building is 109.

KEY (CORRECT ANSWERS)

1.	B	11.	D
2.	C	12.	B
3.	C	13.	D
4.	D	14.	C
5.	B	15.	C
6.	C	16.	B
7.	A	17.	A
8.	D	18.	A
9.	A	19.	C
10.	B	20.	B

21. C
22. F
23. T
24. T
25. F

SOLUTIONS TO PROBLEMS

1. 4(8-1-.5) = 26 hours

2. Each elevator can move 3240 ÷ 18 = 180 passengers per hour, which = 45 passengers per 15 minutes.

3. (335)(6)(12) = 24,120 hours per year.

4. (2825)(.16) = 452

5. (3)(.50) + (8)(.25) + (7)(.10) + (6)(.05) + (9)(.01) = $4.59

6. 1 hr. 40 min. - 55 min. = 100 min. - 55 min. = 45 min.

7. $40 ÷ $33\frac{1}{3}$% = $40 ÷ $\frac{1}{3}$ = $120

8. .750 ÷ .875 ≈ .857

9. Circumference = $(\frac{1}{2}')(\pi)$ ≈ 1.57'

10. 18" ÷ 12" = 1.5. Then, (1.5)(3) = 4.5 lbs.

11. .135 + .040 + .812 + .961 = 1.948

12. (4')(5') = 20 sq.ft. Then, 1600 ÷ 20 = 80 lbs. per sq.ft.

13. (1")(2")(8") = 16 cu.in. Then, (16)(1/4) = 4 pounds

14. 8 men x 3 cars = 50% of work; 24 man-days = 50% of work; 48 man-days = 100%; 24 man-days ÷ 2 days = 12 men per day = 4 extra men

15. ($625)(.90)(.95) ≈ $534

16. 3000 ÷ 150 = 20 people, including the operator. Thus, only 19 passengers are allowed.

17. (8)(5)(4) = 160 hours

18. $200 - 5($6.00+$6.00+$1+$16.00+$5.00) = $30.00

19. (1200)(20%+25%) = (1200)(.45) = 540

20. 9:45 AM - 8:15 AM = 90 min. Then, 90 ÷ 5 = 18 roundtrips

21. (7')(8 1/2') = 59 1/2 sq.ft.

22. False; (20)(.05) = 1, not 2.

23. True. (32+26+10+10+27) ÷ 5 = 21

24. True. (45)(1/5) = 9

25. False. 13 + 19 + 18 + 17 + 21 + 23 = 111, not 109

TEST 3

DIRECTIONS: Each question or incomplete statement is followed by several suggested answers or completions. Select the one that BEST answers the question or completes the statement. *PRINT THE LETTER OF THE CORRECT ANSWER IN THE SPACE AT THE RIGHT.*

1. When 60,987 is added to 27,835, the answer is 1._____
   A. 80,712   B. 80,822   C. 87,712   D. 88,822

2. The sum of 693 + 787 + 946 + 355 + 731 is 2._____
   A. 3,512   B. 3,502   C. 3,412   D. 3,402

3. When 2,586 is subtracted from 3,003, the answer is 3._____
   A. 417   B. 527   C. 1,417   D. 1,527

4. When 1.32 is subtracted from 52.6, the answer is 4._____
   A. 3.94   B. 5.128   C. 39.4   D. 51.28

5. When 56 is multiplied by 438, the answer is 5._____
   A. 840   B. 4,818   C. 24,528   D. 48,180

6. When 8.7 is multiplied by .34, the answer is MOST NEARLY 6._____
   A. 2.9   B. 3.0   C. 29.5   D. 29.6

7. When 1/2 is divided by 2/3, the answer is 7._____
   A. 1/3   B. 3/4   C. 1 1/3   D. 3

8. When 8,340 is divided by 38, the answer is MOST NEARLY 8._____
   A. 210   B. 218   C. 219   D. 220

9. Assume that a helper earns $11.16 an hour and that he works 250 seven-hour days a year. 9._____
   His gross yearly salary will be
   A. $19,430   B. $19,530   C. $19,650   D. $19,780

10. On a certain map, a distance of 10 miles is represented by 1/2 inch. 10._____
    If two towns are 3 1/2 inches apart on this map, express, in miles, the actual distance between the two towns.
    A. 70   B. 80   C. 90   D. 100

11. The area of the triangle shown at the right is _____ square inches. 11._____
    A. 120
    B. 240
    C. 360
    D. 480

12. The sum of 1/3 + 2/5 + 5/6 is

    A. 1 17/30   B. 1 3/5   C. 1 5/8   D. 1 5/6

13. The sum of the following dimensions, 3'2 1/4", 0'8 7/8", 2'6 3/8", 2'9 3/4", and 1'0", is

    A. 9'2 7/8"   B. 10'3 1/4"
    C. 10'7 3/7"   D. 11'4 1/4"

14. If the scale of a drawing is 1/8" to the foot, then a 1/2" measurement on the drawing would represent an actual length of _____ feet.

    A. 2   B. 4   C. 8   D. 16

15. Assume that an area measures 78 feet by 96 feet.
    The number of square feet in this area is

    A. 7,478   B. 7,488   C. 7,498   D. 7,508

16. If a can of paint costs $17.50, four dozen cans of this paint will cost

    A. $837.50   B. $840.00   C. $842.50   D. $845.00

17. The number of square feet in 1 square yard is

    A. 3   B. 6   C. 9   D. 12

18. The sum of 4 1/2 inches, 3 1/4 inches, and 7 1/2 inches is 1 foot _____ inches.

    A. 3   B. 3 1/4   C. 3 1/2   D. 4

19. If a room is 10 feet by 18 feet, the number of square feet of floor space in it is

    A. 1,800   B. 180   C. 90   D. 28

20. A jacket that was marked at $12.50 was sold for $10.
    What was the rate of discount on the marked price?

    A. 10%   B. 15%   C. 18%   D. 20%

Questions 21-25.

DIRECTIONS: Each question consists of a statement. You are to indicate whether the statement is TRUE (T) or FALSE (F).

21. Three-eighths (3/8") of an inch is equivalent to .0375".

22. A floor measuring 12 feet by 9 feet contains 36 sq.ft.

23. A box measuring 18 inches square and 16 inches deep will have a volume of 36 cubic feet.

24. If the charge for a long distance telephone call is 50¢ for the first 5 minutes and 7? for each minute after that, then for 85¢ a person could speak for 10 minutes.

25. If 15 gallons of gasoline cost $14.85 and you use up 10 gallons, then the value of the gasoline which is still left is $4.95.

KEY (CORRECT ANSWERS)

1. D
2. A
3. A
4. D
5. C

6. B
7. B
8. C
9. B
10. A

11. A
12. A
13. B
14. B
15. B

16. B
17. C
18. B
19. B
20. D

21. F
22. F
23. F
24. T
25. T

SOLUTIONS TO PROBLEMS

1. 60,987 + 27,835 = 88,822

2. 693 + 787 + 946 + 355 + 731 = 3512

3. 3003 - 2586 = 417

4. 52.6 - 1.32 = 51.28

5. (56)(438) = 24,528

6. (8.7)(.34) = 2.958 ≈ 3.0

7. $\dfrac{1}{2} \div \dfrac{2}{3} = \dfrac{1}{2} \cdot \dfrac{3}{2} = \dfrac{3}{4}$

8. 8340 ÷ 38 ≈ 219.47 ≈ 219

9. ($11.16)(7)(250) = $19,530

10. 3 1/2" ÷ 1/2" = 7. Then, (7)(10) = 70 miles

11. Area = (1/2)(10")(24") = 120 sq.in.

12. $\dfrac{1}{3} + \dfrac{2}{5} + \dfrac{5}{6} = \dfrac{10}{30} + \dfrac{12}{30} + \dfrac{25}{30} = \dfrac{47}{30} = 1\dfrac{17}{30}$

13. 3'2 1/4" + 0'8 7/8" + 2'6 3/8" + 2'9 3/4" + 1'0" = 8'25 18/8" = 10'3 1/4"

14. 1/2" ÷ 1/8" = 4. Then, (4)(1 ft.) = 4 ft.

15. (78')(96') = 7488 sq.ft.

16. (48)($17.50) = $840.00

17. 1 sq.yd. = (3)(3) = 9 sq.ft.

18. 4 1/2" + 3 1/4" + 7 1/2" = 14 5/4" = 1 foot 3 1/4 inches

19. (10')(18') = 180 sq.ft.

20. $12.50 - $10 = $2.50. Then, $2.50 ÷ $12.50 = .20 = 20%

21. False. 3/8" = .375", not .0375"

22. False. (12')(9') = 108 sq.ft., not 36 sq.ft.

23. False. (18")(18")(16") = 5184 cu.in. = 3 cu.ft., not 36 cu.ft.
    Note: 1 cu.ft. = 1728 cu.in.

24. True. The cost for 10 minutes = .50 + (.07)(10-5) = .85

25. True. $14.85 ÷ 15 = $.99 per gallon. The value of 5 gallons = (5)($.99) = $4.95

BASIC CLEANING PROCEDURES

TABLE OF CONTENTS

		Page
I.	TRASH REMOVAL	1
II.	CLEANING URNS AND ASHTRAYS	5
III.	DUSTING	7
IV.	FLOOR DUSTING	14
V.	VACUUMING (WET AND DRY)	16
VI.	MOPPING (WET, DAMP, SPOT)	18

BASIC CLEANING PROCEDURES

I. TRASH REMOVAL

PURPOSE: To remove waste from patient and tenant areas in order to provide the highest standard of sanitation; protection against fire, pests, odor, bacteria, and other health hazards; and for esthetic reasons.

EQUIPMENT:

Utility cart
Trash cart
Bucket
Germicidal detergent
Plastic liners (small and large)
Cloths
Gloves
Container for cigarette butts

SAFETY PRECAUTIONS:

1. Must wear gloves.

2. Never handle trash with bare hands.

3. Always empty cigarette butts into separate container that has water or sand in it.

4. If liners are not used, do not transfer trash from one container to another transfer trash into a liner. (Shown in Illustration.)

5. Trash must be separated into two categories: General and Special.

PROCEDURE

General

1. Assemble necessary equipment, prepare ger-micidal solution, and take to assigned area.

2. Put on gloves.

3. Pick up large trash on floor, place in trash container.

4. Close plastic liner and secure with tie.

5. Remove liner and place in trash bag on utility cart or place into trash cart, or other trash collection vehicle.

General

PROCEDURE

6. Emerge (dip) cloth into germicidal solution. Wring out thoroughly.

7. Wipe outside and inside of trash container. Dry with second cloth.

8. Replace liner. Liner should extend over top of trash container and fold outward over the upper rim. If plastic liners are not being used, use the Replacement Method-a clean container is exchanged for the dirty one.

9. Proceed with this procedure until all trash is collected or containers are full.

10. Place in utility room or an appropriate storage area until time for disposal.

11. Remove trash from the storage area at the end of the day or at some specified time (by cart or dolly) to dumpsters.

12. If large G.I. cans are used in the specified trash storage area, maintain as listed above.

13. At least once a month, take all trash cans to a specified area and thoroughly wash or steam clean.

14. If using the Replacement Method, dirty trash containers must be washed or steam cleaned daily. Must be stored in inverted or upside-down position to air dry.

15. Clean all equipment and return to designated storage area. Restock utility cart.

PROCEDURE

Special Waste Handling Syringes-Hypodermic Needles-Razor Blades

1. Collect from specified areas (full disposable containers designed for this waste).

2. Place in 20-gallon galvanized container in locked designated area.

3. Call Garage for pick up and disposal when galvanized container is full (10).

Glass and Aerosol Cans

1. Collect from designated areas in marked metal containers.

2. Place in 20-gallon galvanized containers in locked designated area daily.

3. Call Garage for pick up and disposal when container is full.

Pathological Specimen
(Tissue-flesh)

1. This type of waste is handled by a special technologist in the Hospital's Pathological Division.

2. Must be stored in refrigerator until incinerated.

3. Must be incinerated in special incinerator designed for this purpose.

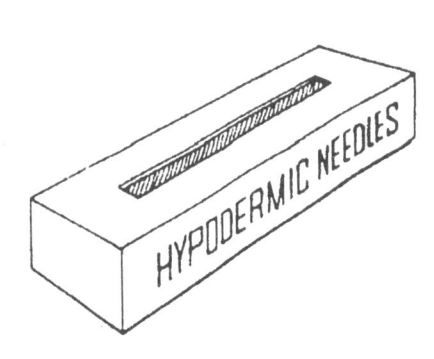

PROCEDURE

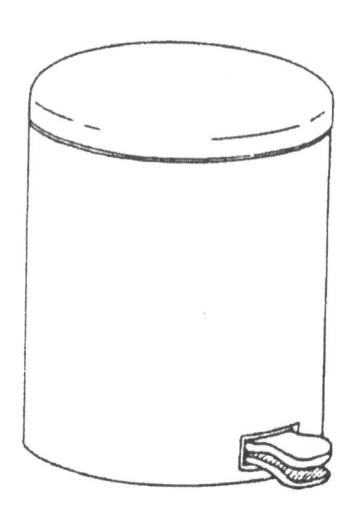

Contaminated

The same procedure is used as for general collection with the following exceptions:

1. Must have covered step-on containers.

2. A second person is required to hold clean liner (top folded over hands for protection).

3. The tied soiled plastic liner is removed from the waste container and placed in a clean plastic liner and then deposited into the regular trash.

4. If in areas that are restricted, must wear protective garments.

II. CLEANING URNS AND ASHTRAYS

PURPOSE: To prevent fire hazards, to control bacteria, and for appearance.

EQUIPMENT:
    Utility cart
    Sifter or slit spoon
    Bucket for sand
    Cloths or Sponges
    Container for cigarette butts
    Gloves
    Buckets (two)
    Counter brush and dustpans
    Germicidal detergent

SAFETY PRECAUTIONS:

1. Wear gloves.
2. Do not place plastic liners on inside of urns.
3. Sweep up all spilled sand immediately.
4. Make sure cigarette butts are placed in special container with water or sand in the bottom.

PROCEDURE

1. Assemble equipment. Prepare solution. Take to designated area.

2. Put on gloves.

3. Empty ashtrays. Dip ashtrays into solution. Wash. Rinse in clear water. Dry. Return to proper area.

4. Continue cleaning other cigarette receptacles. Receptacles can be smoke stands, and/or wall and floor urns with or without sand.

    a. Smoke stands and wall urns:

    (1) Empty cigarette butts into special container (by lifting out inside bucket or unscrewing base from top).

    (2) Wash, rinse, and dry the base, top, bucket and wall attachment.

PROCEDURE

b. Floor urns with sand:

(1) Take out large pieces of trash.

(2) Lift screen to remove cigarette butts and any other waste. Use sifter and spoon for this procedure if screens are not in use.

5. Replace sand if necessary. Sweep up any spilled sand.

6. Dip cloth into germicide solution. Wring out. Wipe off rim and outside of urns. Rinse and dry.

7. Continue this procedure until all urns are completed.

8. Clean all equipment and return to designated storage.

9. At least once a month collect cigarette receptacles. Take to utility room. Remove sand where applicable. Submerge in germicidal solution. Wash thoroughly. Rinse and dry. Replace sand and return to designated areas.

III. DUSTING

PURPOSE: To remove accumulated soil, to control bacteria, for protection, and for appearance.

EQUIPMENT:

    Utility cart
    Treated cloths
    Germicidal detergent
    Gloves
    Furniture polish
    Sweeping tool or Broom
    Extension handle
    Clean cloths
    Buckets (two)
    Vacuum cleaner (Wet and Dry or Back Pack) Broom bags

SAFETY PRECAUTIONS:

1. A fold dust cloth is more efficient than a bunched cloth. When folded properly, a cloth may have as many as 32 clean sides.

2. Use treated cloths or damp cloths when dusting. (Never use a feather duster.)

3. Oily cloths are fire hazards: they must be stored in a covered container.

4. Never shake cloth.

5. Never use circular motion. Dust with the grain.

6. Never use excessive water on wood furniture.

7. Do not take dust cloth from one patient unit to the next.

PROCEDURE

General-Dry

1. Assemble equipment. Prepare solution. Take to assigned area.

2. Put on gloves.

3. Fold treated cloth or damp germicidal cloth. (If using the damp germicidal cloth, use a second cloth for polishing.)

PROCEDURE

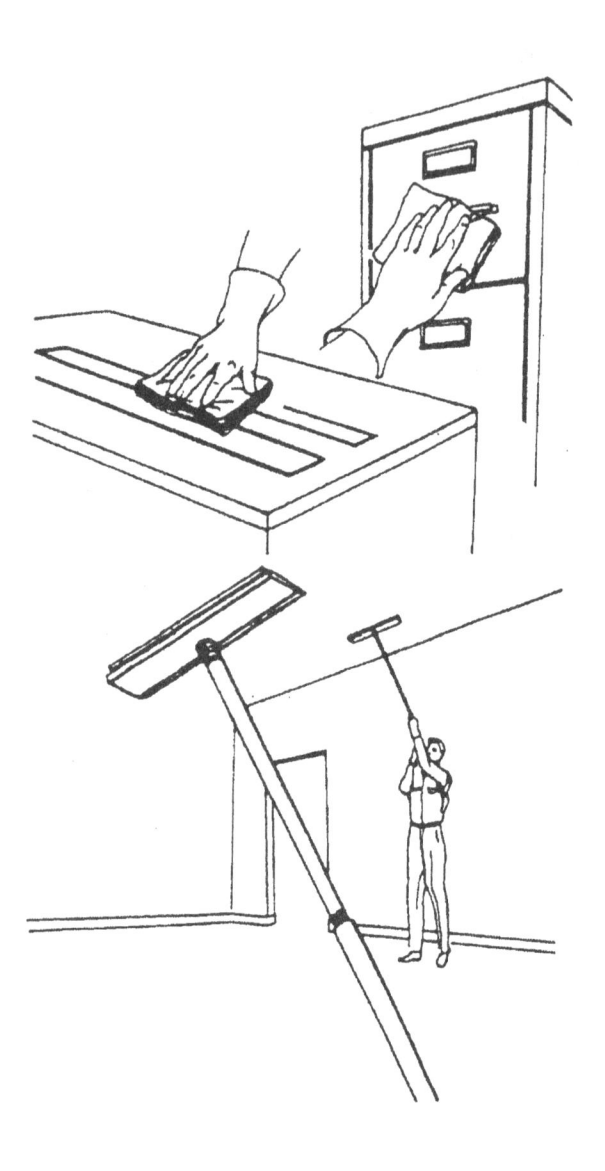

4. Look at area. Begin dusting at a point to avoid backtracking. Use both hands whenever possible. Begin with high furniture and work down to low furniture (for example, dust file cabinets before dusting desk tops).

5. Refold cloth when sides become dust filled or refresh by returning to germicidal solution.

6. Continue dusting until area is completed.

7. Inspect work.

8. Clean equipment and return to designated storage area. Cleaning cloths are placed in liner for laundering; woven treated paper dust cloths are discarded.

Wall and Ceiling Dusting

1. Assemble equipment. Take to assigned area.

2. Move furniture that will interfere with operation to one side of the room. Remove all pictures and other wall mountings and place in a safe area.

3. Put on gloves.

4. Dust ceiling. Start at back of room. Use vacuum or Floor tool or covered broom with extension handle. Place dusting tool against ceiling surface and walk forward to the other end.

5. Turn and overlap stroke. Continue this proc-dure until completed.

6. Dust ceiling both cross-wise and length-wise.

PROCEDURE

7. When ceiling is completed, dust walls from top to bottom. Use full-length vertical overlapping strokes. Include vents, ledges and exposed pipes.

8. When one side of area is completed, replace furniture.

9. Move furniture from other side and continue the dusting procedure until entire area is completed.

10. Replace furniture, pictures and other wall mountings.

11. Inspect work.

12. Clean equipment. Return to designated storage areas. Broom bags are placed in plastic liner/bag for laundering; woven treated paper dust cloths are discarded.

General Comments for Dusting Different Types of Furniture
1. Wooden Furniture:
    a. Dust entire surface.

    b. Apply polish-pour small amount on damp cloth-rub with grain.

    c. Finish polishing by rubbing with dry cloth.

    d. Surface may be washed with natural detergent.

CAUTION: Excessive amount of water should be avoided.

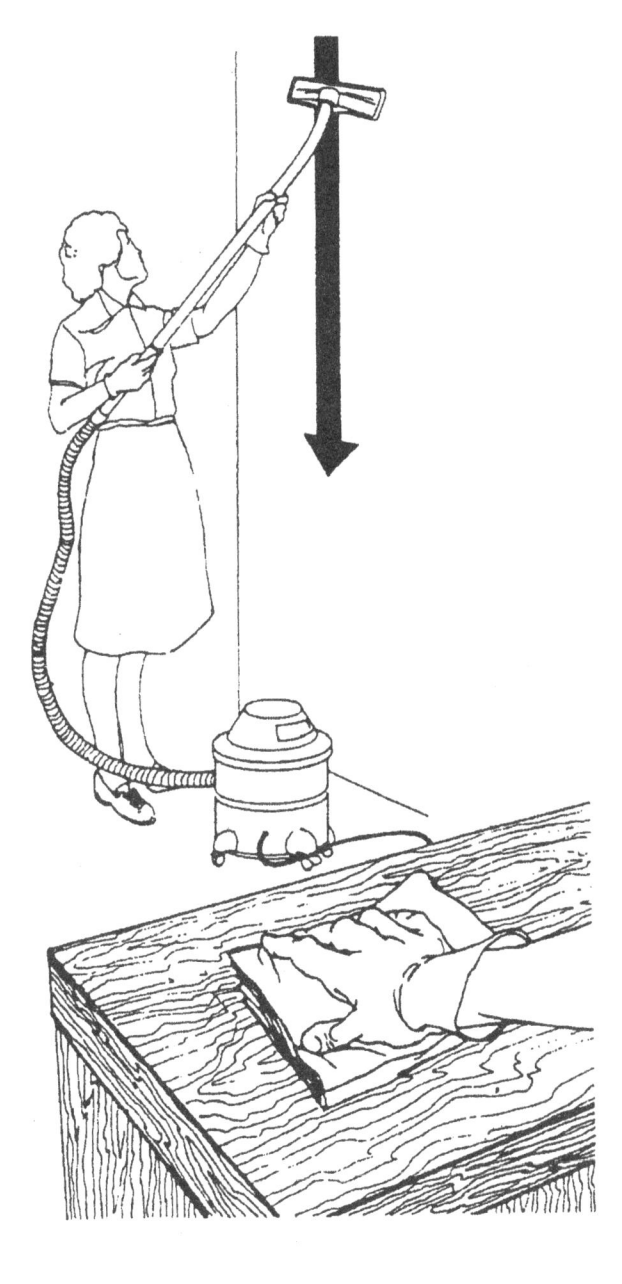

PROCEDURE

2. Metal Furniture:

    a. Dust entire surface.

    b. Surface may be washed and polished.

    c. Apply polish-pour small amount on damp cloth-rub in.

    d. Polish/rub thoroughly with a second cloth.

3. Plastic, Vinyl or Fiber Glass:

    a. Dust entire surface.

    b. Wash with germicidal cleaning solution.

    c. Rinse.

    d. Rub surface dry.

4. Leather:

    a. Damp dust.

    b. Clean with leather polish or saddle soap.

5. Upholstered Pieces:

    a. Vacuum entire surface thoroughly. Use push-pull strokes.

    b. Lift cushion-vacuum both sides, cushion support, and bottom of chair. Do not overlook corners and crevices.

    c. Check carefully for stains and report to supervisor.

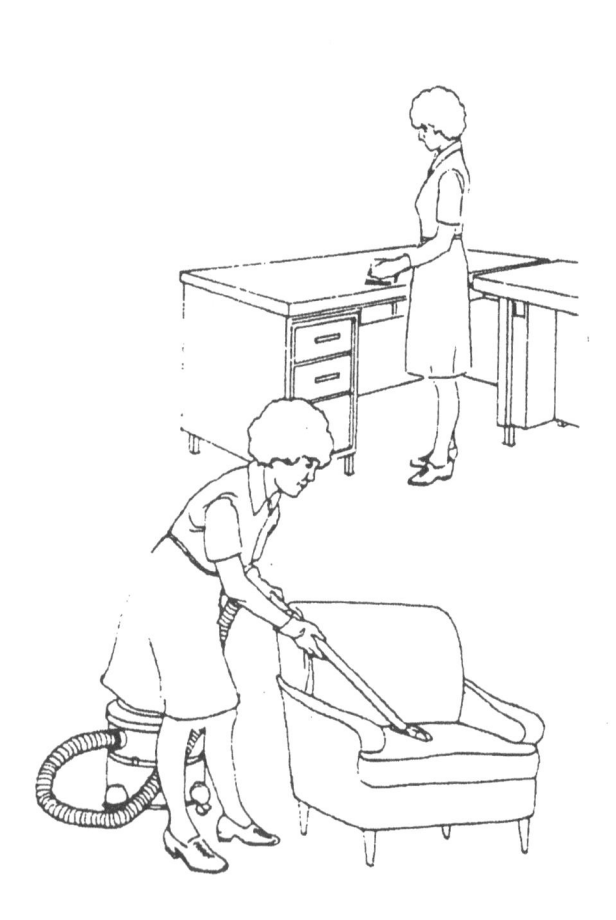

PROCEDURE

Naugahyde:
   a. Elastic:

(1) Ordinary Dirt-Ordinary dirt can be removed by washing with warm water and a mild soap. Apply soapy water to a large area and allow to soak for a few minutes. This will loosen the dirt. Brisk rubbing with a cloth should then remove most dirt. This procedure may be repeated several times if necessary.

In the case of stubborn or imbedded dirt in the grain of the Naugahyde, a fingernail brush or other soft bristle brush may be used after the mild soap application has been made.

If the dirt is extremely difficult to remove, wall washing preparations may be used. Abrasive cleaners may also be used. Abrasive cleaners should be used more cautiously and care exercised to prevent contact with the wood or metal parts of furniture or with any soft fabric which may be a part of the furniture.

(2) Chewing gum-Chewing gum may be removed by careful scraping and by applying kerosene, gasoline or naphtha. If none of these are available, most hair oils or Three-In-One oil will soften the chewing gum so that it may be removed.

(3) Tars, Asphalts. Creosote-Each of these items will stain Naugahyde if allowed to remain in contact. They should be wiped off as quickly as possible and the area carefully cleaned with a cloth dampened with kerosene, range oil, gasoline or naphtha.

(4) Paint-Paint should be removed immediately if possible. Do not use paint remover or liquid type brush cleaners. An unprinted cloth dampened with kerosene, painters naphtha or turpentine may be used. Care must be exercised to keep these fluids from contact with

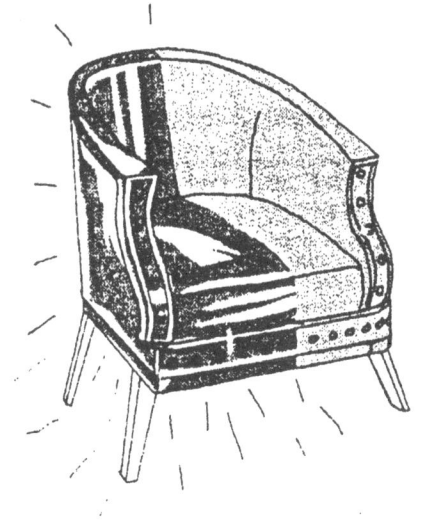

PROCEDURE

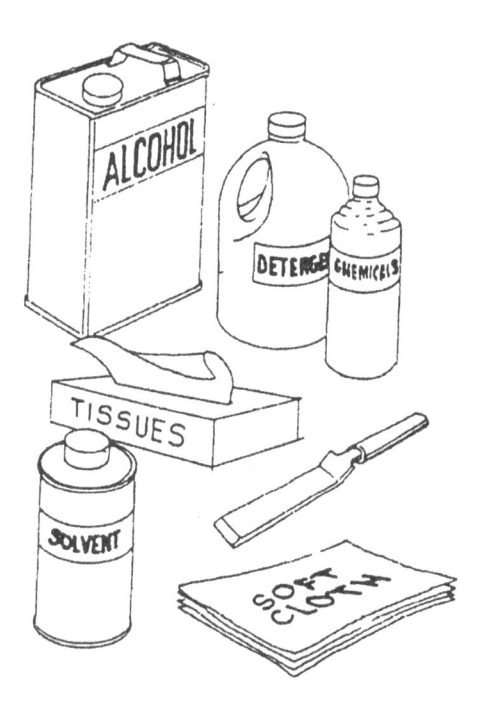

soft fabrics or with the wooden areas of the furniture.

(5) Sulphide Staining-Atmosphere permeated with coal gas or direct contact with hard-boiled eggs, "Cold Wave" solutions and other sulphide compounds can stain Naugahyde. These stains may be removed by placing a clean, unprinted piece of cloth over the spotted area and pouring a liberal amount of 6% hydrogen peroxide onto the cloth and allowing the saturated cloth to remain on the spotted area for at least thirty minutes to one hour. If spot is stubborn, allow the hydrogen peroxide saturated cloth to remain on the spotted area overnight. Caution must be used to see that the hydrogen peroxide solution does not come in contact with stained or lacquered wood and should not be allowed to seep into the seams as it will weaken the cotton thread.

(6) Nail Polish and Nail Polish Remover-These substances will cause permanent harm to Naugahyde on prolonged contact. Fast and careful wiping or blotting immediately after contact will minimize the staining. Spreading of the liquid while removing should be avoided.

(7) Shoe Polish-Most shoe polishes contain dyes which will penetrate the Naugahyde and stain it permanently. They should be wiped off as quickly as possible using kerosene, gasoline, naphtha or lighter fluid. If staining occurs, the same procedure outlined above for sulphide staining using hydrogen peroxide should be tried.

(8) Shoe Heel Marks-Shoe heel marks can be removed by the same procedure as is recommended for paint.

(9) Ball Point Ink-Ball point ink may sometimes be removed if rubbed immediately with a damp cloth using water or

PROCEDURE

rubbing alcohol. If this is not successful, the procedure outlined for sulphide staining may be tried.

(10) Generally stains are found which do not respond to any of the other treatments, it is sometimes helpful to place the furniture in direct sunlight for two or three days. Mustard, ball point ink, certain shoe polishes and dyes will sometimes bleach out in direct sunlight and leave the Naugahyde undamaged.

(11) Waxing or Refinishing-Waxing improves the soil resistance and cleanability of Naugahyde. and any solid wax may be used.

b. Breathable:

U.S. Naugaweave should be treated as a soft fabric and not as a fully vinyl coated fabric. U.S. Naugaweave can be cleaned with foam type cleansers generally used for soft fabrics.

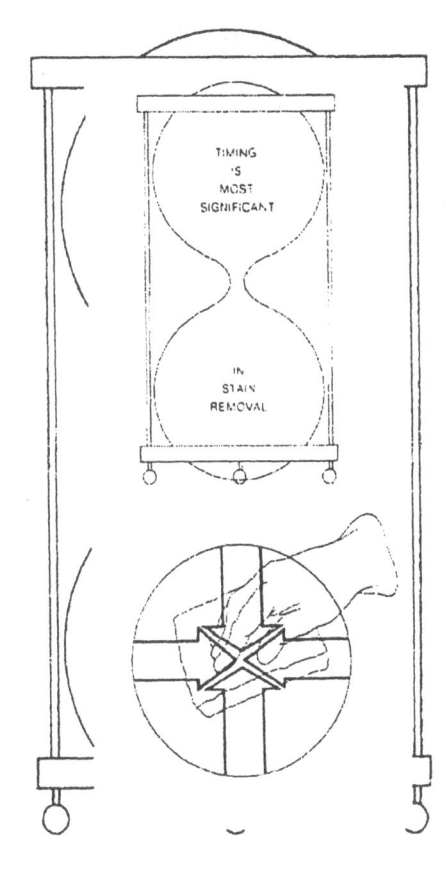

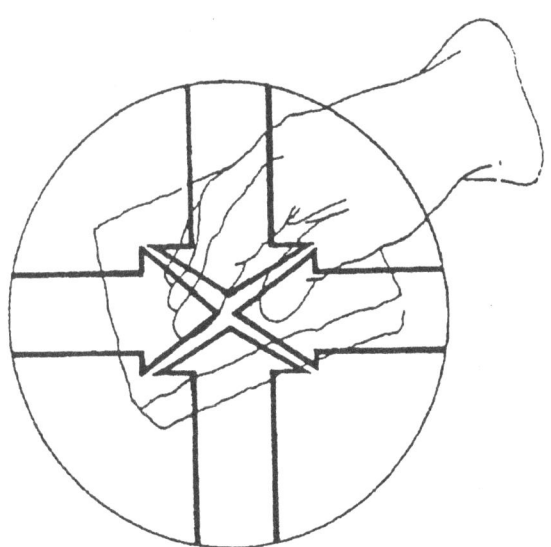

IV. FLOOR DUSTING
(Sweeping/Dusting with covered broom or floor tool with chemically treated disposable floor cloth)

PURPOSE: To remove surface dirt, and make washing easier.

EQUIPMENT:
- Utility cart
- Dustpan
- Treated cloths, or
- Broom bags
- Counter brush
- Sweeping tool, or
- Vacuum cleaner

SAFETY PRECAUTIONS:
1. Never leave piles of dirt and trash in any area.
2. Lift sweeping tool at the end of each stroke. *Do not tap.*
3. Never put waste or sweepings in a patient's waste basket.
4. Keep all equipment out of traffic areas.
5. Use of disposable cloths should be limited to two surfaces (i.e. use two treated cloths per ward, and two Administrative units can be cleaned with one cloth).

PROCEDURE

1. Assemble equipment. Take to assigned area.

2. Move furniture, if necessary.

3. Start dusting/sweeping at far end of room or area and work toward door.

4. Place floor tool on direct line with right toe. Hold handle loosely. Stand erect with feet about eight inches apart. Start dusting/sweeping floor-walking forward. Use a push stroke, lift tool at end of each stroke. Do not tap. Overlap each stroke.

PROCEDURE

5. Continue this procedure until area is completed. Clean under all stationary equipment and furniture.

6. Take up accumulated dirt. Use dustpan and counter brush. Place in plastic liner/trash bag on utility cart.

7. The dusting/sweeping procedure can be performed with the wet and dry vacuum cleaner. *Dusting Isolation units must be performed with vacuum.*

8. Inspect work. Floor should not have any dust streaks. Replace furniture.

9. Clean equipment. Return to designated storage area. Discard disposable treated cloths. If broom bags are used, place in plastic liner/bag for laundering.

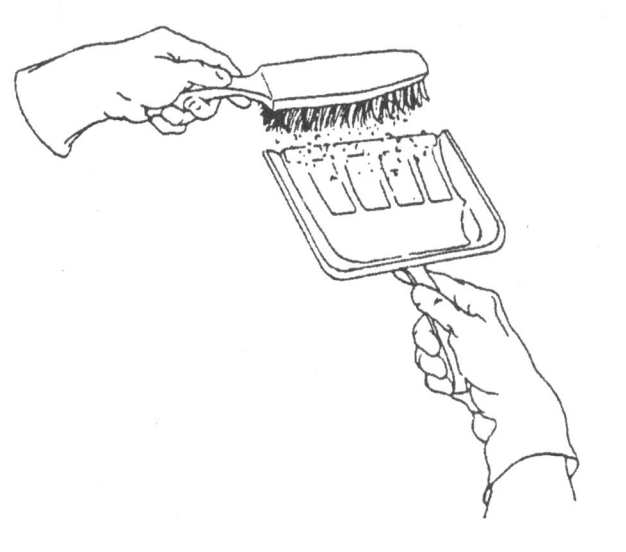

V. VACUUMING
(Wet and Dry)

PURPOSE: To remove dust and dirt and water, to control the spread of bacteria, to aid in reaching difficult-to-reach areas, and for appearance. This operation may be performed on floors, walls, ceiling, rugs, and carpets.

EQUIPMENT:
Upright or tank vacuum cleaner

Wet and dry vacuum cleaner

Back-pack vacuum cleaner

Attachments: Crevice tool, Shelf brush, Pipe brush, Upholstery brush, Walls and Ceiling brush, Dusting brush, and Floor-dry and wet tools.

SAFETY PRECAUTIONS:

1. Empty vacuum when bag is half full.

2. If disposable bag is not in use, empty soil into plastic liner/bag.

3. Never position equipment so that it becomes a tripping hazard.

PROCEDURE

Dry

1. Assemble proper equipment and attachments for the area to be vacuumed:

    a. Upright vacuum for carpet.

    b. Tank cleaner to use on floors, grooves and high cleaning.

    c. Back-pack for stairs, hard to reach areas, walls and ceiling, and drapery.

2. Remove all furniture and other items interfering with the operation.

3. Start in farthest corner of room, area or top of item. Vacuum the surface in a back-and-forth motion.

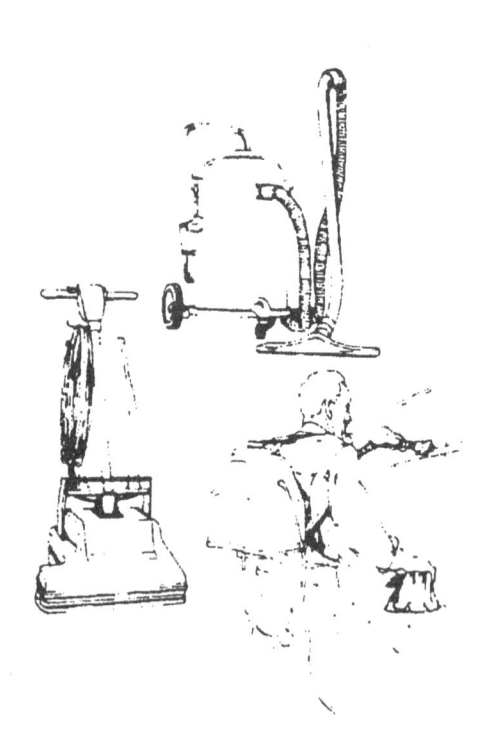

PROCEDURE

4. Empty bag when half full. Continue this procedure until area or item is completed. Change attachments as required.

5. Replace furniture or items.

6. Take equipment to utility room. Empty and clean. Return to designated storage area.

Wet

This procedure is used to remove water. It is considered very effective in the daily performance of different tasks in order to control the spread of infectious organisms. Wet vacuuming is often used in emergencies-flooding, pipe breaks and overflows. See vacuum cleaner guide under Care of Equipment for operation of the wet vacuum.

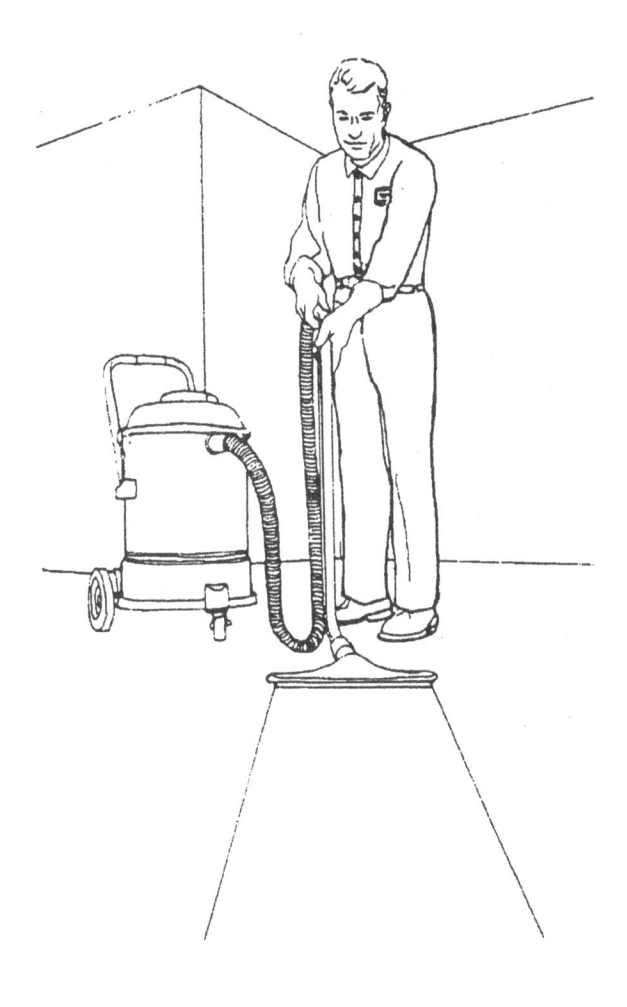

VI. Mopping
(Wet, Damp, Spot)

PURPOSE: To insure maximum cleanliness, to improve the sanitation of the environment, to aid in control of bacteria, and for the appearance of the area.

MATERIALS:

    Utility cart
    Buckets (two)
    Dolly
    Wringers (two)
    Mopheads and Handles (two)
    Nylon abrasive pad
    Caution signs
    Gloves
    Broom-Broom bags
    Sweeping tool-treated cloths
    Wet and dry vacuum cleaner
    Putty knife
    Dustpan
    Counter brush
    Germicidal detergent

SAFETY PRECAUTIONS:
1. Sweep or vacuum before mopping.
2. Post area with "Wet Floor" signs.
3. Mop one-half of corridor at a time.
4. Keep equipment close to walls and away from doors and corners.
5. Excessive water should not be allowed to remain on the floor for any length of time because it will cause damage to nearly all types of flooring material.
6. Begin the operation with clean equipment, mopheads, and clean solution.
7. Change cleaning solution and rinse water frequently (every three to four rooms, depending on size and soilage factors).
8. Solution containers should be conveniently positioned so as not to cause tripping or walking over cleaned areas.

PROCEDURE

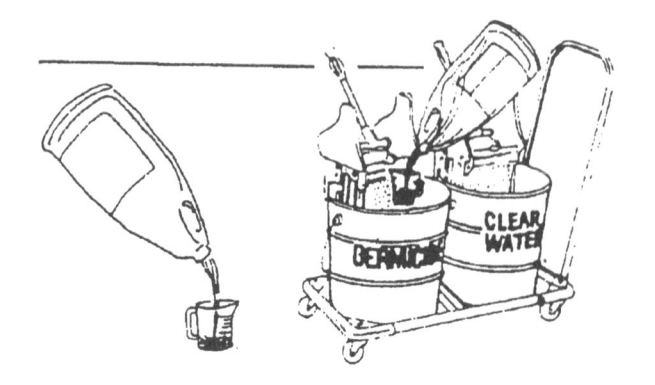

Wet Mopping
1. Assemble equipment. Fill one container two-thirds full with water. Add recommended amount of germicidal detergent. Fill second container two-thirds full with clear water.

PROCEDURE

2. Proceed to designated work area. Post "Wet Floor" signs. Move furniture to simplify operation. Vacuum or dust area with covered broom or tool with treated cloth. Remove gum with putty knife. (Use dustpan and counter brush to remove debris and trash.)
3. Dip one mop into cleaning solution and press out excess water to prevent dripping.
4. First, apply solution on and along baseboard or coving. Use the heel of mophead to clean baseboard and corners. (The putty knife can be used to clean out heavily soiled corners or strands of the mophead wrapped around gloved fingertips is another tool for cleaning the corners. A baseboard scrubber or an improvised abrasive pad on a mop handle can be used to remove built-up soil on baseboards.)
5. Return mop to germicidal solution. Churn thoroughly, wring out and pick up solution off baseboards. Apply rinse water with second mop and dry.
6. Continue with the mopping operation. Take solution mop (with excess water pressed out) and make an eight-inch border around floor area approximately nine feet wide and twelve feet long.
7. Begin at top of area. Place mop flat on floor, feet well apart, place right hand-palm up, almost two inches from end of handle, and left hand-palm down, about fourteen inches on handle. Begin swinging mop from left to right or right to left using a continuous open figure-eight motion. At the end of approximately six to nine strokes (width of strokes depend on height and weight of worker), turn mop over or renew direction by lapping mop (lift mophead and loop it over the strands). Continue this procedure until area is completed. (A nylon pad attached to one side of mophead can be used to remove black marks while performing the daily mopping procedure.

PROCEDURE

8. Return mop to germicidal solution. Churn thoroughly. Wring out and pick up solution. Use same procedure as for applying solution.

9. Dip the second mop into the rinse water, press out excess water and apply rinse water to area. Use same procedure for rinsing as for applying cleaning solution.

10. Dip the second mop again into rinse water, wring out thoroughly and dry floor using side-to-side stroke.

11. Continue the four steps of mopping, picking up, rinsing, and drying until the area has been covered. Change cleaning solution and rinse water frequently.

12. Inspect work: A properly mopped floor should have a clean surface. There should be no water spots. The corners should be clean and baseboards should not be splashed.

13. Wash and dry equipment and return to designated storage area.

14. Mopheads are removed and placed in a plastic bag, and then placed in a regular laundry bag and stored in the designated area to be picked up and laundered.

PROCEDURE

Damp Mopping

Damp mopping is a type of mopping used to remove surface dust. This procedure may be used in place of dry dust mopping. Each time mop is dipped into solution or rinse water, it is wrung out thoroughly. The same motions are carried out in this procedure as are for the wet mopping.

Spot Mopping

Spot mopping is a type of mopping used only when a small area is soiled by spillage (water, coke, coffee, urine and other liquids). Spillage must be wiped up immediately in order to prevent slipping and falling hazards. First, absorb liquid with paper towels or blotters, then mop area.

SPECIAL CLEANING PROCEDURES

TABLE OF CONTENTS

		Page
I.	Drinking Fountain	1
II.	Moving Furniture and Equipment	2
III.	Cleaning Drapery, Venetian Blinds and Window Shades	5
IV.	Glass and Window Cleaning	9
V.	Cleaning Light Fixtures (Fluorescent and Globes)	12
VI.	Wall Washing (Manual and Machine)	15
VII.	Cleaning Elevators	19
VIII.	Entrance and Lobby Cleaning	21
IX.	Stairs and Stairwells, Porches and Back Entrances (Wet and Dry)	24

SPECIAL CLEANING PROCEDURES

I. DRINKING FOUNTAIN

PURPOSE: To control the spread of bacteria and for appearance.

EQUIPMENT:
Germicidal detergent
Paper towels
Buckets (two)
Abrasive cleanser
Bottle brush
Cloths
Gloves

PROCEDURE

1. Assemble equipment. Prepare solution. Take to designated area. Put on gloves.

2. Check water flow.

3. Pour some germicidal solution into bubbler/ mouthpiece and inside surfaces.

4. Scrub bubbler inside and outside with bottle brush.

5. Wash inside surface with paper towel. (Use small amount of abrasive cleanser, if applicable.)

6. Rinse with water from bubbler/mouthpiece. Dry with paper towel.

7. Wash outside surfaces including foot pedal.

8. Rinse and dry.

9. Discard soiled paper towels.

10. Continue with next assignment or clean equipment and return to designated storage area.

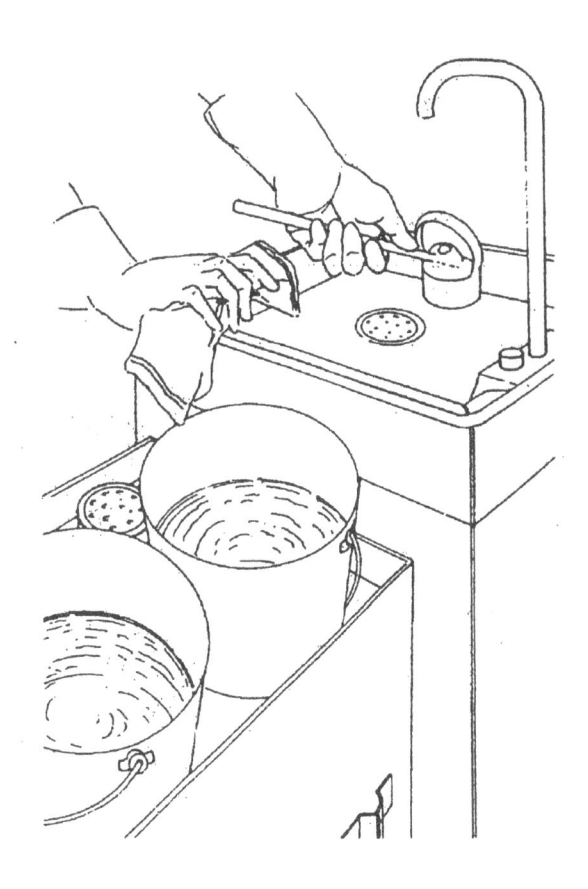

135

II. MOVING FURNITURE AND EQUIPMENT

PURPOSE: To relocate.

However, for proper maintenance purposes, the Housekeeping Section is involved daily with some form of the moving operation which involves moving of furniture and equipment (desks, file cabinets, beds and other items).

EQUIPMENT: Lifting Aids:
 Desk lifter
 File cabinet lifter
 Dolly
 Cart or Table on wheels
 Blanket
 Straps

SAFETY PRECAUTIONS:

1. Secure all locks and safety adjustments on equipment before using.

2. Remove handles or straps that interfere with the operation.

3. Block or lock all wheels on movable carts or tables.

4. To transport objects on movable table or cart, walk down center of hall; stop at corners, watch swinging doors.

5. Do not block vision.

6. Only properly trained individuals should use specialized moving equip- ment.

General

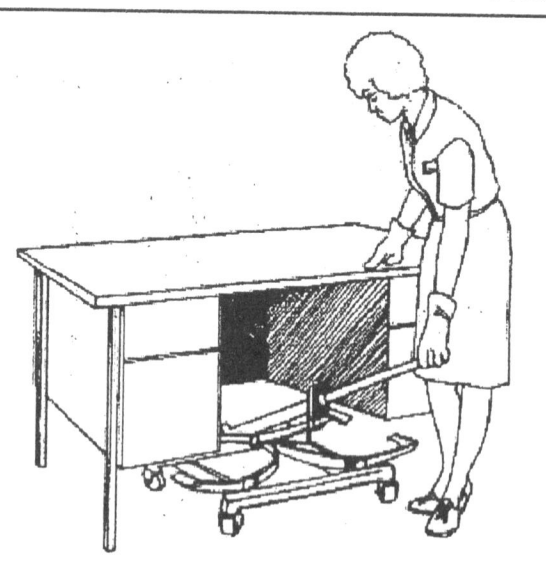

PROCEDURE

1. Assemble necessary equipment and take to assigned area.

2. Prepare the area (move anything interfering with the move).

3. Place lifting aid as close as possible to the piece of furniture or object being relocated.

4. Place object on lifting aid and transport to new location.

5. Return lifting aids and accessories to designated storage area.

PROCEDURE

1. Place under desk and center evenly on arms.

2. Lock. Press down on handle to lift and lock.

3. Remove handle.

4. Move desk to new location.

5. Remove desk lifter. (Insert handle, press down to release safety lock, lower desk into position, and withdraw desk lifter.) Return to designated storage area.

File Cabinet Lifter

1. Adjust bar and lifter head to height of cabinet.

2. Insert lifting blade under file cabinet.

3. Rest lifter head qn top of cabinet.

4. Press lifter tightly against cabinet and adjust arm on the lifter head to fit cabinet top by turning the two wheels.

5. Pull down level on adjustment bar to secure arm and the lifter head.

6. Pivot forward until locked into resting position.

7. Place one hand on bar and the other on handle; press down until cabinet clears the floor.

PROCEDURE

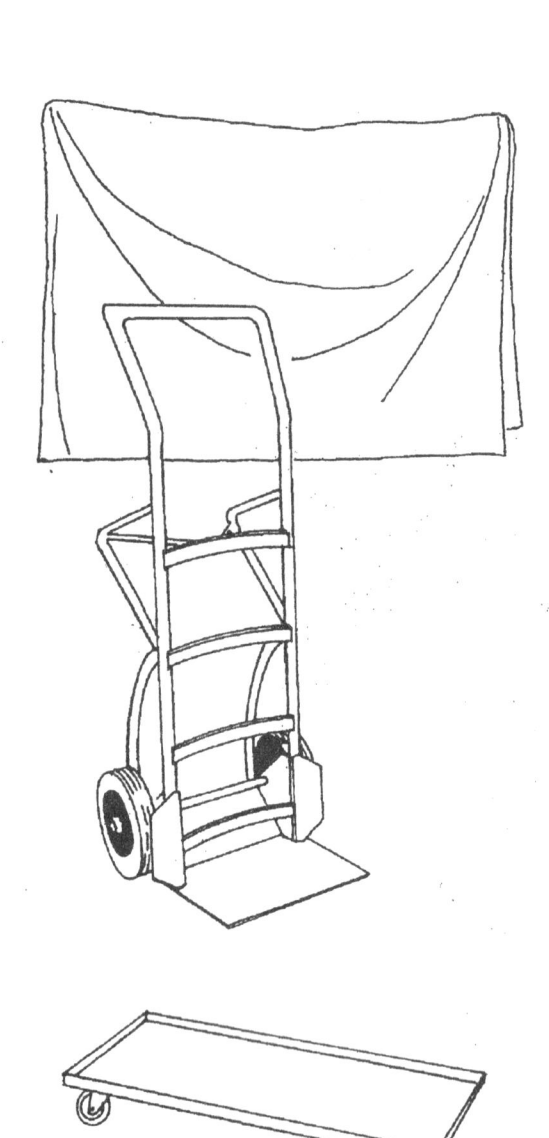

8. Roll into new position.

9. Remove lifter (raise lever arm in upright position, release lifter head by raising the side of the head assembly and remove lifter). Return to designated storage area.

10. To relocate taller cabinets, completely remove the lifter head bar asembly.

**Other Methods
Blankets, Dollies, Carts or
Tables on wheels**

Quite frequently, you may lack the above-mentioned sophisticated equipment. Therefore, you should also know that just by placing a blanket under a desk, table, bookend, file cabinet and other heavy objects, that the item may be pushed or pulled into a new location. If moving over carpeted areas, first place a piece of cardboard down. If using dollies or tables or carts, make sure that furniture or dollies are covered in order to protect from damage.

III. CLEANING DRAPERY, VENETIAN BLINDS AND WINDOW SHADES

PURPOSE: To control bacteria and for appearance.

EQUIPMENT:

    Vacuum cleaner/attachments
    Cart
    Germicidal detergent
    Gloves
    Six-foot step ladder
    Cloths
    Buckets (two)
    Venetian blind brush

SAFETY PRECAUTIONS:

1. Vacuuming should not be done too often, because it weakens the fiber of the fabric.

2. Always cover hands when cleaning Venetian blinds, because of the sharp edges.

PROCEDURE

Drapery

1. Assemble equipment. Take to designated area. Set up ladder and lock.

2. Connect vacuum to nearest convenient outlet.

3. Remove tie-backs and close the draperies.

4. Vacuum. Start at top of cornice or at top of drapery and work down. Use up-and-down motions—overlap.

5. Pull pleats apart to reach all surfaces.

6. Continue this procedure until front of drapery is completed.

7. Pull out drapery and dust the back side. Pull pleats apart to reach all surfaces.

PROCEDURE

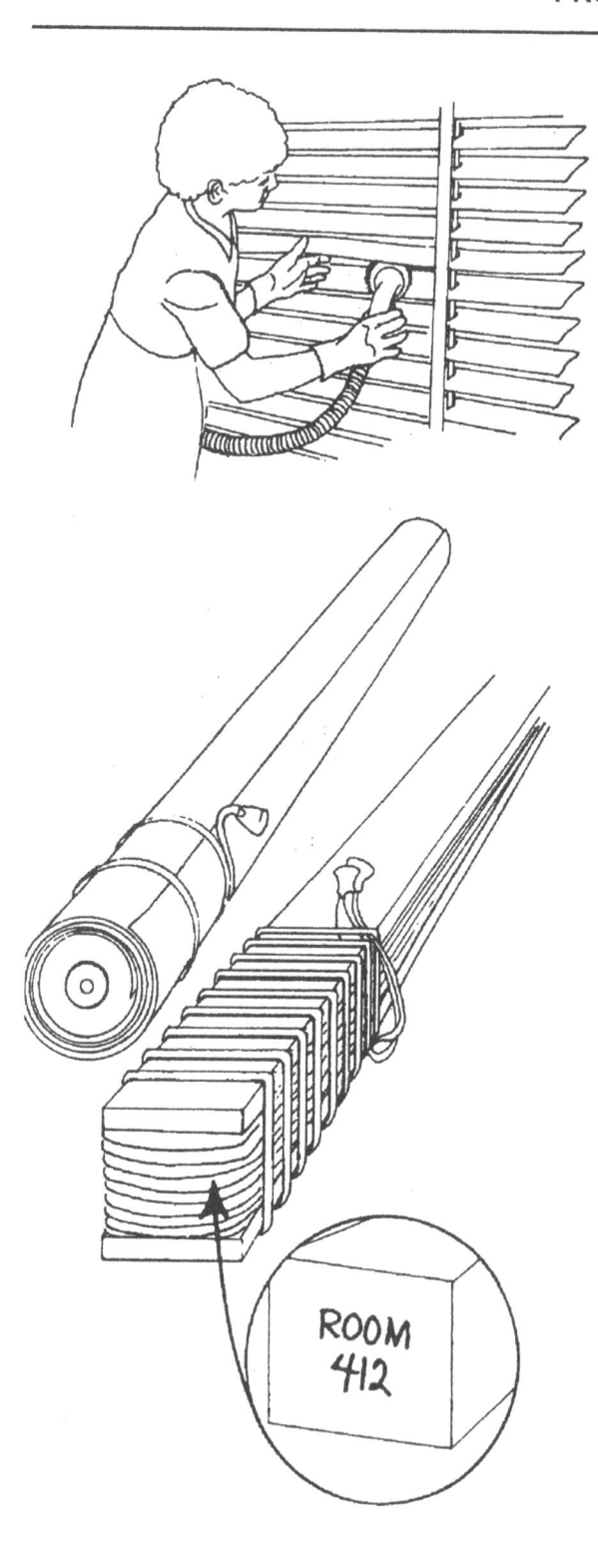

8. Continue this procedure until both panels are completed.

9. Adjust the drapery. Replace ties.

10. Drapery (depending on the type of fabric) is sent out perdiodically to the laundry or dry cleaners. Remove drapes, mark, fold and place in bag. Take to supervisor for cleaning purposes.

11. Clean equipment and return to designated storage area.

Venetian Blinds
(Dusting)

1. Assemble equipment. Take to assigned area. Set up ladder and lock.

2. Lower Venetian blind and place in closed position.

3. Plug in vacuum cleaner. Dust tapes.

4. Start dusting heading (stand on ladder if necessary.) Use side-to-side or left-to-right motion.

5. Dust each slat. Make sure to get behind tapes.

6. Continue this procedure until blind is completed. Dust the other side.

7. Adjust blinds and inspect work.

8. Blind may also be damp dusted by hand.

PROCEDURE

9. Clean equipment and return to designated storage area.

Washing

Blinds may be washed at the window or removed and washed in tub, tank, supersonic machine and/or specialized blind washing equipment. Remember to mark blinds if removed for cleaning.

Washing Blinds by Hand:
1. Assemble equipment. Prepare solution. Take to designated area. Set up ladder and lock. Put on gloves.

2. Lower Venetian blind—vacuum.

3. Place slats horizontal.

4. Wash, rinse and dry tapes.

5. Wash heading. Rinse and dry.

6. Dip cloth in germicidal solution. Wring out. Fold around hand.

7. Take slat in covered hand and use a side-to-side motion—moving left to right, cleaning both sides of the blind at the same time (hold slat with one hand while working with the other hand). Avoid too much water.

8. Rinse and dry.

9. Adjust blinds. Wipe up any spills.

10. Remove equipment. Clean and return to designated storage area.

Wash Away From Window:
1. Assemble equipment. Take to area. Set up ladder and lock. Put on gloves.

2. Remove blinds. Pull blinds to top of frame. Unlock the blind from the frame. Wrap or secure the cord around each end. Mark in an inconspicuous place with indelible marker.

3. Place in cart or on dolly and take to area for washing. The blinds may be hung on special racks for washing and rinse with high pressure unit, or may be scheduled to be washed in the blind louvre washing machine that spray washes and rinses blinds in one operation. Blinds are removed from the machine, hung on racks and allowed to air dry.

4. Pull blinds to top of frames. Wrap or secure cord around each end. Place in cart or on dolly and take back to proper location.

5. Install and adjust blinds.

6. Move equipment. Clean and return to designated storage area.

Window Shades

Window shades require periodic dusting, vacuuming and washing. Most shades are washable. Daily dusting can be accomplished while shade is hanging. It may be performed with a damp germicidal cloth or vacuum cleaner or covered broom.

1. Assemble equipment. Take to designated area. Put on gloves.

PROCEDURE

2. Extend shade full length.

3. Vacuum roller—use side to side motion.

4. Vacuum surface of shade. Use up and down motion. Overlap each stroke.

5. Continue this procedure until shade is completed. If very soiled, repeat procedure using side to side motion.

6. Continue to vacuum opposite side—starting at bottom of shade—hold shade with one hand.

7. Vacuum pull edge—use side to side motion.

8. Vacuum surface—use up and down motion.

9. Roll shade clean on cleaned with one hand and continue the dusting procedure until shade is completed.

10. Adjust shade. Inspect work.

11. Clean equipment and return to designated storage area.

12. Report to supervisor any shade needing repair or replacement.

IV. GLASS AND WINDOW CLEANING

PURPOSE: To remove soil, control bacteria, allow passage of natural light and for appearance.

EQUIPMENT:

    Utility cart
    Ladder (step or platform)
    Buckets (two)
    Cloths or Sponges or Squeegees
    Gloves
    Cleaning agents (Trisodium, Vinegar, Clear water, Alcohol, Commercial glass cleaners, or Synthetic detergents)
    Vacuum cleaner
    Cloths (lint-free)
    Paper Towels

SAFETY PRECAUTIONS:

1. Make sure ladders are in locked position.

2. When using a six-foot or taller step ladder, a second person is required.

3. Place cloth under the bucket to collect spillage.

4. Do not lean out of windows, sit nor stand on window sills or guard rails.

5. Do not place too much water on wooden frames and sashs.

6. Do not wash windows when sun rays are directly on pane.

PROCEDURE

General

1. Assemble equipment, prepare cleaning solution and take to assigned area. Set up as close to work site as possible. (Make sure ladder is on flat surface and is locked and that a cloth is under the bucket to catch spillage.)

2. Prepare window—Remove objects from sill; remove drapery, curtains, shades or blinds, If there are screens or guards, unlock and vacuum.

3. Put on gloves.

4. Vacuum frame and window sills.

5. Wash window frames—starting at top using

143

PROCEDURE

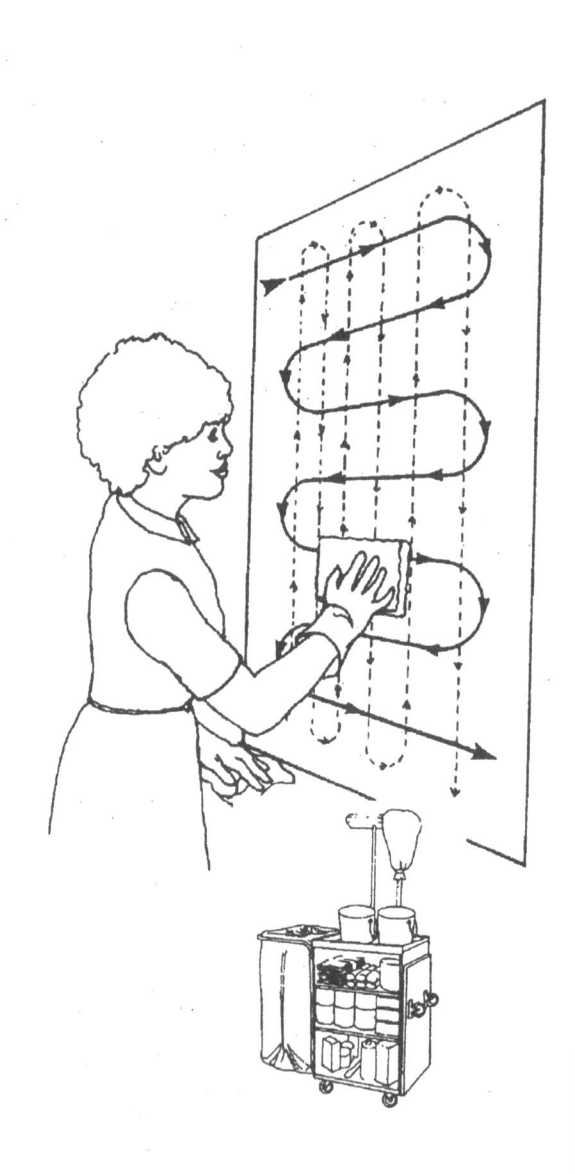

left to right or side to side motion. Then wash the sides using up and down motion.

6. Rinse and dry using same motions.

7. Wash, rinse and dry window sills.

8. Change wash solution, rinse water and cloths. (Clean solution is a necessity.)

9. Dip cloth or sponge into cleaning solution; squeeze out excess water. Start washing at top of window pane (standing to side) using left to right or side to side motion and continue back and forth in one continuous motion until the window is completed. Do not overlook corners. If window panes are very soiled, repeat the washing procedure using up and down motion.

10. Rinse; use the same procedure as washing.

11. Dry with lint-free cloth or paper towel. Use same procedure as for washing. If panes or glass are large or medium in size, use squeegee for drying (using either the "side to side" or "top to bottom" motion) wiping squeegee with cloth after each stroke or when squeegee-pane contact is broken.

12. Continue this procedure until all windows are completed. Then clean equipment and return to designated storage area.

- -

Squeegee Method

1. Apply cleaning solution with sponge or cloth. Use continuous side to side motion.

PROCEDURE

2. Remove water with squeegee. There are two basic motions—*"Side to Side"* and *"Top to Bottom."* Either is acceptable. In the *"Side to Side"* Method, make one continuous stroke starting at bottom of pane with squeegee in flat position and make border. Wipe blade; continue by starting at top of pane (left or right) with squeegee in vertical position; stroke across, and when reaching the opposite side, make a simple half turn overlapping previous stroke. Wipe blade any time squeegee-pane contact is broken. In the *"Top to Bottom"* Method, start at top (left or right corner) of pane and move squeegee to bottom of pane in separate strokes overlapping each stroke. Wipe squeegee blade at the end of each stroke.

3. Wipe up any spills on the sills or frames.

4. Inspect work. Replace items moved from windows and sills.

5. Clean equipment and return to designated storage area.

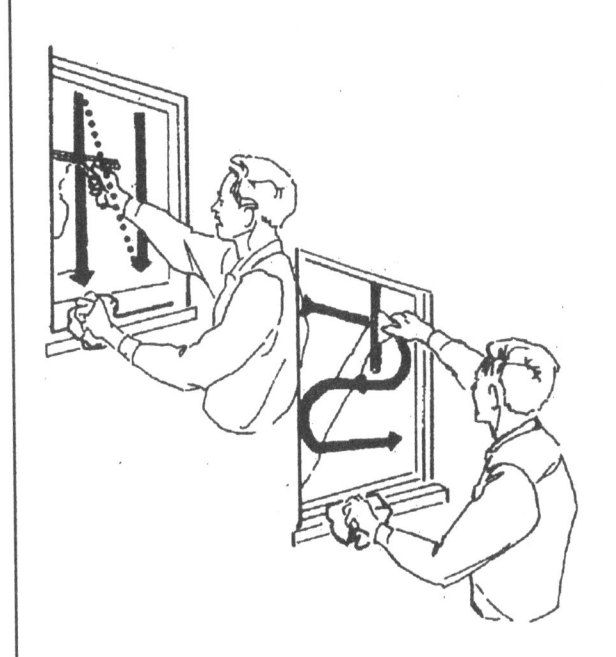

Other Glass Cleaning

Entrance door glass is cleaned daily. Use either the general or the squeegee method. Transoms, partitions and desk tops are cleaned periodically. Use procedure as described in the general method.

V. CLEANING OF LIGHT FIXTURES
(Fluorescent and Globes)

PURPOSE: To control bacteria, assure proper lighting and for appearance.

EQUIPMENT:

- Utility cart
- Cart on wheels
- Ladder (safety or platform)
- Buckets (two)
- Cloths
- Germicidal detergent
- Treated cloths
- Broom block (with extension handle)
- Gloves
- Broom bags
- Vacuum cleaner/attachments
- Screw driver

SAFETY PRECAUTIONS:

1. Always turn off light switch.
2. Schedule when there is least traffic.
3. Do not touch light bulbs while hot or with wet hands.
4. Make sure ladder is locked in position.
5. Do not place fixtures where they can be broken.
6. Move any object interfering with procedure.

PROCEDURE

DRY Fluorescent Light Fixtures

1. Assemble equipment, take to work area. Make sure all lights are off.
2. Move furniture if necessary. Choose either the vacuum cleaner or the covered broom with extension handle.
3. Start at the back of the room. Place cleaning tool against side panel and move forward, using side-to-side motion until you reach the end of the fixture. Then do the other side in the same manner.
4. Continue the process until project is completed.

PROCEDURE

5. Clean equipment and return to storage area. Restock utility cart.

- - - - - - - - - - - - - - - - - - - -

**Globes
Incandescent Light Fixtures**

1. Take assembled equipment and ladder to work area. Make sure all lights are off.

2. Set up ladder and make sure it is locked. If safety ladder is being used, a second person is required.

3. Put on gloves.

4. Dust light fixtures with treated cloth or damp germicide cloth.

5. Clean equipment and return to storage area. Restock utility cart.

- - - - - - - - - - - - - - - - - - - -

**WET
Fluorescent and Globes**

1. Assemble equipment in designated work area or utility room and prepare solution for washing.

2. Take ladder and cart to scheduled area.

3. Turn off lights.

4. Remove side panels (lift up and out).

5. Remove louvre (egg crates) loosening one side at a time.

6. Take to designated area.

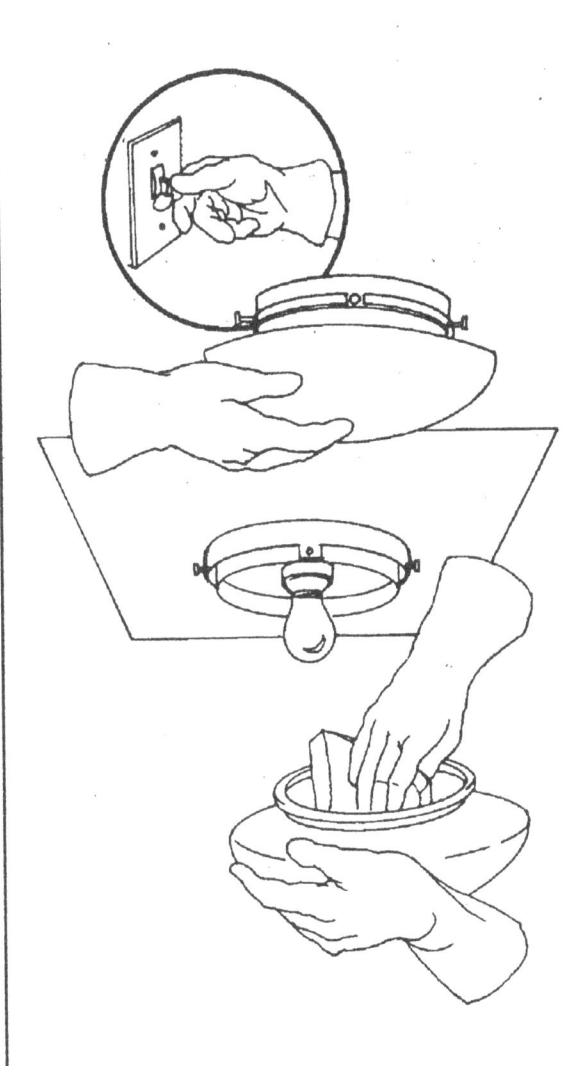

PROCEDURE

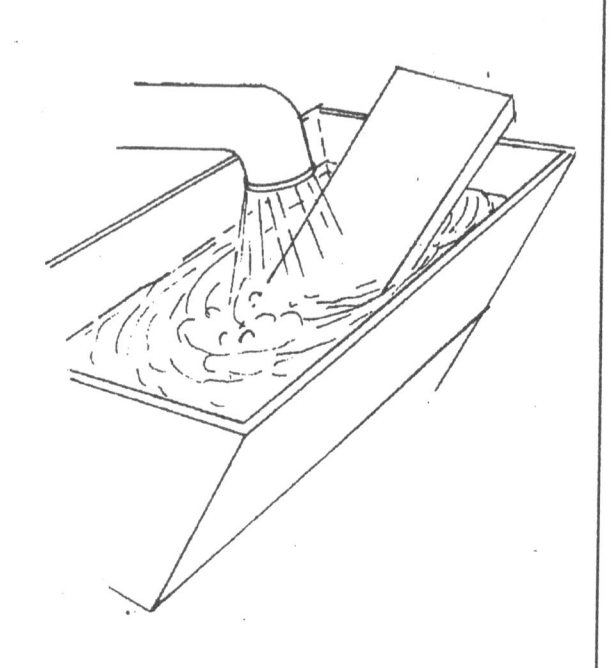

7. Put on gloves.

8. Immerse side panels in prepared solution, wash with soft materials. Don't use any abrasive materials.

9. Rinse in clear water.

10. Dry.

11. Repeat same procedure for "egg crates" and removable incandescent light fixtures (globes). If globes or light fixtures are nonremovable, procedure is to wash, rinse and dry while still attached to the frame.

12. Return light fixtures to their proper area.

13. Attach to frame and make sure that all are securely fastened.

14. Wash and dry all equipment, and return to storage area.

VI. WALL WASHING
(Manual and Machine)

PURPOSE: To remove unsightly soil, control bacteria and for appearance. Walls are also washed for painting purposes.

EQUIPMENT:

- Utility cart
- Platform ladder or
- Step ladder
- Cleaning cloths
- Gloves
- Nylon pad (square)
- Drop cloths
- Trisodium Phosphate or
- Germicidal detergent
- Scaffold
- Sponges
- Buckets (two)
- Vacuum (wet and dry or back-pack), and attachments

SAFETY PRECAUTIONS:

1. Areas must be scheduled and the procedure performed when traffic is the least.
2. Secure locking devices on ladder.

PROCEDURE

Manual

1. Assemble equipment. Prepare solution. Take to assigned area.

2. Move furniture to one side of the room or cover it. Remove pictures and other wall mountings. Place in a safe area.

3. Spread drop cloths under portion of wall to be washed.

4. Set up ladder or scaffold. Secure lock if applicable. Put on gloves.

5. If area has not been dusted, vacuum ceiling and walls.

6. Place buckets on cloth on platform (ladder or scaffold).

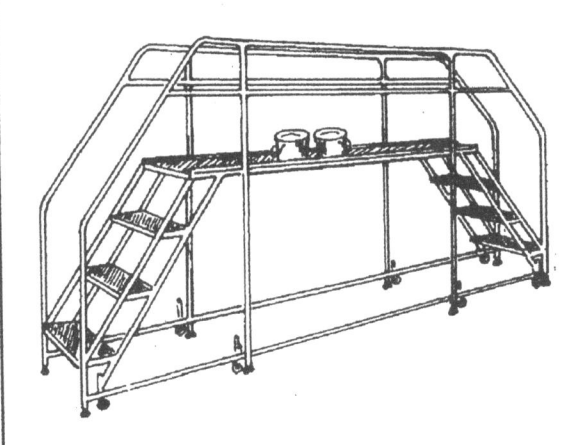

PROCEDURE

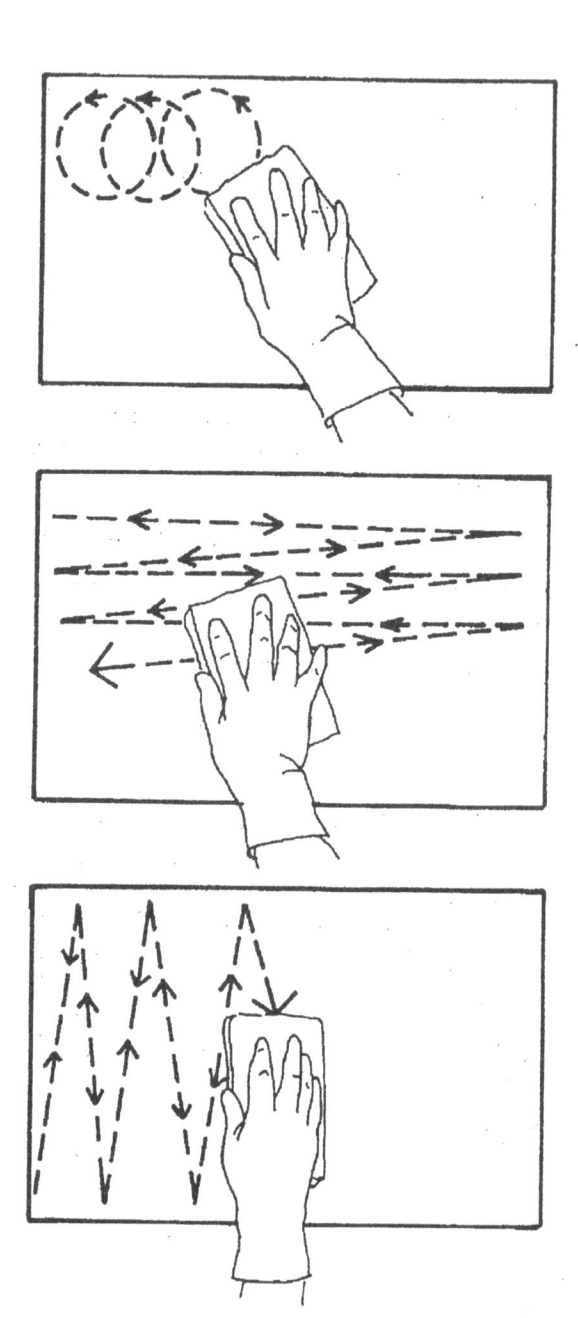

7. Dip sponge into cleaning solution, squeeze out excess water. Take clean cloth to catch drippings.

8. Start at top or bottom. Wash small area. Use circular motion.

9. Dip second sponge into rinse water. Squeeze out excess water. Rinse, use side to side motion.

10. Dry with soft lint-free cloth. Use up and down motion.

11. Continue washing, rinsing and drying until area is completed. Overlap strokes to prevent streaking.

12. Replace furniture. Continue to other side.

13. Move furniture. Continue with the procedure until all walls are washed.

14. Replace all furniture, pictures and mountings.

15. Inspect work.

16. Clean equipment and return to designated storage area.

Machine

The wall washing procedure can be accomplished by machine, thereby saving the institution a great deal of time and labor. The additional equipment necessary to perform this operation includes:

PROCEDURE

Wall washing pressure tanks
Trowels
Wall washing towels
Neutral detergent

SAFETY PRECAUTIONS:

1. Make sure pressure is released before cleaning tanks.

2. Avoid the use of excessive pressure. Excessive pressure will force soil into surface.

1. Assemble equipment. Prepare solution. Take to designated area.

2. Build up pressure in tanks.

3. Place toweling material on trowels.

4. Follow room preparation procedure as in manual wall washing.

5. Dust wall with vacuum.

6. Press solution release levers and thoroughly wet trowels.

7. Begin washing wall. Start by placing trowel in upper corner of wall. Move trowel in a rhythmic side to side motion. Overlap each stroke. Work down the wall by stepping back.

8. Rinse. Use rinse trowel.

9. Dry with third trowel or a clean soft cloth.

10. Continue this procedure until wall is completed.

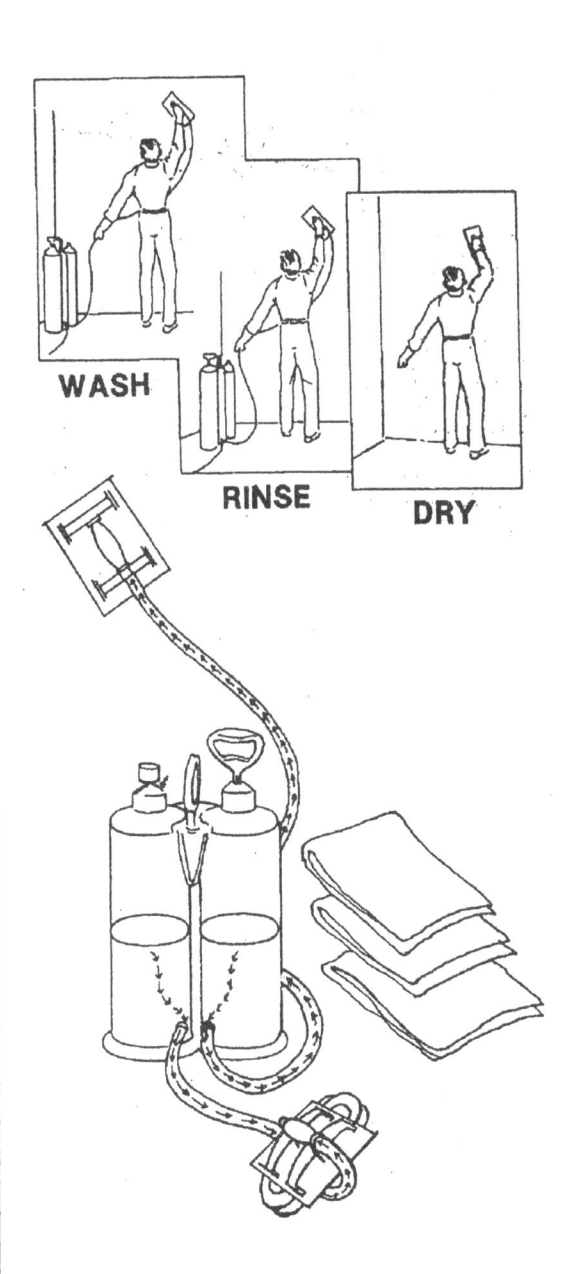

PROCEDURE

11. Replace furniture and other wall mountings. Inspect work. There should be no streaks, surface contrasts or spots.

Remove towels from trowel and place in plastic liner for laundering. Wash, rinse and dry equipment. Rinse tanks and tubings. Dry. Return equipment to designated storage area.

VII. CLEANING ELEVATOR

PURPOSE: To improve sanitation of the environment, control bacteria and for appearance.

EQUIPMENT:

    Utility cart
    Counter brush and dustpan
    Germicidal detergent
    Cloths
    Putty knife
    Stainless steel cleaner
    Electric floor machine
    Buckets and Wringers on dolly (two)
    Vacuum cleaner (wet and dry)
    Four-foot ladder
    Gloves
    Buckets (two)
    Sweeping tool—treated cloth

SAFETY PRECAUTIONS:
1. Take elevator to basement.
2. Put elevator out of order—turn off switch.
3. Do not prop doors open with sticks, buckets, or any other device.
4. Tracks of elevators must be cleaned daily (sometimes more frequently) so that door will open and close properly.

PROCEDURE

1. Assemble all equipment. Prepare solution. Take to designated area.

2. Put on gloves.

3. Vacuum walls, lights, vents, and tracks. Change brushes. Remove gum with putty knife.

4. Vacuum floor or dust with treated cloth.

5. Dip cloth in germicidal solution. Wring out. Spot wash wall areas. Rinse and dry. Wash and dry telephone and box. Wash doors inside and outside. Rinse and dry.

6. Polish all metal surfaces.

PROCEDURE

7. Wet mop floor. Follow wet mopping procedure.

8. Spray buff or buff floor area.

9. Release elevator and continue same procedures until all elevators are completed. Only one elevator should be put out of order at a time.

10. Clean equipment and return to designated storage area.

    NOTE: Once a week, thoroughly clean elevators:
    a. Vacuum thoroughly the walls, ceiling, floors, and tracks.

    b. Wash all walls (interior and exterior), knobs or buttons, control panel, ceiling, vents, ceiling light, telephone, and box. Rinse and dry.

    c. Polish all metal surfaces with recommended polishing agent.

    d. Light scrub floor area.

    e. Apply finish.

    f. Clean all equipment and return to designated storage area.

VIII. ENTRANCE AND LOBBY CLEANING

PURPOSE: to improve sanitation of the environment, to control bacteria and for appearance. The entrance of any building (whether it is a hospital, hotel, home, or business establishment) represents to visitors, potential patients, and others what the interior of the building will be. Therefore, it is very important that these areas are cleaned daily and policed several times each day. The entrance and lobby must be neat and clean at all times.

EQUIPMENT:

- Utility cart
- Gloves
- Cloths or Sponges
- Putty knife
- Plastic liners/bags
- Sifter and slit spoon
- Buckets (two)
- Electric floor machines
- Vacuum cleaner or Sweeping tool
- Glass cleaning agent
- Wet floor signs
- Buckets and Wringers on dolly (two)
- Mopheads and handles (two)
- Automatic scrubber
- Container for cigarette butts
- Squeegee
- Spray bottle
- Deck brush
- Broom and broom bags
- Treated cloths
- Germicidal detergent
- Dustpan and Counter brush

SAFETY PRECAUTIONS:

1. Post wet floor signs.
2. Place equipment near wall area to avoid tripping when not in use.
3. Do not leave electric floor machine unattended and plugged in.
4. Wipe up spills immediately.
5. This operation should be performed during least traffic hours.
6. Clean only half of the lobby at a time. Move furniture.
7. Where urn screens are not in use, use sifter and slit spoon.

PROCEDURE

1. Assemble all equipment. Prepare solution. Take to lobby area.
2. Put on gloves.

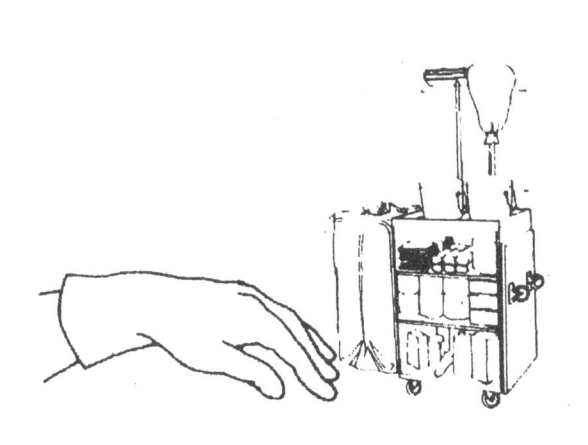

PROCEDURE

3. Clean front entrance. Take broom, counter brush, dustpan and plastic liner to outside area:

   a. Pick up large pieces of trash and place in plastic liner/bag.

   b. Sweep landing and/or steps.

   c. Continue sweeping sidewalk area.

   d. Take up debris with dustpan and counter brush.

4. Return equipment to utility cart.

5. Continue with the cleaning of the lobby:

   a. Post wet floor signs. Move furniture.

   b. Pick up large pieces of trash. Empty trash containers. Wash and dry containers inside and outside. Replace liner.

   c. Empty and wash ashtrays. Clean cigarette urns. Follow urn cleaning procedure.

   d. Take glass cleaning agent and clean cloths or squeegee and wash lobby windows and glass doors inside and outside. Wash any other glass in area at this time. Follow glass cleaning procedure.

   e. Check for cobwebs and remove.

   f. Dip cloth into germicidal solution. Wring out. Damp dust and dry all furniture, window sills, radiators/covers, and other items. Spot wash walls and around light switches. Return cloth frequently to germicidal solution for refreshing.

PROCEDURE

    g. Vacuum or dust floor with sweeping tool or covered broom. Make sure to clean runners or mats—vacuum, hose off, mop or scrub.

    h. Wet mop floor. Follow wet mopping procedure.

    i. Return furniture to proper place and continue with procedure until lobby is completed.

6. Take equipment to utility room. Wash and dry. Return to designated storage area. Restock utility cart.

STAIRS AND STAIRWELLS, PORCHES, AND BACK ENTRANCES
(Wet and Dry)

PURPOSE: To maintain a safe and sanitary environment, to control the spread of bacteria, and for appearance.

EQUIPMENT:

Utility cart
Buckets and Wringers on dolly (two)
Vacuum cleaner (back-pack or wet and
dry), or
Corn broom
Putty knife
Germicidal detergent
Scrub brush
Gloves
Mopheads and handles (two)
Broom bags
Counter brush
Wet floor or Out of order signs (two)
Cloths and Sponges
Buckets (two)
Plastic liner
Deck brush
Dustpan

SAFETY PRECAUTIONS:
1. Report loose treads and banisters and burned out light bulbs.

2. Set up caution signs at *each* doorway.

3. Leave a path open for traffic.

4. When cleaning wide stairs, clean half the width at a time. Leave a dry path for users.

5. Make sure back entrances and stairs are never blocked or cluttered with trash or broken furniture.

PROCEDURE

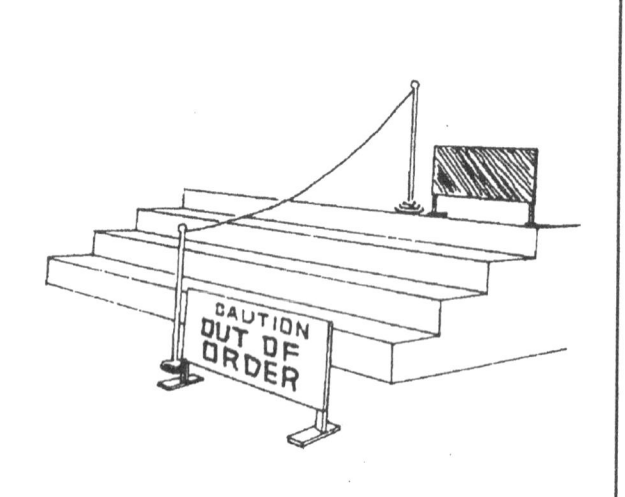

Dry Cleaning

1. Assemble equipment. Prepare solution. Take to assigned area.

2. Place caution sign on the bottom landing.

3. Take second sign, putty knife, and covered broom to top landing.

4. Place sign at top landing.

PROCEDURE

5. Remove any gum. Sweep top landing and work down the stairs. Sweep soil toward closed wall. Use single, continuous, horizontal strokes, and bring down to next step if back of step is closed. However, if back of steps are opened or if steps are opened on each side, counter brush and dustpan are used for this procedure. Sweep each step from both sides to center with counter brush and take up soil in dustpan.

6. Continue procedure until all steps are completed.

7. Sweep bottom landing. Take up trash with counter brush and dustpan. Place in trash bag on utility cart.

8. Dip cloth into germicidal solution. Wring out. Start at bottom and work to top of stairs. Damp dust banister, railing, spindles, radiator, window sills, and ledges.

9. Pick up sign. (Leave sign if wet procedure is being performed.)

10. Continue with the dusting procedure on the opposite side, working down until dusting is completed. (A vacuum may be used to reach difficult areas—ledges, radiators, or to remove cobwebs.)

11. Place caution signs on utility cart. Change cover on broom. Place cover in plastic liner/bag for laundering.

12. Continue to next assignment. If this is the last assignment, clean equipment and return to designated storage area.

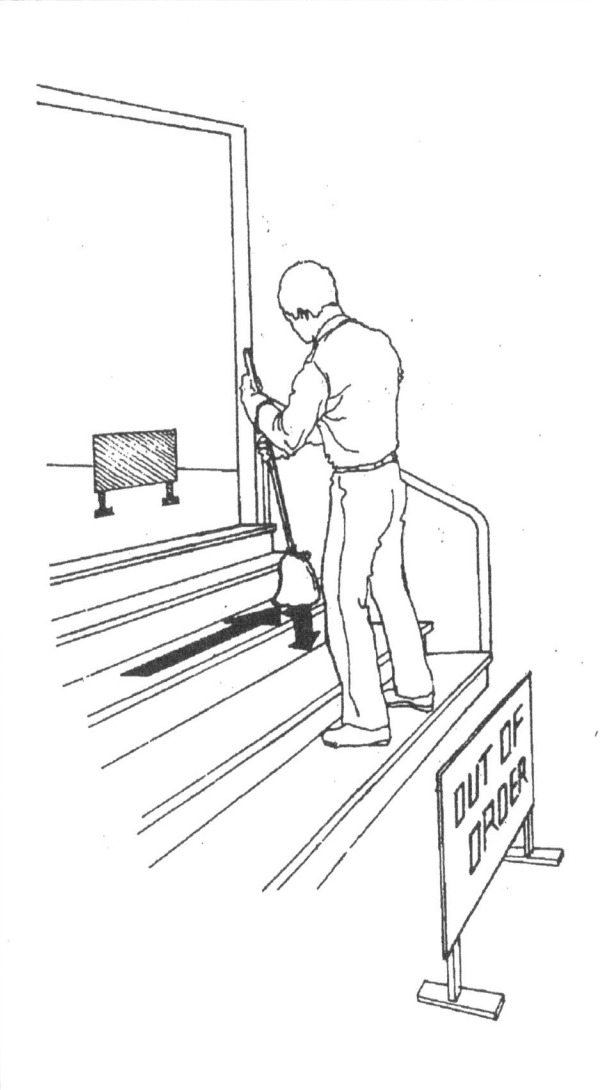

PROCEDURE

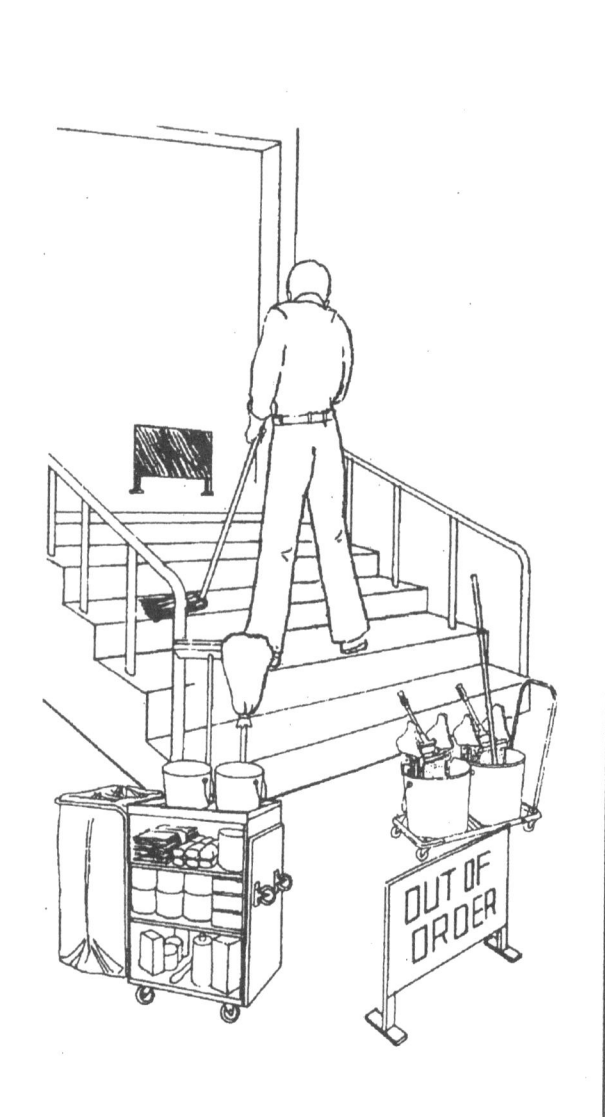

Wet Cleaning
(By Mop)

1. Assemble equipment. Prepare solution. Take to designated area.

2. Sweep stairway with a covered broom.

3. Place buckets on landing. Dip mop into germicidal solution. Press out excess water. Start at top landing and work down.

4. Mop a flight of stairs at a time. Turn mop frequently. Use mop strands to clean corners.

5. Dip second mop into rinse water. Wring out. Pick up soil and solution.

6. Continue this procedure until all steps and landings are completed.

7. Scrub bottom landing thoroughly. Use four-step wet mopping procedure. Apply cleaning solution. Pick up. Apply rinse water and pick up.

8. Take equipment to utility room. Wash, rinse, and dry. Return to designated storage area. Place dust cloths and mopheads in plastic liner/ bag for laundering.

Wet Cleaning
(By Hand)

1. Assemble equipment. Prepare solution. Take to assigned area.

2. Sweep stairway with covered broom.

PROCEDURE

3. Dip sponge into germicidal solution. Squeeze out excess water.

4. Apply solution to treads.

5. Scrub tread with hand scrub brush.

6. Pick up cleaning solution with germicidal solution sponge.

7. Rinse tread. Use second sponge.

8. Pick up rinse water.

9. Continue this process until all treads are completed.

10. Take equipment to utility room. Wash out sponges, brush, and buckets. Return to designated storage area.

Cleaning Wide Stairs
(Dry and Wet)

The procedure for cleaning wide stairs is the same as for narrow stairs with the following changes:

1. Only half of the width of wide steps is cleaned at a time.

2. The dusting procedure is performed before the sweeping procedure.

3. Wide steps are cleaned from bottom up.

BASIC FUNDAMENTALS OF THE MAINTENANCE OF FLOORS

CONTENTS

	Page
FLOOR TYPES	1
BUFFING TECHNIQUE	11
STRIPPING	13
FINISHING FLOORS	18
SPRAY BUFFING	20
CARPET CARE	22

BASIC FUNDAMENTALS OF THE MAINTENANCE OF FLOORS

FLOOR TYPES

I. Resilient—Elastic or Soft Floor

A. ASPHALT TILE

1. Made from asphalt-treated asbestos fibers, with an inert filler (usually limestone) to give it hardness. For darker colored tile, gilsonite (black) asphalt is used. In lighter colors, coal tar resins are used for binders. Ingredients are mixed under heat and transferred to hot rollers, where the mix is rolled into uniform thickness.

2. Precautions. Never use varnish, spirit waxes or solvent-type cleaners. Do not sweep asphalt tile floors with sweeping compounds containing fine oil or petroleum distillities.

B. VINYL TILE

1. Vinyl plastic (resin) is manufactured with vinyl-resin along with color pigments and fillers. It has all the advantages of asphalt tile, plus being more flexible, and almost impervious and immune to damage by petroleum products.

C. RUBBER TILE

1. Is generally made from synthetic, reclaimed, or pure rubber; color pigments; and inert fillers. The mix is fused and used like other rubber products, molded under pressure to required thickness, and then made into sheets of tile. It has the advantages of asphalt and vinyl floors, plus being the most pliable. It recovers from indention and resists cracking.

2. Precautions. Oil, grease, naphtha and similar petroleum products will soften and deteriorate rubber tile. Do not sweep with sweeping compounds containing oils or petroleum distillities. Air and sunlight cause rubber tile to crack or check. Do not use shellac, varnish, lacquer, alkaline soaps, or abrasives on rubber floors.

D. LINOLEUM

1. It is made of oxidized linseed oil, resins, and other filler material thoroughly mixed with ground cork and color pigments. The mixture is pressed out on a backing material (normally burlap) by running the mix through rollers, then curing at high temperature.

2. Precautions. Same as asphalt tile.

E. MASTIC FLOORS

1. Similar to asphalt tile in composition, but ingredients are heated on the job and troweled on, to form a seamless flooring material.

2. Precautions. Same as asphalt tile.

F. CORK FLOORING

1. Is made by compressing or baking cork curlings and ground cork, or by adding synthetic resin binders. The baking causes natural gums and resins in the cork to liquify, thus binding together the cork particles.

GENERAL POINTS TO BE OBSERVED IN MAINTENANCE OF ALL RESILIENT FLOORING:

1. All resilient flooring material should be cleaned and a floor finish applied (either wax or

synthetic) as soon as floor has been allowed to set up. These floors should be cleaned and a finish applied on regular schedule, throughout the life of the floor.

2. Being a semi-soft material, it should be kept free of sand and dirt, which may scratch or discolor the surface.

3. Thorough dusting with a properly treated dust mop is important. To reduce the number of scrubbings necessary, oil and solvent type dust mop treatment should not be used. Damp or wet mopping should be utilized to remove surface soil conditions (mud, water and sand).

4. Spray buffing in heavy traffic areas will maintain these areas looking as well as non-traffic areas. It lengthens the time between stripping. Remember that spray buffing is not a cure for all maintenance problems.

5. Buffing is an absolute necessity in areas where traffic is heavy.

6. The legs of chairs, tables, and desks should be equipped with coasters or glides to prevent denting or marking of floor.

II. Hard Floors

A. CONCRETE

1. Concrete floors are mixtures of cement with varying proportions of sand and gravel. The porosity and smoothness of the surface depends upon the mix and the hardening and finishing process. Color pigments are often added to the topping mix when concrete is used as a decorative floor material.

2. Maintenance for Concrete Floors:

a. Concrete floors protected by concrete sealer and wax will require only dust mopping or floor brushing to keep them clean and attractive. Concrete floors may be cleaned with any mild cleaning solution; however, care should be taken in proper rinsing.

b. If a concrete floor dusts excessively, it should be scrubbed with a neutral soap and sealed. Proper sealing will greatly lengthen concrete floor life, prevent dusting, and make maintenance easier and more economical. When traffic lanes begin to show, the floor can easily be touched up. Properly done, this treatment will not show an overlap.

c. Concrete floors can be waxed rather than sealed. However, better results will be achieved by sealing the floor and then applying a coat of wax. After this treatment, periodic buffing, using a fine nylon disc, will greatly reduce maintenance time, and decrease the frequency of stripping and refinishing.

B. TERRAZZO

1. Terrazzo is one of the oldest flooring materials. It was used in pre-Christian times in many palaces and mansions of ancient rulers and merchants.

2. It is a hard, durable composition material, made up of marble chips and cement matrix. This surface, after hardening for a time, is wet ground under pressure with stone grinders. Because of its pattern, terrazzo does not readily show soil and stays presentable longer than floors of one color.

3. Special Precautions in Maintenance of Terrazzo:

MAINTENANCE OF FLOORS

a. Cleaning materials containing acids or alkalines should be avoided, since the acid or alkali eats into the cement and loosens the marble chips.

b. Avoid abrasive powder cleaners because they encourage "dusting." This type of cleaner actually wears away the floor, and its ill effects are noticeable within a short period of time.

c. Cleaning crystals of a phosphate nature should never be used. A residue remains after the water has evaporated and acts in much the same way as water when it is allowed to stand in a concrete formation and is then frozen. In other words, the crystals fill up porous spots in the cement; and as they dry, they expand. The expansion loosens the marble chips; this is called "spalling."

d. Avoid sweeping compounds containing oil. These will penetrate and discolor terrazzo.

4. Maintenance for Terrazzo Floors

a. In scrubbing a terrazzo floor, do not use steel wool. It is best to use a brush for scrubbing because the steel wool is softer than the terrazzo and may become abraded. Bits of the wool left on the floor will rust and stain the terrazzo. Also, the use of steel wool on terrazzo can result in black carbon marks. Clean terrazzo with neutral, synthetic, free-rinsing liquid detergent. These detergents will leave no unsightly residue that often necessitates special work and materials to remove it.

b. Terrazzo floors should be mopped frequently and rinsed thoroughly. Dirty water will stain if left too long; it leaves a gummy hardened accumulation of film which is not easily removed.

c. The use of a solvent type "water white" sealer on terrazzo will prevent dusting and spalling. However, a heavy surface film of this material allowed to build up will result in severe traffic laning. Color variations in the floor may also appear.

d. Properly applied, colorless, buffable-type terrazzo seal, well-rubbed out, tends to harden the surface, helps hold the marble chips together, and virtually stops penetration of water, stains, oils, gums and other damaging materials. The finish will have a satin-like sheen.

e. Either solvent or water emulsion-type wax can be used on terrazzo. However, only waxes manufacured from light colored products should be used. Solvent-type wax manufactured from waxed having a very dark color, or solvent waxes to which artificial coloring matter has been added, would definitely cause a discoloration of terrazzo. Serious discoloration could also occur if a water wax emulsion made from dark colored waxes is applied to a terrazzo floor.

C. MARBLE

1. Marble is a natural product of crystallized rock, composed of carbonate of lime. Generally, marble used in the interior of buildings for decorative purposes is of the polished, finished type which reflects light because of its glossy surface. This also emphasizes color and marking. Marble used for interior floors may have a "honed" or a "sand" finish.

a. Travertine marble, recognized by its small pits and tarnish-colored surface, requires only cleaning, as does polished marble. Travertine is used generally as wainscot or other trim material.

2. On all types of marble, except the Travertine, sealing is recommended. The primary purpose of this treatment is to provide maximum protection to the marble itself, which is very soft and porous. Ordinary dirt and grease are sealed out of the floor, and because the pits and voids have been filled, the soil is held on the surface and is easy to remove through usual maintenance methods.

3. Marble floors sealed and finished with a good, colorless, buffable type terrazzo sealer can be maintained dry with only occasional mopping. Sealers of solvent cut resin or lacquer nature, used on marble floors, result in traffic laning, uneven appearance of the floor surface, and over a period of time, discoloration of the surface.

4. Special Precautions in Maintenance of Marble:

a. Never use an acid cleaner. It will destroy polish and eventually burn. The end result will be discoloration and disintegration of the marble.

b. Do not use scouring bricks or harsh abrasives. These materials will destroy polish and mar the surface.

c. Bar, powder, or liquid soaps should not be used on marble surfaces. They may form insoluble deposits which accumulate on the surface. This discoloration cannot be readily removed and will become a slip hazard when wet.

d. Never use oily sweeping compounds on marble surfaces. Their use will evenutally discolor the floor.

e. Quick action "lightening" cleaners are apt to be acid in action. The life and finish of the marble will be sacrificed for immediate results.

5. Maintenance for Marble Floors:

a. The secret to beautiful marble is merely keeping it clean after the original sealing treatment. Complicated cleaning agents and procedures will rarely be needed if the marble surfaces are maintained properly and regularly. When complete cleaning is necessary, use a neutral, free-rinsing detergent that will not leave a slippery or unattractive residue.

b. Marble spalling and deterioration can be caused through neglect. Marble is not indestructable, and when neglected, the accumulated dirt and grease can completely deteriorate and damage the surface beyond repair.

D. OXYCHLORIDE

1. Oxychloride, sometimes called magnasite, is similar to concrete. It is produced in many colors. It can be installed with two types of finish. One type of finish is trowelled on. The other type of finish is ground and gives the appearance of being terrazzo. It can be laid over nearly any type of sub-floor and produces a surface which is rather resilient, yet dense and strong. However, magnasite is a somewhat porous and soft material as compared to terrazzo or concrete.

2. Special Precautions in Maintenance of Oxychloride:

a. Avoid use of strong alkalies for cleaning.

b. Acids used in some cleaning materials tend to dissolve oxychloride due to chemical reaction and should not be used.

MAINTENANCE OF FLOORS

c. Avoid excessive use of water. This material is ever-thirsty, and deterioration of the binder will result.

3. Maintenance for Oxychloride Floors:

a. In cleaning, a neutral soap or a non-alkaline detergent should be used. The application procedure is listed under asphalt tile.

b. Oxychloride flooring is porous and may be sealed with a penetrating-type sealer. Sealing will fill the pores of the floor covering, and maintenance work will become easier.

c. When excessively soiled, oxychloride floors should be scrubbed with a floor machine, using a scrubbing brush. However, the excessive use of water will damage some of the fillers, and will also attack the magnesium oxychloride binder and deteriorate it. For this reason, oxychloride floors should be sealed and waxed.

d. Solvent-type wax should be used on this flooring. Oily floor dressings should not be used as they could result in serious discoloration. Sweeping compounds containing organic dyes and free oil could also cause discoloration, and any sand present in the compound could result in the scratching and abrading of the rather soft oxychloride floor.

E. HARD TILE

1. Ceramic tile or "hard tile" is made of finely ground clay and baked to the hardness of stone. The various types include ceramic mosaic, quarry, and clear glaze.

2. Hard tile is naturally durable and resistant to soil defacement; but to get full value from a large investment, it has to have the same care as more susceptible flooring materials. Hard tile can be either glazed or unglazed. Tile used as flooring material is usually unglazed. Glazed tile is normally used as wall surfacings.

3. Special Precautions in Maintenance of Hard Tile:

a. Avoid solutions of strong alkaline cleaners, such as tri-sodium phosphate and sal soda. These cleaners penetrate the cement grout between the tile and upon drying, leave crystallized deposits. Continued use of alkaline cleaners will cause the crystallized deposits to accumulate and swell, causing disintegration of the grout.

b. Do not use steel wool for cleaning hard tile. The tile is harder than the steel wool and will abrade the wool, causing discoloration of the tile. Abrasive cleansers should never be used on the glazed surfaces.

c. Do not use acid cleaners, not because they will injure the tile, but because they will tend to destroy the cement grout. They may also dull glazed or ceramic tile.

d. Oily dust mops and sweeping compounds should not be used for maintenance of hard tile floors.

4. Maintenance for Hard Tile Floors:

a. About the only maintenance process for glazed tile floors consists of dusting and spot washing. Non-alkaline synthetic cleaners are recommended for cleaning.

b. Tile used as a flooring material resists most traffic stains, but it can suffer from the erosive action of abrasion. This means not only the wear and tear from traffic; but also from abrasive cleansers, which in time, will scratch or dull the finish.

c. A penetrating sealer, such as the type used for terrazzo, will prove to be a protection for the surface and will also protect cement grout from undue deterioration. Surface sealers which leave a heavy film of a non-buffable nature should not be used.

d. Waxing a hard tile floor is not recommended because wax may become a safety hazard. Where safety is not a factor, either the water emulsion or solvent wax can be used.

F. WOOD

1. The use of hard wood floors is as old as civilization. Their durability has been an important factor in their wide use. Wood floors, properly maintained, are capable of retaining their natural good looks for a long period of time. Wood can last a lifetime and longer.

2. Special Precautions in Maintenance of Wood:

a. Use a minimum amount of water to maintain wood floors. Excessive water may enter through the ends of the wood and cause swelling or warping.

b. When wood floors are set in mastic, exercise extreme care in the use of sealers, spirit waxes, solvent cleaners, and water.

c. Select and use a maintenance method which eliminates or minimizes the necessity for resanding.

3. Maintenance for Wood Floors:

a. Any good soap, except those strongly alkaline, can be used for cleaning wood floors. However, scrubbing, or even wet mopping will ultimately damage a wood floor.

b. It is most important to understand the adverse effects of water, oil, and alkali soaps on wood. Water raises the grain on wood floors, causes swelling and warping, and in general, creates a rough surface that is difficult to maintain. Where wood floors are bonded to a sub-floor, penetrating water will weaken the bond and cause loosening. In addition, water discolors wood, gives it a musty odor, and causes it to rot. Oil softens wood, darkens it, and creates a sticky surface that picks up and holds dirt. Alkali cleaners can stain and darken wood floors.

c. Wood floors of any type require positive sealing. Seals, manufactured specifically for wood floor application, protect against penetration of moisture, and properly formulated, are resistant to acids, alkalies, and oils.

d. The two general classifications of wood sealers are called surface seal and penetrating seal. The type used depends upon the floor usage.

e. Surface sealers are used for floors which are not subjected to heavy traffic. This type forms a perceptible film on top of the wood while penetrating it to a certain extent, and sealing. The surface seals are preferred for the sake of appearance.

f. The true penetrating sealers protect the wood surface by filling the pores but leave little actual surface. The penetrating seal is better for areas of heavy traffic since its "stain" finish is less subject to marking.

g. Traffic lanes, which show up in time, can be resealed without treating the entire area. The worn areas need only be scrubbed and given a light coating. If sufficient care is used in doing the patching, the former worn spots will not be noticeable.

MAINTENANCE OF FLOORS

h. Waxing, after the seal application, is an ideal treatment to provide maximum appearance and protection. Use of a solvent-type wax is highly recommended. It will prolong the life of the wood surface by reducing the need for mopping.

STAIN REMOVAL FOR RESILIENT FLOORS

A properly maintained resilient floor covering should have sufficient wax or floor finish on the surface to protect it against most water based stains, and many oil- and solvent-based stains. Freshly spilled stains should be wiped up or blotted immediately before they have a chance to dry. Dried stains, being more difficult to remove and usually of questionable origin, may require more than one treatment of different stain removers. Never use a solvent-type cleaner (turpentine, naphtha, dry-cleaning solution) on asphalt or rubber.

GENERAL POINTS TO OBSERVE:

1. Act promptly in treating stains or spots. Stains or spots are most easily removed when fresh. Use the mildest treatment, first. Maybe blotting paper or cold water sponging will remove the stain.

2. Before treatment of the stain, wet the area around it with clear water. This tends to stop the spread of the cleaner. Always work from the outside toward the center to prevent leaving a cleaning ring.

3. Several applications may be necessary before the stain can be completely removed.

4. Water is considered a good solvent. When possible its use is recommended first. In any case, it is always best to use the simplest procedure.

5. It is important to know the surface to be treated and the nature of the stain before trying to remove the stain. If you do not know, leave it alone. Call in an expert.

   a. Is the stain water-borne? If so, water will remove it.

   b. Is the stain alcohol-borne (for example, iodine)? If so, alcohol will remove it.

   c. Is the stain alkali? Then use an acid to neutralize it.

   d. Is the stain acid? If so, use alkali.

MAINTENANCE OF FLOORS

TYPE OF STAIN	TREATMENT
Acids	Clean with diluted general purpose cleaner. Strong acids may require neutralization with ammonia solution.
Adhesives, Flooring	Rub with nylon pad dipped in dilute cleaner. Some mastic adhesives may respond better to concentrated cleaner and nylon pad. Use alcohol on asphalt or rubber.
Alcoholic Beverages	Rub with nylon pad dipped in dilute cleaner. Wine stains might require alcohol or hydrogen peroxide.
Alkalies	Neutralize with acetic acid 5% solution (vinegar), rinse thoroughly, dry and apply polish.
Blood	First, the soiled area should be washed with plain, clear, cold water. Then, a few drops of ammonia should be applied to the area.
Candle Wax	Scrape off with putty knife. Wash with dilute cleaner, rinse, dry and apply polish. Use concentrated cleaner for asphalt and rubber.
Candy	Scrape off with putty knife. Apply diluted cleaner, rub with nylon pad.
Chewing Gum	Scrape off with putty knife. Scraping may be more effective if gum is first frozen with dry ice. Wash with diluted cleaner, rinse, dry and apply polish. Use concentrated cleaner for asphalt and rubber.
Chocolate	Scrape off with putty knife. Rub with nylon pad dipped in dilute cleaner. Rinse, dry and apply polish if necessary.
Cigarette Burns	Rub with coarse, then mild, nylon pad dipped in dilute cleaner. Rinse and dry. Slight indentations may require patching.

MAINTENANCE OF FLOORS

Coffee	Wash with diluted cleaner. A build-up of residue may require the use of mild nylon pad. If stain is old, place over it an absorbent cloth saturated with a glycerin solution. Let stand for about a half hour. Then, reclean with dilute cleaner. A deep stain may require the use of hydrogen peroxide.
Crayon	Scrape off with putty knife. Rub residual mark with nylon pad dipped in solution. Wash with dilute cleaner, rinse, dry and apply polish if necessary. Use concentrated cleaner for asphalt and rubber.
Fruit Juices	Use dilute cleaner. Persistent stains may require hydrogen peroxide.
Grass Stains	See Coffee
Ink, Ball Point	Clean with naphtha and/or alcohol (for asphalt and rubber, rub with nylon pad dipped in concentrated cleaner). Rinse, dry and spot polish.
Ink, Washable	Use diluted cleaner. If ink is soaked into floor, apply an alcohol-soaked blotter for several minutes. Wash with dilute cleaner, rinse, dry and apply polish.
Iodine	Clean with alcohol or an ammonia-saturated cloth. Deep stains may require longer contact with ammonia-saturated cotton. Rinse with dilute cleaner, clear water, dry and apply polish.
Lipstick	Scrape with putty knife. Rub residual stain with nylon pad dipped in concentrated cleaner. Deep stains may require the use of hydrogen peroxide followed by dilute cleaner. Rinse, dry and apply polish if necessary.
Nail Polish	Clean with acetone (use alcohol and nylon pad on asphalt and rubber).
Oil and Grease	Use diluted cleaner, rinse and dry.

MAINTENANCE OF FLOORS

For Persistent Stains

Cover stain with cotton batting soaked in hydrogen peroxide. On top of this, lay cotton batting soaked in ammonia. Repeat treatment as necessary until stain is removed.

Paint .... Use paint remover sparingly. (Do not use solvent on asphalt and rubber. Rub with nylon pad.) Apply diluted cleaner, rinse, dry and polish.

Black Rubber Marks .... Rub with nylon stripping pad dipped in concentrated cleaner. Apply dilute cleaner, rinse, dry and polish. For wood or other non-resilient floors, rub with pad dipped in cleaner or naphtha.

Rust .... Use oxalic acid solution, rinse thoroughly, dry and apply polish if necessary.

Shellac .... Clean with alcohol. Apply diluted cleaner, rinse, dry and polish.

Shoe Polish .... Rub with nylon pad dipped in concentrated cleaner. Apply dilute cleaner, rinse, dry and polish.

Solvents .... Solvents may roughen floor or cause color mixing. Burnish with an abrasive pad or nylon pad. Apply floor polish.

Tar .... See Chewing Gum.

Tobacco .... Apply diluted cleaner. On porous floors use lemon juice and water or equal parts of alcohol and glycerin. It may be necessary to bleach the stain with hydrogen peroxide or a liquid bleach.

Urine .... Apply diluted cleaning solution. If stain is old, use oxalic acid solution followed by cleaner. Rinse, dry and polish if necessary.

MAINTENANCE OF FLOORS

BUFFING TECHNIQUE

PURPOSE: To remove surface soil and renew the protective surface coating.

EQUIPMENT:

    Electric floor machine
    Nylon pads
    Treated cloths
    Brush or Drive assembly
    Sweeping tool, or
    Broom and broom bags

SAFETY PRECAUTIONS:

1. Do not leave machine unattended and plugged in.

2. Handle the machine carefully. Keep both hands on machine.

3. Always remove all cord off hooks and handle before beginning the buffing operation.

4. Check cord and plug for breaks and loose connections.

PROCEDURE

1. Assemble equipment. Take to assigned area.

2. Dust/sweep floors.

3. Tilt machine back on wheels and handle.

4. Straddle handle. Secure brush or drive assembly to drum of machine. Turn counterclockwise to lock.

5. Plug machine into most convenient outlet.

6. Stand machine on brush.

7. Adjust handle to proper height for comfort and ease of handling.

8. Raise wheels.

PROCEDURE

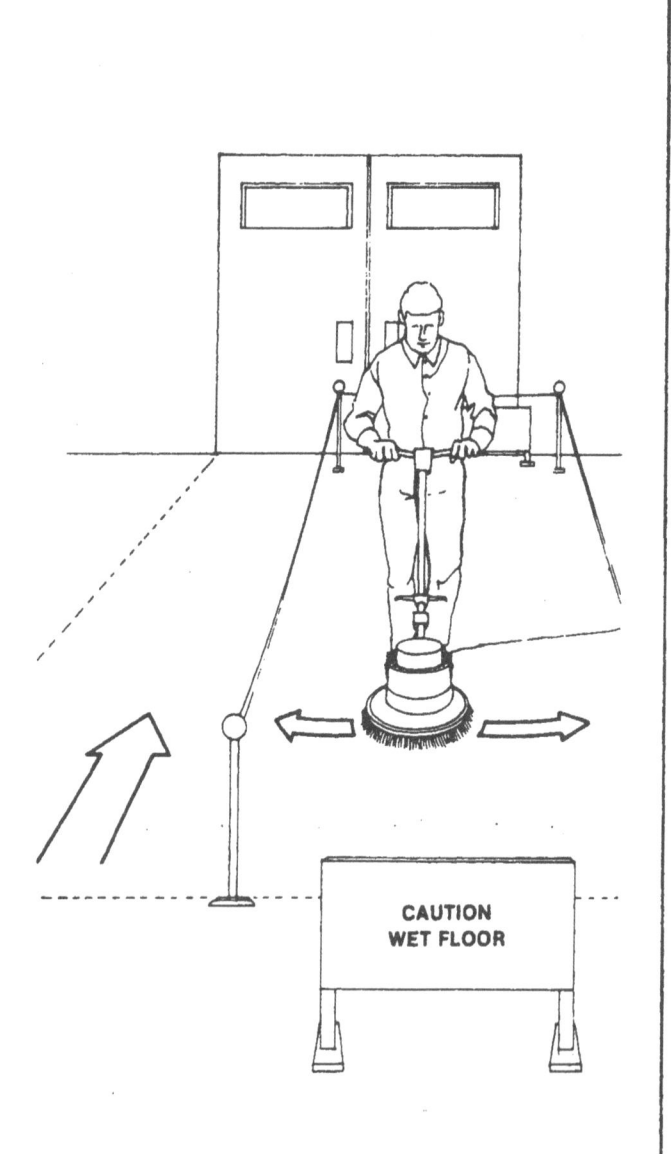

9. Begin buffing:
    a. Place cord over shoulder to keep out of path of machine. Start machine directly in front of the operator.

    b. Press downward on handle to move machine to right.

    c. Raise the handle to move the machine to the left.

    d. Move machine slowly in a left to right and right to left, or side to side arc pattern.

    e. Walk backward which facilitates easier movement of machine. However, it is safer to move forward.

10. Continue this procedure until area is completed.

11. Take equipment to utility room. Remove brush or drive assembly and pads, and wash. Wipe machine and cord off. Return to designated area.

MAINTENANCE OF FLOORS

STRIPPING
(Wet and Dry)

PURPOSE: To remove finish and embedded dirt, and to prepare floor for refinishing. This operation is performed by a combination of chemical action of the cleaning agent and the action of the brush or pad attached to an electric floor machine.

EQUIPMENT:

- Utility cart
- Nylon stripping pads
- Buckets and wringers on dolly (two)
- Mopheads and handles (two)
- Putty knife (long handle)
- Vacuum cleaner (wet and dry)
- Cloths
- Wet floor signs
- Sweeping tool—treated cloths, or
- Broom—broom bags
- Coving brush and handle
- Electric floor machine and attachments
- Drive assembly
- Scrubbing brush with pad holder
- Stripping agent
- Gloves
- Dustpan and Counter brush

SAFETY PRECAUTIONS:

1. Strip floor only on the advice of the supervisor.

2. Always sweep (use sweeping tool or covered broom) or vacuum before stripping.

3. Post area with wet floor signs.

4. Strip a small section (approximately six feet) at a time to avoid standing in solution.

5. Do not use an extension cord that is smaller than cord on machine.

6. Make sure that electric cord is free of any breaks and that the plug and outlets are grounded. Do not remove grounding prong.

7. Authorities state that adapters should not be used on portable electrical commercial equipment.

8. Place electric cord over shoulder to prevent it from becoming entangled in the machine. Hold a loop of the cord in hand so that a sudden motion will not jerk the cord and break wires.

PROCEDURE

Wet

1. Assemble equipment. Prepare solution. Take to designated area.

2. Put area out of order. Post wet floor signs.

3. Move furniture and disconnect all electrical appliances and equipment.

4. Vacuum or dust area with sweeping tool or covered broom. Remove debris with dustpan and counter brush.

MAINTENANCE OF FLOORS

PROCEDURE

5. Scrub baseboards. Use coving brush, baseboard cleaning attachment, or improvised nylon pad on mop handle to remove built-up soil from baseboards in areas where applicable.

6. Apply stripping solution to floor surface with mop. Allow to stand for two to three minutes.

7. Begin scrubbing far enough from walls to prevent the splashing of soil and solution.

8. Carry solution on floor with motion of the machine. Move slowly, but continuously—using a side-to-side, overlapping, arc pattern. Cover a six-foot path. If floors are pitted or dented, scrub in a criss-cross pattern. Turn machine slightly on edge, either to the right or left, (heeling) to remove "hard to remove" marks.

9. Pick up soil and solution. Use mop or wet vacuum. In extremely soiled areas, it may be necessary to repeat the above procedures.

10. Rinse floor and baseboards. Apply enough rinse water to completely remove all soil and solution.

11. Pick up rinse water with mop or wet vacuum.

12. Re-rinse floor surface with clear water several times in order to free surface of detergent. This is important because detergent harms some types of floor surfacing.

13. Continue entire procedure until area is completed.

14. Take equipment to utility room. Wash and dry. Wash off machines, cords, brushes, and pads. Return all equipment to designated stor-

MAINTENANCE OF FLOORS

PROCEDURE

age area. Restock utility cart. Place mopheads in plastic liner/bag and place in laundry bag; then store in designated area to be picked up and laundered.

Dry

This procedure at Saint Elizabeths Hospital is performed in restricted areas only and should be used only upon the direction of the supervisor.

ADDITIONAL EQUIPMENT:

Nylon stripping pad (coarse, aggressive, loosely woven)

Aerosol dry stripping agent

Spray attachment unit

SAFETY PRECAUTIONS:

1. Do not discard aerosol cans with regular trash.

PROCEDURE:

1. Assemble equipment. Attach spray unit to floor machine. Prepare mopping solution.

2. Prepare area—move furniture, unplug electric appliances and equipment.

3. Sweep or dust floor with covered broom or floor tool. Pick up debris and discard.

PROCEDURE

4. Dip mop into cleaning solution. Wring out thoroughly.

5. Damp mop area.

6. Shake aerosol stripping agent.

7. Snap can into spray unit. Keep dot on valve rim pointed down.

8. Apply stripping agent to floor (only enough for complete pad spread).

    a. Move machine *forward* and spread foam on first pass.

    b. Slowly move machine back over the same area to strip on second pass.

    c. Slowly move machine back over same area to burnish dry on third pass.

    d. Slowly move machine over same area on the fourth pass, applying stripping agent to new area—completing the four-step operation of the dry stripping system. (If the area is not dry on fourth pass, too much stripping agent was used.)

9. Move forward into next area. Overlap previous strokes and continue the four-step operation of spreading, stripping, and burnishing until area is completed.

10. Dust floor. Use *untreated* covered broom or floor tool. Pick up soil.

11. Dip mop into rinse water. Wring out thoroughly.

12. Damp mop area.

13. Apply floor finish as normally required.

MAINTENANCE OF FLOORS

PROCEDURE

14. Wash nylon pad immediately. Wash and dry all equipment and return to designated storage area.

FINISHING FLOORS
(Sealers and Floor Finishes)

PURPOSE: To fill pores and cracks, prevent stains and deterioration, to provide protective coating and leveling to surface, to reduce maintenance, and to restore floors to their original finish.

EQUIPMENT:

    Synthetic sealer
    Synthetic Finish
    Electric floor machine
    Plastic liners
    Buckets and Wringers on dolly (two)
    Mopheads and handles (two)
    Cloths

SAFETY PRECAUTIONS:

1. Do not save contaminated/soiled solution. Discard.

2. Never pour any part of the used solution back into the container.

3. Never pour or drip finish on floor.

4. Remove spills and splashes of sealer or finish immediately. If allowed to dry, will not be able to remove.

PROCEDURE

1. Assemble equipment. Place plastic liners in buckets. Fold over rim and under handle. Take to assigned area.

2. Place mophead into one bucket. Pour sealer on mophead. Wring out mophead. Continue pouring small amounts of sealer onto mophead and wringing out until mophead is saturated. (This eliminates the waste of product.) Wring out. (Make sure mop does not drip.)

3. Apply two thin coats of sealer to floor surface. Apply first coat crosswise, and apply second coat lengthwise for complete coverage. Allow time for complete drying between coats.

4. Place second mophead into second bucket. Pour floor finish on mophead. Wring out mophead. Continue pouring small amounts of finish

MAINTENANCE OF FLOORS

PROCEDURE

onto mophead and wringing out until mophead is saturated. Wring out.

5. Apply three thin coats of floor finish to surface. Apply first coat crosswise, second coat lengthwise, and third coat crosswise for complete coverage and surface leveling. Whenver mop pulls or drags during application, return to solution. Allow time for complete drying between coats.

6. To make surface very hard and level/smooth, buff with polishing pad after each application, or complete the procedure, and buff floor after one hour drying time. (Do not use brush—will remove finish.)

BE CERTAIN THAT YOU:

Take equipment to utility room. Wash thoroughly. Place mophead into plastic liner/bag and place in laundry bag. Return equipment to designated storage area.

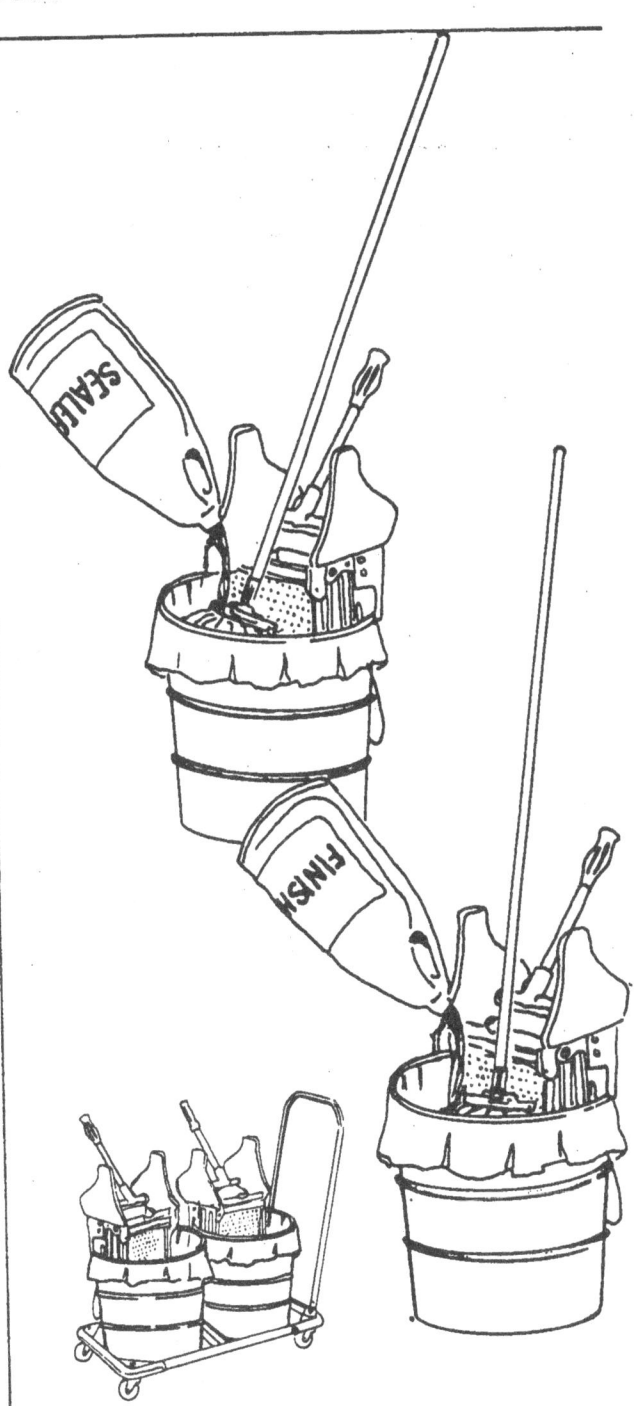

SPRAY BUFFING

PURPOSE: To maintain floor to optimum level. Also good for patching floors before they reach the point of needing a major refinishing job. Spray buffing is the basic method for maintaining resilient floors.

EQUIPMENT:

    Electric floor machine
    Aerosol cleaning agent, or
    Synthetic floor finish
    Nylon Pads (thick, loosely woven, aggressive)
    Sweeping tool
    Spray attachment unit, or
    Hand spray
    Brush with pad holder attachment, or
    Driving pad assembly
    Dustpan and Counter brush

SAFETY PRECAUTIONS:

    Same as for general buffing.

PROCEDURE

1. Assemble equipment. Attach spray unit to floor machine. Take to designated area.

2. Move furniture.

3. Sweep floor with covered floor tool. Pick up soil.

4. Shake aerosol cleaning agent. Snap can into spray unit.

5. Move floor machine to area, begin buffing as usual.

6. When black marks, spots, soil scuffs or scratches appear in the path of the buffer, spray a light mist on the areas. (If spray bottle is used, spray finish upward into air so that it falls to the floor in a mist instead of a stream.)

7. Buff same area until soil/damage is removed and shine appears. The machine will move

MAINTENANCE OF FLOORS

PROCEDURE

---

freely at first, then the area will become tacky or sticky before the shine appears.

8. Continue this procedure until area is repaired/clean. If area is too damaged, light scrub the area and apply thin coats of finish.

9. Remove pad or brush. Place in plastic liner. This procedure keeps pads/brushes moisted and makes cleaning easier.

10. Take equipment to utility room. Wash pads and place on flat surface or hang on peg to dry. Wipe off equipment and return to designated storage area.

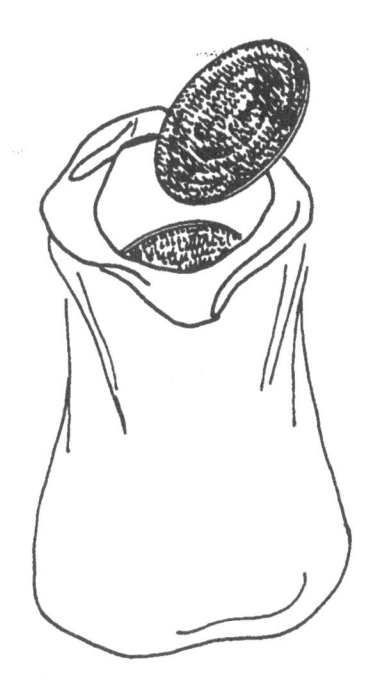

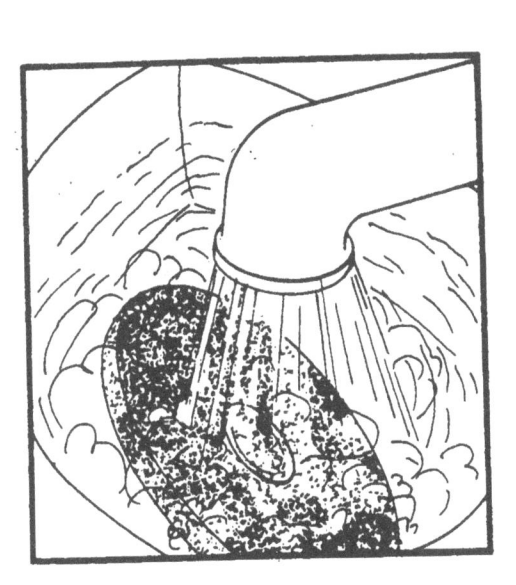

CARPET CARE
Cleaning and Spot Removal

PURPOSE: To remove dust, dirt, and grit particles, control bacteria, extend the life of the carpet and for appearance.

EQUIPMENT:

    Suction vacuum cleaner (Pile-lifting, upright machine with a brush and beater bar)
    White nylon hand brush with handle
    Shampooing machine
    Bucket and funnel
    Plastic boots or liners
    Wet and dry vacuum cleaner
    Shampooing agent
    Spot removing kit

SAFETY PRECAUTIONS:

1. Damp floors and uncleaned spills cause rot and mildew. Therefore, avoid soaking the carpet.

2. The steps to carpet care are:

    a. Vacuum

    b. Shampoo

    c. Remove spot

    d. Vacuum. Do not take any short cuts.

3. Release pressure in solution tank before removing cap.

4. Never wear shoes with dyed soles.

5. Protect carpet from rust stains. Use aluminum foil, cardboard, or plastic furniture coasters under legs of furniture.

PROCEDURE

1. Assemble equipment. Prepare solution. Pour into shampoo tank. Replace cap. Take to assigned area.

2. Move furniture. (If furniture cannot be moved out of area, move furniture to center of room. Vacuum, shampoo, remove spots, and vacuum perimeter. Replace furniture. Clean center of area/room.)

3. Vacuum with upright heavy duty pile lifting machine. Use three straight back-and-forth motions over the same area. (To prepare carpet for shampooing with regular vacuum, six back-and-forth strokes are required.)

MAINTENANCE OF FLOORS

PROCEDURE

4. Continue this procedure until entire carpet is vacuumed.

5. Shampoo carpet. Start in far corner of the room and work toward door. Set pile selector. Build up foam, and wait until foam appears around head of shampooing machine.

6. Take hand brush and shampoo along wall edges and corners.

7. Move machine in a forward and backward, or push and pull motion. Work across carpet, overlap each stroke.

8. Drop down to next area—overlap previous area. Continue procedure until carpet is completed.

9. If foam is brownish, vacuum immediately with wet vacuum; repeat shampooing procedure.

10. Remove any remaining spots.

11. Allow to dry.

12. Vacuuming *is a must in order to remove soil*.

13. Raise the pile with brush or machine.

14. Replace furniture. Aluminum foil, cardboard, or plastic furniture coasters may be placed under legs of furniture to avoid rust stains.

15. Take equipment to utility room. Clean. Hose off brush, wheels, and underneath shampoo machine. Wipe off exterior cabinet, and dry. Empty wet and dry vacuum. Wash and dry. Wash brush. Return all equipment to designated storage area.

USE AND CARE OF
EQUIPMENT, MATERIALS, AND SUPPLIES

CONTENTS

		Page
1.	GENERAL POINTS TO BE OBSERVED	1
2.	USE AND CARE OF NON-AUTOMATIC/MANUAL EQUIPMENT	3
3.	USE AND CARE OF AUTOMATIC EQUIPMENT	9
4.	HELPFUL SERVICE HINTS FOR WET AND DRY VACUUM	13
5.	HELPFUL SERVICE HINTS FOR FLOOR MACHINES	14
6.	HELPFUL SERVICE HINTS FOR AUTOMATIC SCRUBBERS	15

USE AND CARE OF
EQUIPMENT, MATERIALS, AND SUPPLIES

1. GENERAL POINTS TO BE OBSERVED:

The institution has invested a large amount of money in expensive modern equipment, materials, and supplies in order to help fulfill the housekeeping goals. Therefore, it is the responsibility of each employee to keep the equipment in good working condition and use materials and supplies economically.

Storing of equipment is part of the Housekeeping Aid's job in caring for equipment. Some institutions have storage areas or utility rooms located in each department or on each floor. Others have central equipment rooms near housekeeper's office. These areas are equipped with hooks, racks, shelves, sinks, and floor drains for the cleaning and storing of equipment, material and supplies.

The storage area must be maintained daily and every item must have a place.

Care of equipment, materials, and supplies are divided into two groups: care of non-automatic/manual equipment, and care of power-operated (electric or battery) equipment. However, there are several general points to be observed on the care and upkeep of all equipment, materials, and supplies.

1. Follow manufacturer's instructions for operation and maintenance.

2. Provide a preventive maintenance program (routine and systematic inspections and repairs).

3. Replace equipment, materials, or supplies promptly when faulty or ineffective.

4. Keep equipment clean at all times.

5. Use materials and supplies economically.

6. Provide adequate and proper storage area for equipment, materials, and supplies.

7. Use each piece of equipment only for its intended purpose.

8. Report faulty, damaged, or ineffective materials or equipment to supervisor.

PURPOSE: To maintain equipment in good working condition; to insure faster, easier, and more efficient performance; to control bacteria and for appearance.

EQUIPMENT:

    Germicidal detergent
    Cloths or Sponges
    Buckets (two)
    Gloves

SAFETY PRECAUTIONS:

1. Never pour used sealer or finish back into clean solution containers.

2. Brushes should never be stored on the bristles or left on machines.

3. Do not use more of an item than is necessary to efficiently perform the task.

4. Make sure pressure is released from wall washing tanks before cleaning.

192

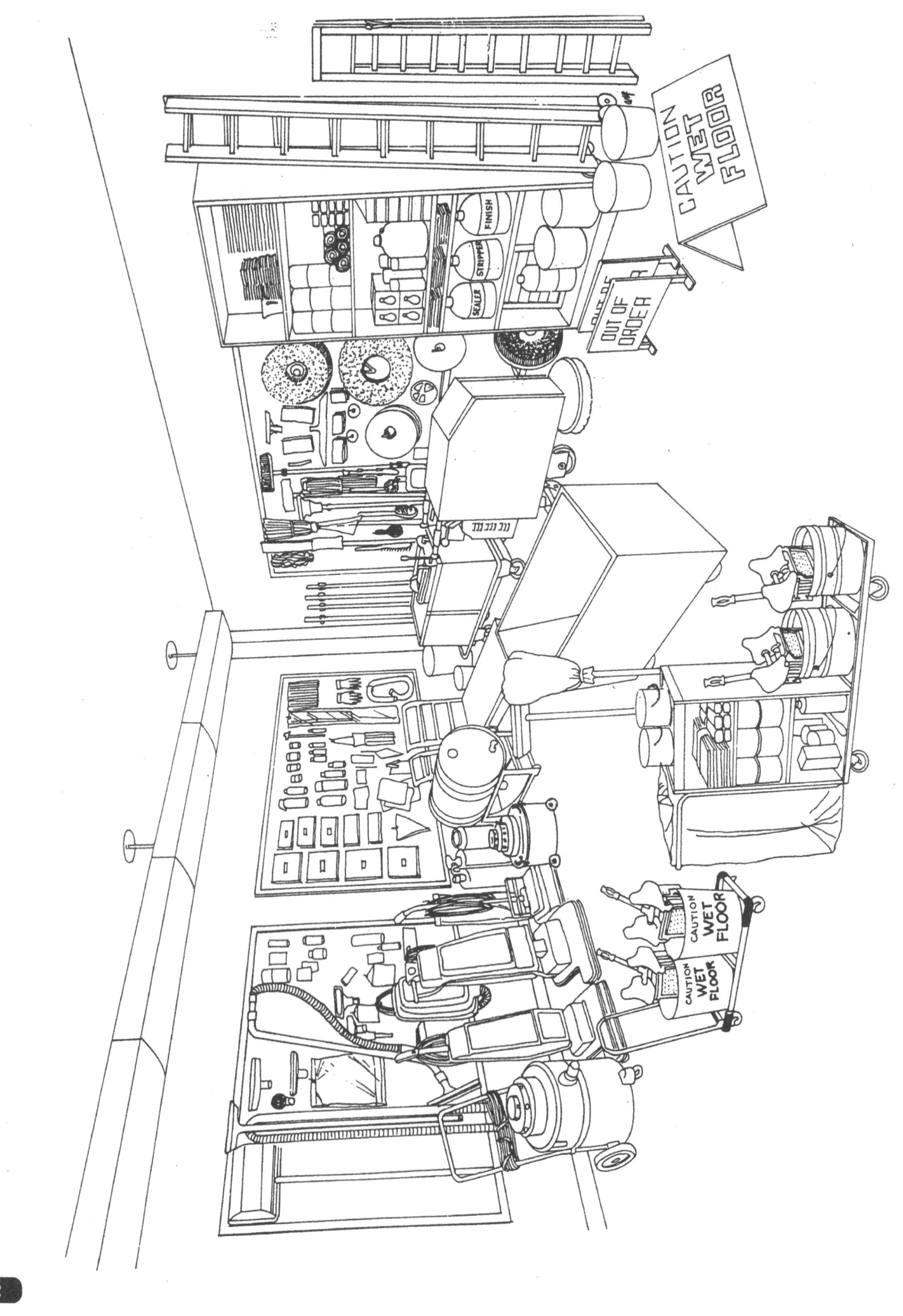

USE AND CARE OF EQUIPMENT

5. All equipment must be cleaned at the end of the day and returned to designated storage area.

2. **USE AND CARE OF NON-AUTOMATIC/MANUAL EQUIPMENT:**

Included in this type of equipment are items used in housekeeping duties that are entirely moved or operated by hand. This includes everything from brushes to wall washing pressure tanks.

EQUIPMENT:

    Utility carts
    Brushes of all types:
      a. Counter
      b. Sweeping
      c. Toilet
      d. Deck and other Scrub brushes
      e. Radiator
      f. Scrub and Polish
      g. Pot
      h. Nylon hand brush
      i. Coving or Baseboard

    Dustpans
    Screens, sifters and slit spoons
    Caution signs
    Squeegees
    Buckets (small and large)
    Dollies
    Wringers
    Mopheads
    Nylon pads
    Sweeping floor tools
    Extension handles
    Trash carts
    Wall washing pressure tanks
    Corn brooms

Ladders
Gloves
Sealers
Strippers (bulk and portioned)
Finishes (bulk and portioned)
Germicidal detergents (bulk and portioned)
Polishes (furniture, stainless steel)
Treated cloths
Dust cloths
Soaps
Plastic liners
Carpet sweepers
Putty knives
Hose (water)
Measuring cups
Mopping tanks
Spray units
Toilet tissue
Paper towels
Bottles (plastic)
Trash containers

PROCEDURE

Utility Carts

1. Wipe off all shelves with germicidal cloth at the end of the day. Dry.

2. Place plastic liner on top shelf to keep from rusting.

3. Use it daily in performing duties as assigned.

4. Keep shelves neatly stocked with all supplies and equipment.

Brushes

1. Clean at the end of the day.

2. Comb with a stiff fiber brush or comb and wash under running water. Shake out excess water.

3. Store by hanging on rack—free from touching any surface or store on block/wood part of brush.

4. Do not use until brushes are dry.

5. For maximum wear and effectiveness, brushes with removable handles should be rotated at least once a week.

6. Always hang broom up. Never stand on the straws.

Bottles
(Plastic spray bottle)

1. Clean exterior with paper towel dipped in germicidal solution. Dry.

2. Return to utility cart.

3. A trigger type must be taken apart regularly and washed and rinsed thoroughly.

Carpet Sweepers

1. Empty into plastic liner after each use. Place liner in trash collection container.

2. Remove strings and debris from brush and wheel.

3. Damp wipe the sweeper.

Caution Signs
(Wet floor, Out of order)

1. Damp wipe and dry after each use.

2. Periodically, thoroughly wash, rinse, and dry.

Cloths
(Treated and Cleaning)

1. Treated:
   a. Use all surfaces of the woven treated paper before discarding.

   b. Treat own cloths by spraying lightly with solution and allow to stand overnight in covered container. May be discarded or laundered.

2. Cleaning:
   a. Rinse frequently during use.

USE AND CARE OF EQUIPMENT

PROCEDURE

b. At the end of the day or at the end of the bathroom cleaning procedure, place cleaning cloths in plastic liner, then into a regular laundry bag for laundering.

c. Never leave cloths lying around.

Dustpans

1. Clean at the end of the day. Wash with germicidal solution.

2. Rinse and dry.

3. Hang on hook on cart so that it will not become bent or damaged.

Extension Handles

1. Use as an aid for high dusting.

2. Wipe off daily.

Floor Sweeping Tools

1. Use a disposable cloth.

2. Use all surfaces possible.

3. Damp wipe handle and foot frame daily.

4. Wash tool once a week with germicidal detergent.

5. Hang up on utility cart when not in use.

Germicidal Detergents and Strippers

1. Used in the cleaning operation to remove soil.

2. Do not over use—will destroy flooring surfaces.

3. Use recommended amount only.

4. Read label before using.

Gloves

1. Wash outside of gloves under running water (while on hand) at the end of the day.

2. Remove and wash inside. Wipe dry.

3. Hang across a smooth surface to dry.

Hose
(With cut-off nozzle)

1. Rinse off rubber or plastic hose.

2. Roll in a three-foot circle to prevent kinking. Drain water while rolling.

3. Hang hose on a rack or peg in storage area.

Knives
(Putty—short and long)

1. Wipe handle and blade with germicidal solution at end of day. Dry.

2. Return to cart.

6   USE AND CARE OF EQUIPMENT

PROCEDURE

Ladders
(Safety and Platform)

1. Wipe off after each use with germicidal solution.

2. Rinse and dry.

3. Return to designated storage area.

Measuring Cups

1. Rinse immediately after use.

2. Dry.

3. Store so that it will not be damaged.

Mops—Dust

1. Do not use to mop up spills.

2. Remove loose soil from mop frequently—by vacuum if possible.

3. Remove mophead at end of day, place in plastic bag and take to designated storage area for laundering.

Mops—Wet

1. Cut off loose and uneven yarn strands.

2. Never twist or squeeze mop extra hard—such action will break fibers and destroy the mophead.

3. Remove mophead at the end of bathroom cleaning and at the end of the day.

4. Place in plastic bag and into laundry bag and take to designated storage area for laundering.

Mopping tanks, Buckets, Wringers and Dollies

1. Remove any loose mophead yarn, string, or foreign matter.

2. Wash, rinse, and dry daily. Invert small and medium size buckets to dry.

3. Keep the equipment in good repair. Report any defects to supervisor.

4. When necessary, add a few drops of oil to casters.

5. Avoid hitting the mopping unit against other objects and walls.

6. Replace bumper strip when needed.

7. Do not allow a cleaning solution to remain in the bucket when the bucket is not in use.

Small Buckets or Pails

1. Empty contents.

2. Wash, rinse, and dry.

3. Turn upside down to dry.

USE AND CARE OF EQUIPMENT

PROCEDURE

Polishes

1. Used on furniture, stainless steel, wood and metal.

2. Use only the recommended amount.

3. It is very annoying to get polish on one's clothes; so, thoroughly rub the surface to remove excess polish.

- - - - - - - - - - - - - - - - -

Paper Towels and Toilet Tissue

1. Replacement supplies.

2. Always place in containers—not in window sills or on top of cabinets.

- - - - - - - - - - - - - - - - -

Screens, Sifters/Slit Spoons

1. Wash and shake off excess water.

2. Dry. Handle so as not to bend screen.

3. Place on hook on utility cart or other designated storage area.

- - - - - - - - - - - - - - - - -

Nylon Pads

1. Wash pads under running water. Rinse.

2. Hang or store on flat surface until dry.

Plastic Liners

1. Used to line trash containers.

2. Must be replaced daily.

3. Do not use for any other purpose than intended.

- - - - - - - - - - - - - - - - -

Sealers, Finishers

1. Items used to protect flooring.

2. These items are very expensive.

3. Use liners in buckets when using sealer and finish.

4. Never pour solution on floor.

5. Wipe up spills or drips immediately.

6. Never waste the product. Pour just enough on mophead in bucket to wet mophead, which should eliminate any material being left over.

7. In case there is a small amount left over—discard it. Do not pour into clean solution—solution will sour.

8. Mopheads should be placed in plastic liner/bag for laundering.

9. Wash, rinse, and dry buckets, wringers, dolly, mops and mop handles used in these operations.

PROCEDURE

Soaps

1. Used for hand washing and bathing.

2. Must rinse before using.

3. Not used for cleaning inanimate surfaces.

Sponges

1. Place in germicidal solution. Wash thoroughly. Squeeze out excess water.

2. Rinse. Squeeze out excess water.

3. Place on flat surface to dry—do not hang on nails.

Squeegees
(Small or large)

1. Wash squeegee blades in germicidal solution.

2. Rinse. Drain off excess water.

3. Wipe dry and return to utility cart or storage area.

4. Do not store with squeegee blades down.

Spray Units

1. Used for spray buffing and dry stripping.

2. Wipe off with germicidal solution.

3. Rinse spray nozzles.

4. Do not let material harden on nozzle.

Trash Containers

1. Used to receive or hold waste.

2. Handle containers so as not to scratch, puncture or bend them.

3. Wipe trash container inside and out daily. Replace liner.

4. Once a month—collect trash containers, take to utility room, and thoroughly wash, rinse and dry or steam clean.

Trash Carts

1. Used for general collection of trash.

2. Take to utility room. Wash inside and outside thoroughly. Let drain.

3. Rinse and let drain.

4. Wipe dry.

Wall Washing Machines/Pressure Tanks

1. Empty at the end of the operation.

2. Rinse tubing and inside of tanks.

3. Wipe off outside with germicidal detergent. Dry.

4. Store in designated storage area.

USE AND CARE OF EQUIPMENT

3. USE AND CARE OF AUTOMATIC EQUIPMENT:

Automatic equipment is equipment that is power operated either by electricity or battery. This type of equipment is very expensive and must be properly maintained to insure good service and maximum efficiency. Therefore, keep this equipment free of dirt, and oiled properly and keep screws and nuts tight. Automatic equipment is usually divided into three categories: floor machines, vacuum cleaners and automatic scrubbers.

EQUIPMENT:

Single disc floor machines—with or without spray attachments
Drive assemblies
Square buffers—Attachments (Plates and baseboard scrubbers)

Shampoo machines
Automatic scrubbing machines
Vacuums
   a. Suction
   b. Back-Pack
   c. Wet and dry
   d. Pile lifter
   e. Upright

Vacuum attachments—wand, hose, crevice tool, brushes—floor, wall, ceiling, upholstery, carpet and attachments for wet floor operation

Battery operated sweepers
Automatic mop assemblies

PROCEDURE

Floor Machines

1. Used for scrubbing, stripping and polishing of large or small areas quickly. Also used for special application—such as spray buffing and dry stripping.

2. Never attach brush by running machine over it and allowing it to lock.

3. Never leave machine unattended. Disconnect when not in use.

4. Machine is cleaned at the end of the day or after completion of assignment.

a. At the work site, tilt machine back on handle. Remove brush and pad or drive assembly and place in plastic liners/bags.

b. Rinse machine in upright position. Damp wipe cord with germicide cloth. Wind cord on handle or storage hooks as it is being wiped. Inspect for defects and report to supervisor.

c. Take equipment to utility room. Remove brushes, pads and/or drive assembly from plastic liners/bags. Wash thoroughly under running water. Store on flat surface or hang on peg to dry. DO NOT

PROCEDURE

USE AGAIN UNTIL DRY.

d. Wash handle and exterior surface of machine. Dry.

e. Tilt on handle and rinse the underside of the brush housing with clean water. Dry.

f. If a solution tank is used—rinse tank and feed lines/tubing. Dry.

g. Store equipment in designated storage area.

h. Never store machines on brushes. Store in tilted position.

Extension Cords

1. If an extension cord is used, make sure it is the same size as on the equipment so that the proper amount of current is carried to machine.

2. Do not yank on an electric cord to pull the plug from the outlet.

3. Damp wipe cord with germicidal solution. Dry.

4. Wind loosely and hang or lay in a safe place.

Vacuum Cleaners
(Upright, Wet and Dry, Back-Pack)

1. Used to remove soil from floors and carpeting, window sills, ledges, screens, vents, blinds, upholstery, walls and ceiling; and to pick up water—scrub, rinse, overflow, flooding.

2. Empty upright vacuums when bag is half full

a. Outer bags may be cloth, mole skin or paper.

b. Cloth and Moleskin Bags may be vacuumed, but never washed. Discard disposable bags.

c. Damp wipe handle, hose, and cord with germicidal solution. Dry.

3. Clean wet and dry vacuum at the end of the day.

a. If used for dry purposes:

(1) Make sure machine is set up with flannel and paper liners.

(2) To clean, remove hose, head assembly, and cloth filter. Leave paper filter in place.

(3) Tilt machine back on handle and wheels. Pull out bag so that it hangs outward.

(4) Continue raising machine until it is resting on handle. Slap tank several times to dislodge all dirt.

(5) Remove bag by sliding elastic band off the lip of the tank. Place in a plastic liner. Tie and discard.

(6) Wash tank inside and outside with germicidal solution. Rinse and dry.

(7) Wash all attachments. Rinse and dry.

(8) Wipe off cord and rewind on handle, not around head assembly.

(9) Wipe off head assembly.

(10) Check impaction filter. Not necessary to remove after each usage, unless torn, dam-

USE AND CARE OF EQUIPMENT

PROCEDURE

aged or wet. Supervisor should set a specific time for changing (for example, every 30 days).

(11) Take equipment to designated storage area. Leave head assembly off tank, turn on side for airing and drying purposes.

b. If used for wet purposes:

(1) Make sure machine is set up for the wet operation.

(2) Remove flannel and paper liners and insert the cyclonic separator which has a float that shuts off the suction of the machine when tank is filled to maximum level.

(3) To clean, remove hose, head assembly, and lift out cyclonic separator.

(4) Wheel machine to area with drain or low sink. Tilt tank back on handles to empty. (Some of these have drain valves.)

(5) Rinse two or three times with clean water to remove sludge.

(6) Wash, rinse and dry tank and accessories.

(7) Store in designated storage area.

(8) If impaction filter is wet—allow to dry. Sterilize or autoclave before using again.

Automatic Scrubbers/Sweepers

Used for scrubbing, stripping, buffing, and sweeping large areas. In order for machines to work properly, they must be charged daily in a well ventilated room. Battery must be checked regularly and distilled water added when water is below internal plates or triangle. Battery cover must be left opened when charging. Do not smoke in area when machine is being charged.

1. Automatic Scrubber
   a. To clean, take equipment to utility room. Empty—open dump valve or fold tanks over drain.

   b. Flush tanks, wheels and squeegee. Use a hose to perform this task.

   c. Wash exterior surface with germicidal solution.

   d. Rinse and dry.

   e. Take to designated storage area.

   f. Make sure windows are open.

   g. Report any defects, damages or necessary repairs to supervisor.

2. Powered Sweeper
   a. To clean, take to utility room. Remove and empty trash pan.

   b. Shake down filters—remove and empty pan.

   c. Remove brushes—comb, wash, rinse and shake well. Dry.

   d. Wash exterior surface with germicidal solution. Rinse and dry.

   e. Wash pans. Rinse and dry.

   f. Replace all parts.

   g. Take to designated storage area.

PROCEDURE

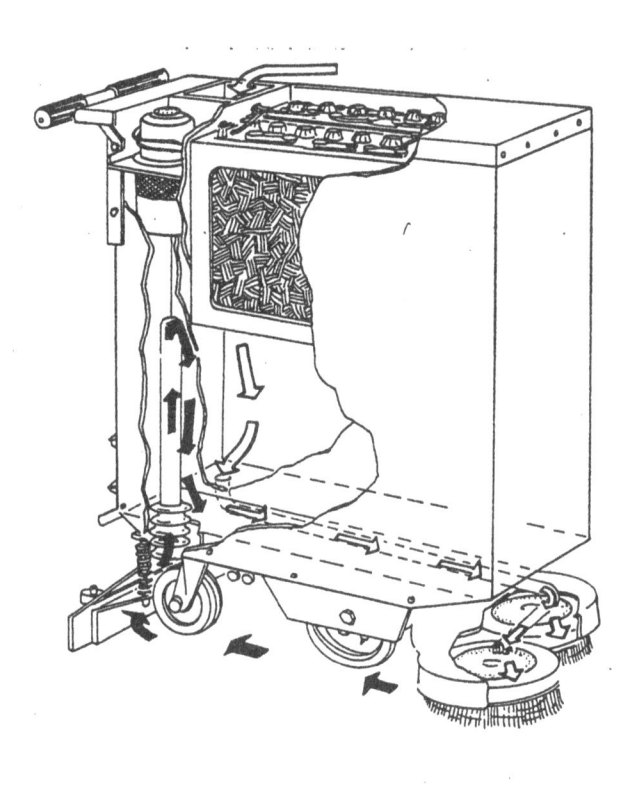

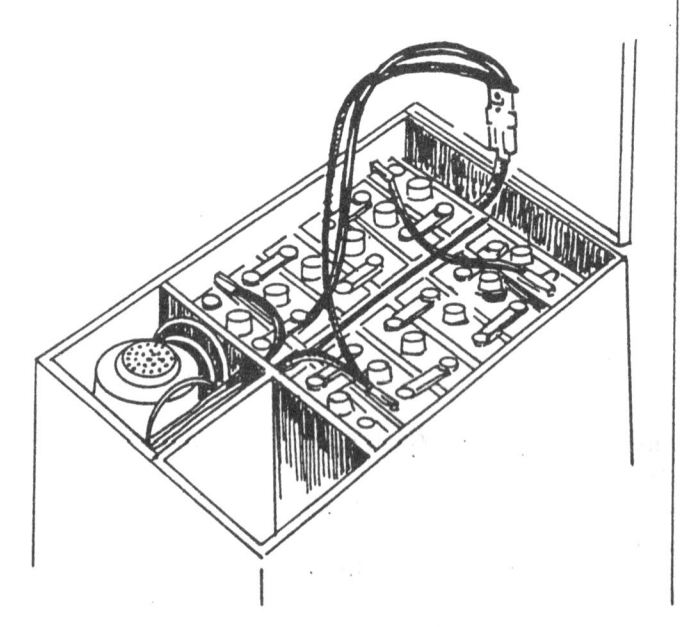

h. Check battery—leave cover open.

i. Connect for charging.

j. Make sure windows are open.

k. Report any defects or necessary repairs to supervisor.

USE AND CARE OF EQUIPMENT

4. HELPFUL SERVICE HINTS FOR WET AND DRY VACUUM:

1. Always operate vacuum on the proper voltages as outlined on the data plate.

2. After using for dry applications, remove the disposable paper bag (5 to 9 gallon units only), and mitten flannel filter and clean before reusing. For added convenience, keep a supply of disposable paper bags on hand (5 and 9 gallon units only)—they may be obtained from your authorized distributor.

3. If air movement is interrupted in your vacuum, check the dust filter to make sure it's clean. To see if hose has become clogged, remove hose from machine and test suction at machine intake. Sometimes a clogged tool will be the culprit, so check tools periodically.

4. For wet work, remove the disposable paper bag and dust filter, then place the water separator in the tank (5 and 9 gallon units only). In the 10 gallon models, install the wet filter and water shut off.

5. After using machine for wet work, and before putting it away, clean tank inside and outside; clean tools thoroughly.

6. Store machine in clean dry place.

7. The suds supressor bar at the tank inlet should be checked and replaced, if necessary, after 125 gallons of solution have been picked up. Suds supressor bar is replaced by removing inlet deflector and sliding new bar into place. These bars may be obtained from authorized distributor (for 5 and 9 gallon units only).

8. Many tools are available for the wet and dry vacuum. Contact your authorized distributor for additional tools.

SERVICE DIAGNOSIS:

1. Motor will not start
   a. Possible causes:

   (1) Power source or outlet dead

   (2) Vacuum switch faulty or damaged

   (3) Excessively worn brushes

   (4) Wire shorted or broken

   b. How to correct:

   (1) Activate source or check cord

   (2) Replace switch

   (3) Replace brushes

   (4) Replace wires

2. Little or no suction
   a. Possible causes:

   (1) full tank—wet shut off closes fan inlet

   (2) Clogged attachment inlet, hose or vacuum inlet

   (3) Clogged filter bag

   (4) Tank gasket seal leaks

   (5) Exhaust air outlet covered

USE AND CARE OF EQUIPMENT

b. How to correct:

(1) Empty tank

(2) Remove lodged materials

(3) Clean filter bag

(4) Position seal properly

(5) Remove obstruction

3. Machine noisy
   a. Possible causes:

   (1) Vibration or resonating of metal parts

   (2) Dirty filter

   b. How to correct:

   (1) Secure all mountings firmly

   (2) Clean filter

4. Motor runs hot or smells warm
   a. Possible causes:

   (1) Motor cooling air intake or exhaust clogged.

   (2) Motor overloaded with mist or suds.

   (3) Dirty filter

   b. How to correct:

   (1) Clean air intake and exhaust passages

   (2) Empty tank; install new suds suppressor

   (3) Clean filter

5. HELPFUL SERVICE HINTS FOR FLOOR MACHINES:

   SERVICE DIAGNOSIS:

   1. Machine wobbles—hard to control.
      a. Possible causes:

      (1) Brush bristles distorted resulting in brush being uneven

      (2) Switch housing not tight on handle tube

      (3) Handle tube not connected firmly to machine hose

      (4) Pads or brushes worn unevenly

      b. How to correct:

      (1) If brush is new, soak in water for several hours, remove from water, shake off excess water, rest brush on flat surface on back with bristles pointing upward.

      (2) Tighten bolts securing housing to handle tube, tighten set screws. If housing is still loose, drill and tap new hole in housing, insert pointed set screw and tighten firmly.

      (3) Check all mounting bolts for tightness, insert washers for shims if necessary.

      (4) Replace with new pad or brush.

   2. Motor will not run
      a. Possible causes:

      (1) Unplugged at wall

      (2) Unplugged between motor and handle cable

      (3) Fuse blown or circuit breaker tripped

USE AND CARE OF EQUIPMENT

(4) Cable wires severed

(5) Switch burned out

(6) Wires detached at switch

(7) Motor burned out

b. How to correct—follow these steps

(1) Visibly check all connections to be sure the plugs are securely plugged into the appropriate receptacle.

(2) Check fuse or circuit breaker. Replace or reset if necessary.

(3) Visibly, and carefully, check cable for wire breakage.

(4) Unplug motor from handle cable and connect motor directly to wall receptacle through use of an adequate gauge extension cord (at least 14-2). CAUTION: Remove brush or pad holder from machine before plugging into power source.

(5) If after #4 above motor does not operate, remove motor from machine and take it to your distributor, or an electrical repair station designated by your distributor for repairs.

(6) If after #4 above motor does operate, the problem lies between the motor and the wall receptacle. Remove switch box cover plate and ascertain that all electrical connections are secure.

(7) Remove cable from the terminals on the switch and replace with an extension cord (preferably 14-3) to determine if wires have been severed inside the cable.

(8) Replace switch.

3. Runs hot
   a. Possible causes:

(1) Motor overloaded. Machine does not have sufficient power for the job. (Example—dry spray-buff cleaning with abrasive pads.)

(2) Air intake ducts clogged with dust and lint.

b. How to correct:

(1) Secure the proper machine for the job or use the same machine with pads of less abrasive material.

(2) Remove drip cover and shroud. Use forced air to blow dust and lint from motor.

6. HELPFUL SERVICE HINTS FOR AUTOMATIC SCRUBBERS:

SERVICE DIAGNOSIS:

1. Motor will not start
   a. Possible causes:

(1) Battery charge condition very low—check with hydrometer

(2) Battery connectors loose or disconnected

(3) Loose or broken wires

b. How to correct:

(1) Recharge batteries fully before beginning operations.

(2) Fasten battery connections securely.

(3) Fasten all wires securely and tape.

2. Machine will not move
   a. Possible causes:

   (1) Clutch requires adjusting

   (2) "V" belt slipping

   (3) Battery charge condition very low—check with hydrometer

   b. How to correct:

   (1) Adjust clutch per "Clutch Adjustment" instructions.

   (2) Adjust "V" belt tightness.

   (3) Recharge batteries fully before beginning operations.

3. Machine streaking a cleaned floor
   a. Possible causes:

   (1) Foreign materials lodged under rear squeegee blade

   (2) Insufficient water flow to brushes

   (3) Worn squeegee blades

   (4) Squeegee out of adjustment

   (5) Worn brushes or pads

   b. How to correct:

   (1) Raise squeegee and clean squeegee blade.

   (2) Clean fine filter screen in tank and examine lines for a flow restriction.

   (3) Replace squeegee blade.

   (4) Adjust per instructions.

   (5) Replace brushes or pads.

4. Solution not being properly picked up
   a. Possible causes:

   (1) Vacuum motor wired for 12 or 18 volts and too much solution being laid

   (2) Clogged pick-up tube

   (3) Air leaks around vacuum motor mount

   (4) Ball check (water shut-off) sealing vacuum motor opening to tank

   (5) Clogged filters

   (6) Drain valve not completely closed

   (7) Pick up tube plug or suds suppressors not seated properly

   b. How to correct:

   (1) Use 24-volt switch position.

   (2) Remove lint accumulations and clean tube through plugged hole in tank at top of tube.

   (3) Seal all leaks.

   (4) Clean ball check (water shut-off) assembly and replace.

   (5) Replace filters.

   (6) Close valve.

   (7) Securely seat pick-up tube plug.

USE AND CARE OF EQUIPMENT

5. Short operating time
   a. Possible causes:

   (1) Battery charge condition very low—check with hydrometer

   (2) Continuous heavy motor load due to special brushes

   (3) Constant brush operation—210 lb. position

   b. How to correct:

   (1) Recharge batteries fully before beginning operations.

   (2) Use special brushes requiring heavy motor load only for particular application.

   (3) Use locked brush cleaning operations sparingly.

6. Machine pulls to one side
   a. Possible causes:

   (1) Squeegee dragging only on one side

   b. How to correct:

   (1) Adjust per instructions.

7. Machine creeps
   a. Possible causes:

   (1) Clutch out of proper adjustment

   (2) Clutch cable binding in wound wire casing

   (3) Clutch collar sticking

   b. How to correct:

   (1) Adjust clutch per "Clutch Adjustment" instructions.

   (2) Lubricate clutch cable and casing.

   (3) Lubricate clutch.